Energy Made Easy

Energy Made Easy

*Helping Citizens Become
Energy-Literate*

Ronald Stein / Todd Royal

Copyright © 2019 by Ronald Stein / Todd Royal.

Library of Congress Control Number: 2019910931
ISBN: Hardcover 978-1-7960-4984-8
  Softcover 978-1-7960-4983-1
  eBook 978-1-7960-4982-4

All rights reserved. No part of this book may be reproduced or transmitted in any form or by any means, electronic or mechanical, including photocopying, recording, or by any information storage and retrieval system, without permission in writing from the copyright owner.

Any people depicted in stock imagery provided by Getty Images are models, and such images are being used for illustrative purposes only.
Certain stock imagery © Getty Images.

Print information available on the last page.

Rev. date: 08/08/2019

To order additional copies of this book, contact:
Xlibris
1-888-795-4274
www.Xlibris.com
Orders@Xlibris.com
800502

CONTENTS

Preface vii
Introduction xi
Chapter 1   Energy Density 1
Chapter 2   Prosperous Societies and Energy 10
Chapter 3   World Wars I and II Were Both Won With Energy 29
Chapter 4   Paris Accord Plans to Reduce Greenhouse Gases
                   Miss the Mark 45
Chapter 5   How China and India View Energy 62
Chapter 6   Renewable Electricity 83
Chapter 7   Electrical Grid 118
Chapter 8   Electric Vehicles 139
Chapter 9   Requirements for a Carbon-Free Society 148
Chapter 10 Energy and National Security 166
Chapter 11 The Weaponization of Energy 187
Chapter 12 Climate Change 205

Author Biographies 231
Endnotes 235
Index 321

Preface

Congresswoman Alexandra Ocasio-Cortez (AOC) has done the world a favor through her proposed, "Green New Deal." She has highlighted the challenges of energy, electricity, and how we power the world. Our book – *Energy Made Easy* brings simplicity and clarity to complex issues that AOC and Presidential candidates are bringing up on a daily basis. From global warming to electrical grids this book addresses energy in layman's terms to help citizens become energy literate.

For the last decade, Ronald Stein with over fifty year's experience, as a certified professional engineer (P.E.), has become the private business spokesperson for the energy and infrastructure industries. Having over 100 published Op Ed articles that provide energy literacy for citizens, private industry, and government leaders. Ron shows how energy is the primary drivers of our daily lives and global economy.

Todd Royal began his career in the energy sector after having his master's thesis titled, "Hydraulic Fracturing and the Revitalization of the American Economy," published in the U.S. Library of Congress in 2015. With over a 130 articles and scholarly works on energy, geopolitics, national security, foreign policy, and California politics published globally in featured publications such as USA Today to Modern Diplomacy, Todd's work can be viewed on Twitter @TCR_Consulting

Together, we've summarized in-depth research into a book that can be carried in your briefcase, taught in classrooms, viewed in corporate boardroom PowerPoint's, or help government leader be informed about all thing's energy related.

The following chapters summarize many of those energy subjects into concise areas to give the readers an easy guide to energy in layman's terms. 1. Energy Density, 2. Prosperous Societies and Energy, 3. World War I and II were both won with energy, 4. Paris Accord plans to reduce greenhouse gasses miss the mark, 5. How China and India View Energy, 6. Renewable Electricity, 7. Electrical Grid, 8. Electric Vehicles, 9. Requirements for a Carbon Free Society, 10. Energy and National Security. 11. The Weaponization of Energy, and 12. Climate Change.

Energy is multifaceted, but we've tried to allow the reader to grasp enough knowledge quickly so they can participate in discussions with friends and fellow workers, or question or agree with AOC the next time she is on CNN.

As an added benefit to the reader, each chapter is a stand-alone chapter on an energy subject. The readers may not be interested in the entire spectrum of energy but can selectively pick and choose hot energy topics trending on current news or social media coverage.

It is dangerous and delusional to believe anything can be explained in sound bites, much less energy. This book will make you look at energy and ELECTRICITY in a new, fresh way, and perspective that is desperately needed with the upcoming U.S. Presidential election and global events taking place in China, Russia, Iran, Africa, India, and South America.

Energy is at the forefront of everything that touches our lives. Ron likes to say and Todd as well, "that humanity enjoys the thousands of products that come from a barrel of crude oil!" Therefore, it is delusional to think that society is going carbon-free or the get-off-the-fossil-fuel-crowd has any intellectual insight into this fact without believing there movement is anything other than a political organization attempting to elect officials who buy into taxpayer subsidies and write offs when their shenanigans fail.

The purpose, creation and importance of this book is revealed every day when we turn on lights, go on an airplane or brush our teeth. Energy is everywhere. And this is where Ron and Todd with this book will simply talk about energy issues in a way and with insight backed up by thorough research that will make you, the reader, wonder and question energy and electricity in a way you never imagined.

So much can be said about energy, and Ron and Todd are going to illuminate the electrical grid, climate change, and how energy builds prosperous societies, as a few examples of what lies ahead. Their expertise on all matters of energy will make this an easy read, but also a page turner that shows example after example backed up with heavy research to think about, question, or believe in how energy matters in every part of our lives in the 21st century.

We look forward to hearing from you and speaking further about **Energy Made Easy.**

Ronald Stein, P.E.
Founder and Ambassador for Energy & Infrastructure

Ronald.Stein@PTSadvance.com
Twitter: @PTSFounder

Todd Royal
Independent public policy consultant in Los Angeles focusing on the geopolitical implications of energy

ToddRoyal@yahoo.com
Twitter: @TCR_Consulting

Introduction

The world is using more energy, including electricity, than ever before. According to the International Energy Agency (IEA), "energy consumption in 2018 grew at its fastest pace in a decade." Seventy percent of all gains came from fossil fuels, and the technologies needed to slash carbon emissions and fossil fuel usage are not yet on track to accomplish that task, the IEA said.

Reliable energy means a better quality of life for the world's societies. Economies and human lives run on energy, and on electrical energy, in particular.

A crucial challenge for humanity is to find alternative sources of energy that can replace the benefits fossil fuels have provided us over the last two centuries.

Figure Intro-1

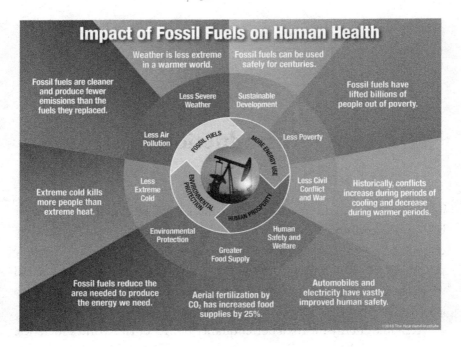

Electricity by itself cannot support the military, airlines, cruise ships, supertankers, container shipping, and trucking infrastructures. Nor can electricity alone, and especially that generated solely from renewable sources such as wind and solar, provide the thousands of products from petroleum that are essential to our transportation infrastructure, our electricity generation, our cooling, heating, manufacturing, agriculture—indeed, virtually every aspect of our daily lives and lifestyles.[1]

United States (U.S.) energy from fossil fuels (coal, natural gas, and petroleum) increased from 78 quadrillion BTUs in 2017 to 81 quadrillion BTUs in 2018. The 2018 increase was the largest in energy consumption, in both absolute and percentage terms, since 2010.[2] This illustrates the point that when economies grow, energy use increases.

The U.S. Energy Information Administration (EIA) projections to 2040 show that fossil fuels will continue to dominate future global demand, although renewables and nuclear energy will siphon off some electricity generation from fossil fuels. The EIA also reports that nuclear power will be needed to meet climate goals.³

Figure Intro-2

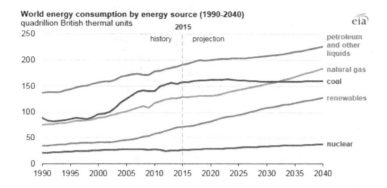

Source: U.S. Energy Information Administration, International Energy Outlook 2017-2018.⁴

Fossil fuels will have a large role in the future for clean energy. All the components of electric vehicles, and renewables, are manufactured from fossil fuels.⁵ See Figure Intro-3 below.⁶

Figure Intro-3

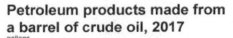

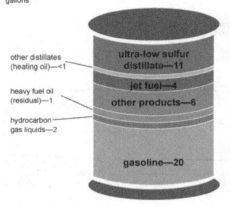

According to a 2018 report from Global Data, a leading data and analytics firm, "China, India and the United States (US) are major driving forces behind the growth of global electricity transmission and distribution conductors' market."[7]

There are billions of people today who are still without reliable electricity and thus forced to burn cow dung and rotted wood for energy.[8] As an example, 600 million Africans do not have electricity, or reliable sources of electricity, to run their hospitals, turn on the lights, or cook their food.[9] To solve these kinds of urgent energy problems requires an understanding about the origin and nature of electricity, its reliability, scalability, and whether the electricity sources being contemplated are cost-effective.

Energy at its core should empower individuals, nations, and, yes, entire continents. The density of an energy source has been shown to be an effective tool for measuring its efficiency in generating electricity. So far, the United States has been the only modern industrialized nation to meet the Kyoto Protocol for increased use of energy-dense natural gas over burning coal.[10]

Understanding energy will help us formulate the best energy policies to bring billions of people out of crippling poverty, lowered life expectancies, and even protect them from the allure of terrorism.[11] There is an opportunity to alleviate poverty and war if every person on the planet can be given access to scalable, reliable, affordable, abundant, and flexible energy.[12] When basic facts are ignored or shoved aside for political gain, however, rational energy discussions no longer happen.

A recent major study concluded that oceans were rising. This study had serious mathematical miscalculations and other biased issues that have since come to light.[13], In fact, oceans are not rising.[14] The final months of 2018 provided additional examples of prejudiced conclusions in regard to energy and electricity, which included highly publicized presentations that ignored or overlooked pertinent facts.

NASA data showed that global temperatures "dropped sharply over the past two years from February 2016 to February 2018."[15] Yet reporters were assigned to write about a group wanting to carve President Donald Trump's face into a glacier, apparently to prove climate change was occurring.[16] Major media outlets chose not to cover the global cooling story by investigative journalist Aaron Brown of Real Clear Markets.[17] If the planet is indeed cooling, or warming, or even somewhere in between, then what are the plans to counter these changes? How do governments, economies, and global citizens react to that change? It is only by avoiding political hyperbole and sticking to a rational discussion of decipherable facts that we as a nation (and you as readers) can make informed decisions about energy.

Amid the impressive amount of graphs, charts, tables, and prognostications on global energy issues, certain stubborn and irreducible facts must be faced—like this one: "the percentage of total global primary electricity demand provided by wind and solar is 1.1%."[18] Even by the year 2050 according to most energy industry estimates, renewables will be unable to eliminate fossil fuel's role in our lives. As an example, coal usage "increased 4.3 per cent in 2018 and consumption rose 1.4 per cent, the fastest increase for either since 2013," according the *2019 British Petroleum (BP) Statistical Review of World Energy.*[19] Most of this growth came from the Asia-Pacific region, and even coal use in the United States grew by 6.9 percent in 2018, due to strong foreign demand, which caused global coal exports to grow by 6.5 percent.[20]

A rational response to these realities would be to re-examine our energy needs and available solutions without increasing regulations and imposing top-down government controls that will likely punish middle-class and blue-collar workers.

All too often, lawmakers rely on fear tactics to compel public compliance on a given issue, and all too often with the end goal of gaining more power, more money, and more regulatory control over those who put them in office. Alarmism over global warming, climate change, etc., is at the forefront of these fear tactics, but such alarmist conclusions are openly rebutted by such circulations as the Oregon Petition Project, published by the Oregon Institute for Science and Medicine that was signed by more than 31,000 American scientists, with more than 9,000 signatories with doctorates.[21] These scientists have strong reservations as to whether man is causing the earth to warm. Unfortunately, fear by government climatologists and their apologists has taken over the energy and electricity debate. The unvarying message, whether openly stated or subliminally intended, seems to be: *"I'm from the government, and I'm here to help."*

And these scare tactics keep changing: "As the global warming bubble deflates, another scare is being inflated—species extinction." Remember in 2006 when Al Gore got everyone's attention by projecting the impending extinction of polar bears? He has gone silent of late on polar bears simply because their numbers keep rising and may indeed have quadrupled.[22]

Even the remarkable Germans have increased emissions via German Chancellor Angela Merkel's *"Energiewende"* policy, which consists of transitioning the German economy away from nuclear and fossil fuels into renewable electricity.[23] What has actually occurred, with increased building and use of coal-fired power plants to meet Germany's electricity needs, is reminiscent of the bad old days of East German reliance on highly polluting lignite, or *braunkohle*.[24]

The Germans haven't yet attempted to use the clean coal technology being tested and tried by the Chinese, South Koreans, and Japanese.[25] If renewable electricity is the future, then it is time to build a better solar panel, wind turbine, electric vehicle, and begin the process of inventing a smart grid that can store and disperse power on intermittent weather days and dark nights.

The get-off-fossil-fuel leaders like former Vice President Al Gore, former California Governors Jerry Brown and Arnold Schwarzenegger, and billionaire environmental activist Tom Steyer are crusading on behalf of intermittent, dilute, low-energy-density renewables in their quest to "save the world." These men's luxurious lifestyles would end once a total reliance on renewables-only eliminated the cornucopia of products that make and move so many things in our advanced societies.

Economies around the world would collapse, infrastructures would eventually deteriorate, and the prosperity of growing populations would dwindle away. And please note: Emerging countries such as China and India, along with Africa, have never indicated that they would allow lack of pipelines carrying oil and natural gas, domestic politics against fossil fuels, or sensitivity to the above-mentioned Western environmentalists to keep them from achieving the First World status enjoyed by the U.S., the EU, and Asian nations like South Korea, Japan, and Taiwan.[26]

Make no mistake. The jet engine and diesel engine that fuel (pun intended) all forms of modern transportation would be virtually eliminated by dependence on renewable electricity. And there would be other unintended and catastrophic consequences that these four influential men have obviously never considered. These would include widespread deaths from weather and a lack of chemicals derived from refined crude oil that currently feed the planet.

We will attempt to educate, providing the latest technical expertise and solid research, and then let readers decide for themselves. Too often energy policies are mandated after climate catastrophes that make headlines. If weather produces a downpour, forest fire, flood or heat wave, remember climate change isn't always the reason.

This leads to bad energy policies and a tendency to embrace "climate hysteria."[27] Environmental concerns and the need to keep powering our modern economy are not mutually exclusive endeavors.[28] *Energy Made Easy* isn't intended to be a How-to-Manual or Energy for Dummies, but a tool for policymakers and everyone involved with energy, which is YOU. We hope you enjoy the read, as we've attempted to provide the public with more energy literacy and a look at energy in a fresh, new way.

Ronald & Todd

Chapter One

Energy Density
By Ronald Stein

Summary

The energy available from deep-earth minerals/fuels is abundant, affordable, reliable, and, equally important, continuous and uninterruptable. Because of all these wondrous properties, this kind of energy has made it possible for us to reduce infant mortality, extend longevity, and "make products and move things" anywhere in the world via planes, trains, ships, and land vehicles. It is also thanks to the energy extracted from deep-earth minerals that we have been able virtually to eliminate deaths from diseases and extreme forms of weather.

Intermittent electricity from less-energy-dense renewables like wind and solar, on the other hand, requires huge land resources and the construction of unsightly wind and solar farms that destroy vegetation, trees, and wildlife while lowering home values.

The two prime movers that have done more than any other invention for the cause of globalization—the diesel engine and the jet turbine—both get their energy manufactured from the energy density of deep-earth minerals/fuels. Without these awesome engines, there would be no modern transportation. And without transportation, there is no commerce.

Energy Density

Given all the hype over renewable sources to generate intermittent electricity, the numbers I am about to cite, all readily available from the Energy Information Administration (EIA),[29] are remarkable in that they reveal a continuing bias toward nonrenewable sources. The energy-density sources of oil, natural gas, and coal still dominate the fuel mix of U.S. consumption. And yet, over the past six decades, tens of billions of dollars have been spent on renewable and alternative intermittent electrical generation schemes, such as wind energy, solar energy, corn and other biofuels, along with electric cars. The result of all this investment in all these renewables has been only a modest gain in market share in comparison to oil, natural gas, and coal.[30]

It may be easier to comprehend the U.S. Energy Information Administration projections[31] that dependency on energy from fossil fuels continues into the future when you understand that renewables are incapable of providing any of the thousands of products from fossil fuels that are part of all our lifestyles. Nor can renewables supply the fuels needed by the militaries, airlines, cruise ships, supertankers, container shipping, and trucking infrastructures, let alone the jet and diesel engines that are the basis of modern transportation. In addition, all the components of the EV (electronic vehicle) and renewable industries are manufactured from chemicals and by-products derived from the extraction and refining of fossil fuels.

In other words, despite these huge investments, renewables' share of the energy market has been shrinking.[32] What's happening? While conspiracy theorists may prefer to believe that Big Oil, Big Coal, and Big Nuclear are stifling the growth of renewables, the simple truth is that coal, oil, natural gas, and nuclear can satisfy the four energy imperatives: power density, energy density, cost and scale,[33] while renewables fall woefully short of meeting those imperatives.

Back in 1949 nearly 91% of America's total primary energy came from oil, natural gas, and coal.[34] The balance came from renewables, with hydropower being a dominant contributor. By 2008 the market share for coal, oil, and natural gas, along with nuclear, had grown to

92.5% of total primary energy in the U.S. with the small remainder coming from renewables.

Per the U.S. Energy Information Administration Annual Energy Outlook of 2009, with projections of Energy Consumption by Sector to 2030,[35] the energy-density superiority of fossil fuels (that are abundant and readily available) to support the prosperity[36] we're enjoying from that energy supply source (that "makes thousands of products and moves things"), continues to be part of the world's energy mix.[37]

While wind and solar renewables are attempting to make significant and growing contributions to electrical generation, they are nowhere near supplanting oil, natural gas, coal, and nuclear. The reasons are many, beginning with their intermittent nature—meaning, of course, that when the wind doesn't blow or the sun doesn't shine, then wind turbines and solar panels are useless. They also have low-power-density generating capabilities that must always be backed up by fossil fuel or nuclear, and their land-consuming needs have prevented them from being a major player in supplying electricity. Until these technological constraints are overcome, renewables will continue being a media-friendly niche source of energy to electricity.[38]

Figure 1-1

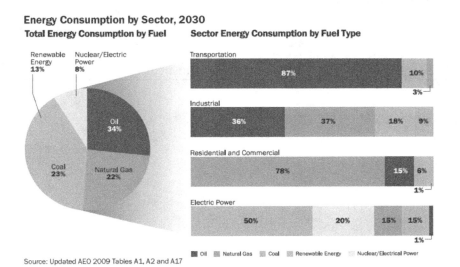

Observations of Figure 1-1

Fuel Source Supply projections to 2030 (shown on the left circle)	Infrastructure Demand projections to 2030 (shown on the right-side bar charts)
Oil 34%	Majority for the Transportation infrastructures and the Industrial infrastructure.
Natural Gas 22%	Primarily split among Residential and Commercial, Industrial, and continuously uninterruptable Electricity Generation, with some to Transportation.
Nuclear 8% and Coal 23%	100% is for continuously uninterruptable Electricity Generation and for the Industrial Sector.
Renewables Electricity 13%	Electricity Generation of _intermittent_ electricity and for Sectors of Industrial, Transportation, and Residential and Commercial. However, electricity alone does not support the transportation infrastructures and, thus, commerce.

Figure 1-2

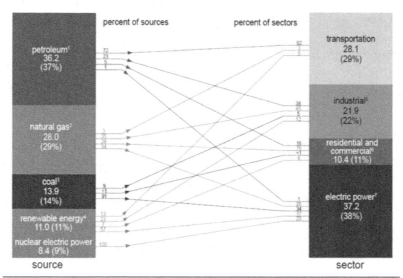

Observations of Figure 1-2

Energy consumption by SOURCE in 2017	Energy consumption by SECTOR in 2017
Petroleum	72% of petroleum goes to the Transportation Sector, but that represents 92 % of Transportation Sectors' demands, and 23% of Petroleum goes to the Industrial Sector to meet 38% of the demand in that sector.

Natural Gas	Almost equally split among Sectors of Industrial 35%, Residential and Commercial 28%, and continuously uninterruptable Electric Power 34%, with a small amount to the Transportation Sector.
Coal	91% of coal goes to the Electric Power Sector, but that represents only 34% of Electric Power Sector's demands.
Renewables Energy	The majority of 57% of Renewable Energy goes to *intermittent* Electric Power demands but is only 17% of the demand in that sector. Again, electricity alone does not support the transportation infrastructures.
Nuclear	100% of Nuclear goes to the Electric Power Sector, but that only represents 23% of continuously uninterruptible Electric Power demand with Natural Gas at 26%, Coal at 34%, and Renewable Energy at 17%.

In California, to meet 100% clean energy by 2045,[39] significant growth in renewables will be required to replace the electricity generation by nuclear and natural gas,[40] as the nuclear power plant at Diablo Canyon will be closing in 2025.

In comparing categories, bear in mind that the average amount of time that power is being produced varies among them, so that total energy obtained is not a simple function of power rating.

Recently, in California, the San Bernardino County Board of Supervisors slammed the brakes on big solar projects,[41] thereby highlighting a challenge California could face as it seeks to eliminate the use of fossil fuels and natural gas to generate electricity. San Bernardino locals soundly voiced their objections to those land-devouring, ecosystem-disrupting, unsightly monstrosities that lead to higher electricity prices and lower property values for nearby residents. The verdict, once again, was NIMBY (Not In My Back Yard)! So, with fewer and fewer places to locate these renewables farms, what's next?

In the increasingly likely event there will not be enough land permitted to build those huge intermittent electricity farms, and with continuously uninterruptible electricity generation now supplied by nuclear and natural gas rapidly vanishing from the grid, California's electricity will have to be imported from other states in order to make up the deficiencies of limited in-state generation. Such electricity imports will obviously come at a premium price for lower-income and blue-collar workers.

And what of the massive amount of electricity needed to charge the estimated 25 or 30 million electric vehicles in California? The utility companies have thus far had little to say about the alarming cost projections or how the state's residents would be impacted by the obviously higher rates authorized by California's Public Utilities Commission (PUC). And it's not just the total amount of electricity, but also the transmission and fast-charging capacity that will need to be built at current filling stations.

A Canadian engineer recently ran the numbers involved in the switchover to EVs and concluded that, in order to match the number of cars that a typical gasoline filling station today can service in a busy 12-hour period (2,000), an electric filling station would require 600 of the 50kw chargers. Even that conservative estimate would require a $24-million investment for each station just for the cheapest chargers. But there's more involved than expense.

For those 600 chargers, the station would need about 30 megawatts of power from the grid. If you think that seems like an incredible amount of electricity, you're right. Thirty megawatts are enough juice to power roughly 20,000 homes. In other words, powering these service stations of the future will require about the same amount of electricity as a city of 75,000 residents! Oh, and by the way, all that electricity, unlike off-hour home recharging, happens during peak-usage daylight hours. I see brownouts and blackouts in California's future. Carry a bag lunch. This could get ugly.

In addition to the huge investments at the electric service stations, utility companies will have to spend gazillions of dollars building a new grid, or merely billions to upgrade the current grid to prevent it from crashing. These mandated investments, naturally, will further drive up the cost of electricity for everyone just so a few elites can drive Teslas and the like.

Even at fast-charging stations, to fully charge an EV can take anywhere from 30 minutes to eight hours, depending on how much of a charge (empty to full or just topping off) the vehicle needs. The added cost of lounge areas that charging stations would need to install and maintain, or the holding areas for vehicles fully charged and waiting for customers to return from offsite dining, shopping or work, will be passed on to the consumer.

Since fossil fuels of oil, natural gas, and coal are energy-dense, portable and storable, with many useful by-products that create thousands of spinoff industries, there is no simple way to move from oil, coal, and natural gas to exclusive renewable electricity. Particularly, as has been pointed out, because the manufacture of all renewables also requires massive amounts of fossil fuels and other natural resources with proportionately little energy return. Some basic comparisons of energy density will help put things in perspective.

Aside from being an intermittent source of electricity, wind has very low energy density. In terms of manufacturing wind and solar devices, development may be constrained by the availability of materials, the cost of mining them, or the reclamation/decommissioning costs. An additional challenge is that even if unit prices of wind and solar devices drop, the costs of integrating wind and solar to the conventional grid and necessary build-out of new transmission lines runs into the billions.

There's no question that electric vehicles have some positive attributes: low refueling costs, no air pollutants at point of use, i.e., no tailpipes on the EVs, and quiet operation. But the crucial question remains, are they actually "clean and green"?[42]

EVs employ the marketing term "clean and green" because, after all, the vehicles have no tailpipes. But it has been pointed out, and accurately, that the EV exhaust outlets do exist, just many miles away. They exist at the mining operations for the lithium and cobalt used in the batteries, and at the power plants that produce the continuously uninterruptible power to charge those batteries. And the "tailpipes" also exist at the refineries that manufacture the chemicals and by-products that are the basis of all the products used in making each EV.

And, despite their promise, all-electric cars continue to be hampered by the same drawbacks that have haunted them for a century: high costs, limited range, slow recharge rates, lack of recharging stations, and a battery life of approximately ten years (as compared to conventional cars with their typical durability of 50-plus years).

Although modern lithium-ion batteries provide a fourfold improvement in energy density when compared with their older lead-acid cousins, they cannot hold a candle (no pun intended) to gasoline, as gasoline holds eighty times as much energy density than the lithium-ion battery. For today's EVs, the lithium-ion battery used in the Tesla weighs in excess of 1,000 pounds, while the iPhone battery is only 0.026kg.

As mentioned by the U.S. Energy Information Administration (EIA) in its Annual Energy Outlook of 2009, with projections of Energy Consumption by Sector to 2030,[43] and the EIA energy consumption projections to 2050 by fuel,[44] electricity by itself, especially intermittent electricity from renewables, cannot and will not power the world. Electricity alone cannot support the militaries, airlines, cruise ships, supertankers, container shipping, and trucking infrastructures. Nor can intermittent electricity from wind, solar, or batteries supply the many petroleum-sourced products that are demanded by every transportation and electricity generation infrastructure, products that are used in medications, cooling, heating, manufacturing, and agriculture and that, in so many ways, have become indispensable to our modern lives and lifestyles.

Chapter Two

Prosperous Societies and Energy
By Ronald Stein

Summary

For the seventy-five years since the end of World War II, we have enjoyed an era of relative peace and global prosperity. In fact, the economies of today's world are still being shaped by the post-World War II order, thanks to the interconnected economic trading systems put in place by the United States and its Allies after 1946.

Less well noted is the decisive role played by energy in that global war (and in World War I), as well as energy's equally significant role in giving birth to the relative peace and prosperity of the modern era. Historians, it seems, tend to overlook the demonstrable truth that World War II was won definitively by the Allies because they had more deep-earth minerals/fuels than did the Axis powers of Germany, Italy, and Japan, the resources required to fuel their militaries—i.e., to move planes, ships, troops, and supplies.

But understanding the centrality of energy in world affairs is absolutely essential to our coming to grips with the great global challenges that face us today and in the future. Simply stated, our prosperous world would never have come into being if the United States and its Allies did not have reliable, scalable, abundant, and affordable oil, natural gas, diesel and aviation fuel, and the market economies in place to exploit those energy resources.

Prosperous Societies and Energy

The abundant lifestyles so many of us enjoy depend on readily available energy that "makes products and moves things." These lavish, taken-for-granted benefits are traceable to two prime movers, which, more than any other factors, have made possible the everyday miracles of global commerce: the diesel engine and the jet turbine. Both of these fantastic modern workhorses get their energy manufactured from crude oil. The object lesson: Without transportation, there is no commerce.

Energy has transformed the horse-and-buggy world of less than two hundred years ago into today's global economy, supplying the insatiable power demands of militaries, airlines, cruise ships, supertankers, container shipping, and trucking infrastructures. In the span of two centuries, man has virtually eliminated weather-related deaths,[45] greatly extended life expectancies, and drastically reduced childbirth-related fatalities.

And, please note, the following industries are <u>increasing</u>, not <u>decreasing</u> their annual needs for fossil fuels to "make products and move things." For example:

- AIRLINES are accommodating 4.1 billion passengers per year with projections to 7.8 billion by 2036:[46]
  - ✓ Worldwide, there are currently more than 40,000 airports[47] of which more than 1,200 are commercial airports.[48]
  - ✓ Currently, there are about 39,000 planes in the world[49]—including all commercial and military planes.
  - ✓ Airlines are consuming more than 225 million gallons of aviation fuels <u>per day</u>[50] to move almost 10 million passengers (and other things), and those statistics are also increasing every year.

- Boeing, one of the world's biggest aircraft manufacturers, says that 39,620 new planes will be needed over the next 20 years. If accurate, the number of aircraft in the world will be 63,220 by 2037.[51]
- The number of airplanes that are in flight on average at any given time[52] worldwide is in the thousands (and all of them can be viewed at the app http://www.flightradar24.com/).
- Passenger projections for 2036 are in excess of 7 billion.[53]

- **CRUISE LINERS** are accommodating 25 million passengers per year:
  - More than 310 cruise liners[54] are consuming around 80,000 gallons of fuel <u>per day</u>, per liner.[55]
  - As a side note, the many billions of vehicle trips to and from airports, hotels, ports, and amusement parks are increasing each year.
- **MERCHANT SHIPS** (about 60,000) are currently involved in commercial maritime transport[56] moving products around the world:
  - Merchant ships' fuel consumption is more than 200 tons of fuel <u>per day</u> per ship.[57]
- **TRUCKING**: More than 15 million commercial vehicles are moving products in America alone.[58]
  - Their fuel consumption is in excess of 140 million gallons of fuel <u>per day</u>.[59]
- **VEHICLES** to move people around the world:
  - There are currently an estimated 1.2 billion vehicles on the world's roads with projections of 2 billion by 2035.[60] By some estimates, the total number of vehicles worldwide could double to 2.5 billion by 2050.
  - Registration of electric vehicles is projected to be, percentagewise, only in the single digits, around 5 to 7 percent. If projections come to reality by 2035, 5 to 7 percent of the 2 billion vehicles would equate to 125 million EVs on the world's roads. The bad news, environmentally speaking, is that would also represent more than 125 <u>billion</u>

pounds of lithium-ion batteries that will need to be disposed of in the decades ahead.
- MILITARY energy needs worldwide are increasing, country by country, each year:
  ✓ The military's planes, ships, vehicles, troops and armories are also increasing each year.
- SPACE TRAVEL and exploration:
  ✓ International participation in the space program is increasing each year. The Saturn V rocket that launched the Apollo spacecraft was 363 feet tall and weighed 6.2 million pounds, the weight of about 400 elephants.

From the above statistics, it's easy to project the negative impacts of getting off fossil fuels on the following industries and infrastructures, all of which are driven by the energy density of oil, coal, and natural gas:

- All medications and medical equipment that are made with the chemicals from crude oil.
- Commercial aviation that is currently accommodating 4 billion passengers annually.
- Cruise liners that have been accommodating more than 25 million passengers annually.
- Merchant ships that move merchandise worth billions of dollars daily.
- The military presence through which nations historically project their strength and feel protected one from another.
- Fertilizers that facilitate growth of much of the food that feeds billions annually.
- Vehicle manufacturing, all parts of which are based on chemicals and by-products from fossil fuels.
- Asphalt used for road construction.

As our industrial societies evolved out of the horse-and-buggy days (when life expectancies were in the 40- to 50-year range, infant mortality rates were high, and weather-related deaths were catastrophic), we established a standard of living based on fossil fuel-driven infrastructures. Jet and diesel engines supply our military and transportation needs, while medications, vaccines, fertilizers, and thousands of other essential products are manufactured from the chemicals and by-products of crude oil. Our economies also make significant use of the power density aspects of the fossil fuel commodities of coal, oil, and gas.[61]

Here is a partial list of the thousands of fossil fuel products that intermittent electricity from wind and solar are <u>incapable</u> of manufacturing:

> Medications, vaccines, cosmetics, iPhones, fertilizers, refrigerators, jet fuel, computers, calculators, pharmaceuticals, air conditioners, heaters, solvents, diesel, motor oil, bearing grease, floor wax, ballpoint pens, football cleats, sweaters, boats, insecticides, bicycle tires, nail polish, fishing lures, dresses, tires, golf bags, cassettes, dishwashers, tool boxes, shoe polish, caulking, petroleum jelly, CDs and CD players, faucet washers, antiseptics, curtains, basketballs, soap, antihistamines, purses, shoes, dashboards, cortisone, putty, dyes, pantyhose, refrigerants, percolators, life jackets, rubbing alcohol, linings, skis, TV cabinets, shag rugs, tool racks, car battery cases, epoxy, paint, mops, slacks, umbrellas, yarn, hair colorings, roofing, toilet seats, lipstick, denture adhesive, ice cube trays, synthetic rubber, speakers, plastic wood, electric blankets, glycerin, tennis rackets, dice, nylon rope, candles, house paint, roller skates, surfboards, wheels, aspirin, safety glasses, antifreeze, football helmets, clothes, toothbrushes, ice chests, footballs, detergents, vaporizers, heart valves, parachutes, enamel, dishes, cameras, anesthetics, artificial turf, artificial limbs, dentures, folding doors, cold cream, drinking cups, car enamel, shaving cream, golf balls, toothpaste, gasoline, ink, dishwashing liquids, paint brushes, telephones, toys, unbreakable

dishes, antiseptics, dolls, car sound insulation, tires, motorcycle helmets, linoleum, tents, refrigerator linings, paint rollers, electrician's tape, model cars, glue, roller-skate wheels, trash bags, soap dishes, permanent press clothes, hand lotions, clothesline, dyes, soft contact lenses, shampoos, food preservatives, fishing rods, oil filters, combs, transparent tape, upholstery, disposable diapers, sports car bodies, salad bowls, awnings, ammonia, dresses, safety glass, hair curlers, pajamas, VCR tapes, eyeglasses, pillows, vitamin capsules, movie film, loudspeakers, ice buckets, credit cards, crayons, insect repellents, water pipes, roofing shingles, fishing boots, balloons, shower curtains, garden hoses, plywood adhesive, milk jugs, beach umbrellas, rubber cement, sunglasses, cold cream, bandages, drinking cups, guitar strings, false teeth, toothbrushes, perfume, luggage, wire insulation, fan belts, shower doors, carpeting, LP records, hearing aids, wading pools.

The energy resources vital to all of us in our daily lives can be summarized with a simple acronym, T E C H M A P:

Transportation:	cars, trucks, freight trains, planes, trains, ships, roads
Electricity	lighting, refrigerators, heaters, computers, phones, TV's
Cooking	ovens, stoves, microwaves, barbeque grills
Heating	homes, businesses, warehouses, vehicles, public spaces
Manufacturing	lubrication, packaging, processing, delivery
Agriculture	framing, ranching, all food products
Products	medical care, sanitation, lubrication, education, technology

The developed countries have enjoyed the benefits to human activities, lifestyles, and prosperity afforded by fossil fuels for the last couple of centuries, but almost half the world[62]—over three billion people in underdeveloped countries—live on less than $2.50 a day. At least 80% of humanity lives on less than $10 a day, and in those countries income inequality is widening. In 2005, the wealthiest 20% of the world accounted for 76.6% of total private consumption. Incredibly, the poorest 40 percent of the world's population accounts for 5 percent of global income. The richest 20 percent accounts for three-quarters of world income. Water problems affect half of humanity.

- There are approximately 11,000,000 child deaths every year, of which more than 70 percent are attributable to six causes: diarrhea, malaria, neonatal infection, pneumonia, preterm delivery, or lack of oxygen at birth. About 29,000 children under the age of five—21 each minute—die every day, mainly from preventable causes.[63]

When you include fatalities of "other than children," the numbers get even worse:

- 8,000,000 world cancer deaths[64] per year.
- 5,000,000 tobacco-related deaths per year,[65] and current trends show that tobacco use will cause more than 8,000,000 deaths annually by 2030.
- 4.2 million deaths every year as a result of exposure to ambient (outdoor) air pollution.[66]
- 3.8 million deaths every year as a result of household exposure to smoke from dirty cook stoves and fuels.[67]
- 2.3 million women and men around the world succumb to work-related accidents[68] or diseases every year according to the International Labor Organization estimates; this corresponds to over 6,000 deaths every single day. Worldwide, there are around 340 million occupational

accidents and 160,000,000 victims of work-related illnesses annually.
- 1.23 million world traffic deaths[69] per year.
- 270,000 pedestrians killed[70] on roads each year.
- 190,900 premature deaths caused by drugs[71] (range: 115,900 to 230,100). Opioids account for most drug-related deaths[72] and in most cases such deaths are avoidable.

After that slice of morbidity, I'd like to present a tad of relatively good news by looking at the safety of nuclear power reactors.[73]

From the outset, there has been a strong awareness of the potential hazard of both nuclear criticality and release of radioactive materials from generating electricity with nuclear power. As in other industries, the design and operation of nuclear power plants aim to minimize the likelihood of accidents and avoid major human consequences when they occur.

- Nuclear-related deaths: Worldwide total (not annually, but from inception of nuclear) nuclear deaths[74] including Three Mile Island (March 1979), Chernobyl (April 1986), and Fukushima (March 2011) are <u>less</u> than 200.

To put the above numbers into perspective, of the many millions who die each year from starvation, diseases, weather, air pollution, driving, working, walking, and overdosing, nuclear-related deaths have been less than 200 worldwide, not annually, but from inception of the industry.

There have, to date, been three major reactor accidents in the history of civil nuclear power—Three Mile Island (March 1979), Chernobyl (April 1986), and Fukushima (March 2011). One was contained without harm to anyone; the next involved an intense fire without provision for containment; and the third severely tested the containment, allowing some release of radioactivity. These are the only major accidents to have occurred in more than 17,000 cumulative reactor-years of commercial nuclear power operations in 33 countries.

Today there are about 450 nuclear reactors[75] operating around the world. Additionally, there are 140 nuclear-powered ships[76] that have accumulated 12,000 reactor years of "safe" marine operation.

The evidence over six decades shows that nuclear power is a safe means of generating electricity. The risk of accidents in nuclear power plants is low and declining. The consequences of an accident or terrorist attack are minimal compared with other commonly accepted risks. Radiological effects on people of any radioactive releases can be and have been avoided.

Getting off fossil fuels, the primary supplier of energy to the numerous infrastructures listed above, will mean turning off the energy supply to all those TECHMAP resources. This, in turn, could lead to shorter life spans, diminished transportation infrastructures, and more weather-related deaths. Not to belabor the point, but intermittent electricity from renewables is simply incapable of providing the collective energy demands of those vital infrastructures.

Interestingly, the primary economic reasons that oil refineries even exist are to manufacture the aviation, diesel, and gasoline fuels for our military and transportation industries. From one 42-gallon barrel of oil about 19.4 gallons of gasoline are manufactured. The rest (over half) is used to manufacture the chemicals and by-products that are part of our daily lifestyles.[77]

It may sound shocking, but there are actually no economic reasons just to manufacture the chemicals and by-products from crude oil that are the basis of the thousands of products[78] that have transformed people's lives for the better and that have become indispensable to transportation infrastructures, electricity generation, cooling, heating, and agriculture.

The focus of this chapter, thus far, has been on the energy needs of prosperous societies, but what of the world's poor and less prosperous societies? Economic development requires access to more than just electricity; it also requires access to affordable, abundant, and reliable energy, which has been the defining characteristic of every developed nation.

Many of those living in undeveloped nations[79] that lack electricity, power, or energy, will at some point be seeking to acquire the same standard of living enjoyed by those in developed countries, those who are the fortunate beneficiaries of fossil fuels that provide them the cornucopia of products not only for their daily lives, but for their national infrastructures. And the dilemma faced by these energy have-nots is compounding daily as the world's population grows from the current 7.7 billion to a projected 9.7 billion in 2050.[80]

Developing countries tend to have many common characteristics. For example, with regard to health risks, they commonly have: low levels of access to safe drinking water, sanitation and hygiene; energy poverty; high levels of pollution (e.g., air pollution, indoor air pollution, water pollution); a high proportion of people with tropical and infectious diseases; high incidence of road traffic accidents. Too often, there are also widespread poverty, low education levels, inadequate access to family planning services, and correspondingly shorter life expectancies, higher infant mortality rates, and greater numbers of weather-related deaths.

For developing countries to attain any semblance of the prosperity enjoyed by developed countries, we can say with absolute certainty that the world isn't using too much fossil fuels, <u>it's not using enough</u>. More consumption of everything manufactured from crude oil by the world's energy-poor would help save the lives of hundreds of thousands of impoverished people every year. These are people who currently die premature deaths due to indoor air pollution caused by burning low-energy-density biomass (such as straw, dung, twigs, wood, and leaves) to cook their food and heat their homes.

High-energy societies, on the other hand, enjoy a much higher standard of living than do their low-energy counterparts, and these gains have led, understandably, to expectations of continued improvements.

With a robust economy, the good news is that we can "afford" to micromanage almost anything, but the bad news is that the costs associated with such micromanagement are being born by rich and poor alike; and may be contributing to the growing homeless and poverty population percentages in the nation. Blue-collar workers, for instance, absorb a disproportionate share of energy costs relative to their total earnings.

The renewable sectors of wind and solar, like every other infrastructure, are dependent on the products manufactured out of crude oil for all their components so they can produce emission-free intermittent electricity for blue-collar workers.

But renewable electricity simply cannot support the energy needs of the military or medical industries, nor supply the fuels needed by planes and ships, and by the jet and diesel engines that are the basis of our transportation systems. In addition, even the components of the EV and the wind and solar renewable industries are all manufactured from chemicals manufactured from fossil fuels.

Figure 2-1

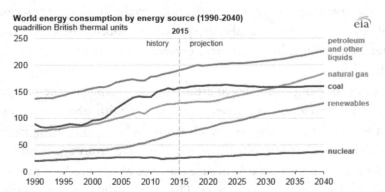

Observations on Figure 2-1

Petroleum and other liquids	Projections to 2040 reflect the continued domination for fossil fuels to support the jet and diesel engines which are the basis of transportation, and the numerous products manufactured from fossil fuels that are the basis of every infrastructure.
Natural gas	Increasingly being used for continuously uninterruptible electricity generation.
Coal	Diminishing worldwide for continuously uninterruptible electricity generation, as natural gas and intermittent electricity from renewables provide the supply. Reflects the populations of India and China joining an energy society that continues to decrease its coal usage and increase its use of electricity from renewables like wind and solar.
Renewables	Continuous gains to provide _intermittent_ electricity to the grid, but electricity alone cannot support our transportation infrastructures.
Nuclear	Light increase worldwide for generation of continuously uninterruptible zero-emission electricity.

'Clean Energy'

The phrase is commonly used—or overused, to be quite honest about it. All of us, even those who understand that oil, natural gas, and coal run the world, often refer to wind and solar as "clean" without even questioning it. It is, however, definitely time to do some questioning.

What is it that makes wind and solar so clean and fossil fuels so dirty? Mostly perception and hype. With wind and solar, you don't see anything getting burned (perception) like you do with oil, natural gas, and coal. And it's the burning that creates pollution (hype).

But is that really true of wind and solar? We "feel" like they're clean because we don't burn them. Well... at least not directly. But let's drill down a bit. These industries aren't born of unicorns and pixie dust. Producing solar panels and windmills requires a lot of mining for resources, especially for rare-earth minerals.

China owns 95% of the rare-earth market, and the Chinese government, last anybody checked, isn't all that protective of the environment. Their mining projects are creating giant, toxic and radioactive lakes.[81] It's a serious problem, one they will be dealing with for decades to come.

Even though California and the federal government both have transparency in their supply chain laws (starting with The California Transparency in Supply Chains Act SB 657[82] and followed by the U.S. With Business Supply Chain Transparency on Trafficking and Slavery Act of 2014 HR 4842),[83] the richest and most powerful companies in the world are still making excuses for not investigating their supply chains of lithium and cobalt for their lithium-ion batteries and are continuing to power their manufactured EVs with "dirty batteries." For example, the lithium-ion battery for the Tesla weighs in excess of 1,000 pounds, while the iPhone battery is only 0.026 kg.

And what about land use for electricity generation?[84] The U.S. Energy Information Administration (EIA) estimates that natural gas and coal use about 12 acres of land per megawatt of electricity produced. Solar and wind gobble up four and six times that amount of land, respectively. What's so clean about that? Not much. Better check "land use" off the environmental "virtue" list.

There are other environmental impacts to consider. Industrial wind and solar projects kill a lot of wildlife. Wind turbines alone are estimated to kill 600,000 birds and a million bats each year. And bats are very important to our ecosystem because they are essential to pollination. Wind and solar farmers can acquire an eagle "take" permit from the U.S. Fish and Wildlife Service (USFWS) that allows the site to participate in the nationwide killing of as many as 4,200 bald eagles annually.[85]

In addition, wind turbines cause visual blight and have negative health impacts on the people who live around them.

New York pediatrician Dr. Nina Pierpont studied the effects of wind turbines in North America and Europe and found that humans are affected by low-frequency noise and vibrations from wind turbines through their ear bones, much as fish and some amphibians are affected by undersea sound waves. For susceptible persons, extended exposure can even cause psychosis.

In 2008, Professor Arnold Wilkins, emeritus professor, Department of Psychology, University of Essex, discovered wind turbines can trigger epileptic fits and seizures[86] if the light flickers more than three times a second. Skeptics would say turbines don't usually move that fast. However, a farm of turbines can cause multiple shadows to flicker even faster than the minimum risk speed, depending on the angle of the sun.

Keep in mind that deep-earth minerals/fuels have been running the world since they began fueling the industrial revolution some 200 years ago, and they still carry more than 80 percent of the load per the EIA Energy International Outlook.[87] Wind and solar currently contribute less than three percent to our energy use. For that small amount of power, we are forced to deal with a significant amount of environmental nastiness.

The point of all this is not to dismiss or even disparage wind and solar, but to talk about them in a way that sheds some light on the false perceptions pushed upon us by many in the media and academia (not to mention the political realm). It is patently false to say deep-earth minerals/fuels are "dirty" while wind and solar are "clean."

For the thriving societies that have robust economies, various sources of energy, and numerous infrastructures that support those economies, the flowchart below from Lawrence Livermore National Laboratory helps to explain how energy integrates with the various infrastructures and their individual energy-consumption needs.

Energy is all about SUPPLY and DEMAND. The Lawrence Laboratory energy chart shows the energy sources on the left, i.e., the SUPPLY, and the consumption by infrastructure on the right, i.e., the DEMAND. Obviously, if there was no energy DEMAND by humanity, there would be no need for SUPPLY of the different types of energy as can be seen in the Energy Flow Chart: Charting the Complex Relationships Among Energy, Water, and Carbon.[88]

Figure 2-2

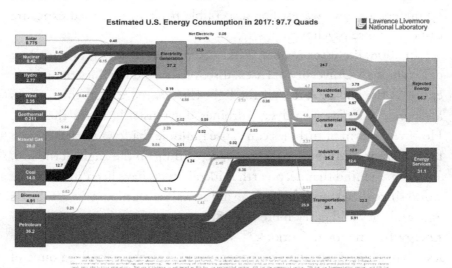

Observations of Figure 2-2

Source Supply (shown on the left side)	Infrastructure Demand (shown on the right side)
Petroleum	Majority used for the Transportation infrastructures and some to the Industrial infrastructure.
Natural Gas	Primarily split between continuously uninterruptible Electricity Generation and Industrial, with some to Residential and Commercial infrastructures.
Nuclear and Coal	100% is for continuously uninterruptible. Electricity Generation.
Renewables of Solar and Wind	100% is for Electricity Generation of *intermittent* electricity.

Social Innovation Creates Prosperous Societies[89]

Economists estimate that between 50 and 80 percent of economic growth comes from innovation and new knowledge of energy. Fossil fuel energy continues to be essential for manufacturing chemicals and by-products as the basic ingredients to things such as medications, air conditioners, heaters, buildings, and clothing which protect us from nature's hazards. Societies with fossil fuels have more clean water and better sanitation and have also reduced climate-related deaths by 98 percent over the last 80 years.[90]

- Extreme heat
- Extreme cold
- Floods
- Droughts
- Blizzards
- Hurricanes
- Earthquakes

- Tornadoes
- Tsunamis
- Volcanic eruptions
- Animals
- World domination of energy

U.S. Representative Alexandria Ocasio-Cortez ("AOC") wants us to construct a super-electrical grid to run the entire country. But many of our vital industries and services cannot run on electricity alone. The long list includes the medical industry, the military, airlines, container shipping, cruise liners, and the makers of the many thousands of essential products from fossil fuels.

Looking back just a few short centuries, we see how far we've come since the horse-and-buggy days. Fossil fuels now impact everyone's standards of living, providing us with medications, cosmetics, plastics, fertilizers, and thousands upon thousands of other essential products, along with affordable transportation from jet engines, diesel trucks, and automobiles that have been the primary cause of globalization.

And lest we forget, back in those "bad old" horse-and-buggy days, life was hard and dirty, with far too many weather-related deaths and a life expectancy somewhere in the forty-plus area.

Kicking our fossil fuel "habit" would reverse much of the incredible progress made over the last few centuries. Many of the products that we currently derive from fossil fuels—products that renewable electricity generation simply cannot provide—would vanish from our stores and supply chains or be rendered no longer affordable for most of us. Likely examples include medications, cosmetics, plastics, fertilizers, and transport by planes, ships, and motorized vehicles.

The growing prosperity made possible through the use of fossil fuels has reduced infant mortality, extended longevity (to more than 80 years), and contributed to a dramatic increase in the world's population. It has allowed us to move anywhere in the world via planes, trains, ships, and motor vehicles, while virtually eliminating deaths from extremes of weather.

There is no question that getting off-fossil fuels would reduce fossil fuel emissions, but it would also drastically impact the lifestyles that we've become accustomed to. More alarmingly, in this brave new fossil-fuel-free world, <u>surprisingly few of us would live beyond 40-plus years.</u> So, perhaps, one unintended "benefit" of our getting off-fossil fuels might be the virtual elimination of all those unfunded pension liabilities we keep reading about. Not a very good trade-off for a reduced life span.

The get-off-fossil-fuel leaders like Al Gore, billionaire environmental activist Tom Steyer,[91] former California Governors Jerry Brown and Arnold Schwarzenegger, and current Governor Gavin Newsom are all beating their drums for intermittent renewable electricity[92] from wind and solar to "save the world." Their impassioned campaign seems strangely oblivious of the fact that 100 percent of the industries that use fossil fuels to "make products and move things" in order to support economies around the world are *increasing*, not *decreasing*, their usage demand each year.

Our world has become accustomed to the continuing improvements to the standard of living provided by elaborate infrastructures (including the military) that support the prosperity of growing populations. But too few of us have been informed that these wonderful life improvements are all dependent on energy derived from fossil fuels.

The public, especially the homeless and poverty[93] populations that have paid dearly for the increasing micromanagement of our emissions and renewables, deserves to know the costs being incurred to reduce our minuscule contributions to the world's greenhouse gases.

Now consider this: With all the complexities of the oil-refining processes,[94] the Bureau of Labor Statistics shows that the downstream-energy-refining-sector has reduced injuries for more than 20 years. The Bureau of Labor Statistics charts show that the petroleum-refining sector of health and safety to be one of the safest industries to work in.[95]

Figure 2-3

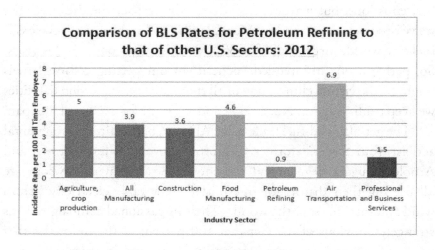

Observations of Figure 2-3

According to the BLS, as you can see, it's safer to work in a refinery than an office building!

Until electricity storage technology can support intermittent electricity from wind and solar, the world will continue to need redundant fossil fuel backups for those windless and cloudy days in order to provide continuously uninterruptible electricity to the economy.

As discussed earlier in this chapter, the U.S Energy Information Administration (EIA) graphical projections of energy consumption by source to 2040[96] and the Lawrence Laboratory flowchart of U.S Energy Consumption in 2017,[97] electricity alone, especially intermittent electricity from renewables, has not, and will not, run the economies of the world. Simply put, electricity by itself is unable to support the energy demands of the military, airlines, cruise ships, supertankers, container shipping, and trucking infrastructures. Nor can intermittent electricity from wind, solar, or batteries supply the many products from petroleum that are demanded by every transportation infrastructure, electricity generation, medications, cooling, heating, manufacturing, and agriculture that are the basis of everyone's standard of living.

Chapter Three

World Wars I and II Were Both Won With Energy
By Todd Royal

Summary

A widely recognized reason for the global prosperity and relative peace enjoyed by the West over the past seventy years is that the Western Allies won both World War I and World War II. Often overlooked, as a decisive factor in the Allies prevailing in both wars is that they had more deep-earth minerals/fuels to mobilize their militaries than did the Central Powers in 1914-1917 or, less than two decades later, the Axis Powers of Germany, Italy, and Japan.

Our prosperous world would never have come into being if the United States and its strategic Allies had not possessed reliable, scalable, abundant, flexible, and affordable oil, natural gas, diesel and aviation fuel energy resources to mobilize their militaries.

Today, the post-World War II order continues to shape today's world as a consequence of all the interconnected economic trading systems put in place by the United States and its Allies after 1946.

Figure 3-1

World War I Map[98]:

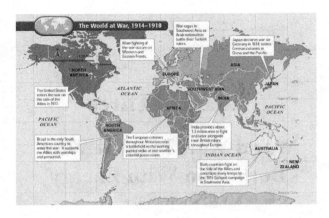

Figure 3-2

World War II Map[99]:

Britain, France, the Soviet Union, and the United States of America on one side, and the three Axis Powers of Germany, Japan and Italy on the other.

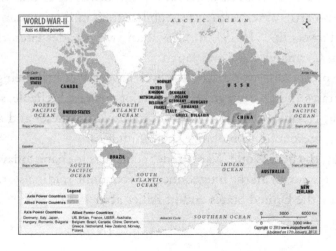

Description: Map shows the Axis and Allied power countries during World War II.

Introduction

Joseph Stalin once said: *"The war was decided by engines and octane."*

Winston Churchill agreed with Stalin on the critical importance of fuel: *"Above all, petrol governed every movement."*[100]

The two most devastating wars in the history of mankind (WWI & II) were won with enormous amounts of oil, coal, natural gas, and aviation fuel used by the victorious Allied nations and armies to move ships, planes, tanks and armor, trucks, troop carriers, weaponry, and anything else needed to assault and occupy nations. Since there are thousands upon thousands of books that have been written on the two world wars, the focus of this chapter will be confined to the energy aspects of Allied victory, specifically the significant contributions of oil in our winning WWI and oil's absolutely decisive contribution to Allied victory in WWII.

If the Allies had not won WWII, the world would be living under some form of totalitarian terror from the Nazis, Imperial Japanese, Fascist Italians, or Communist-Socialist Russians. We can thank oil and abundant energy for our current international order, and for the blessing of going more than seventy years now without another world war.[101]

Energy in the form of nuclear weapons that were used twice in WWII has been the sole reason why the world has averted a third, and even deadlier world war since 1946. Whatever else this concentrated form of energy has or has not accomplished, it has made unlimited worldwide warfare obsolete (though, of course, regional conflicts with conventional weapons persist). If Nation A attacks Nation B or a host of other nations, bundled energy in the form of nuclear weapons can annihilate cities, states, nations, continents, potentially even the entire world. Energy is saving mankind from itself.

The tragedy of the First World War can be summed up as the sacrifice of the ordinary man. The majority of the 15 to 20 million killed were male soldiers. This ghastly toll decimated European societies, and the European insistence on human rights and equality under the law has never been the same.

In the aftermath of the Great War, Europe underwent a deep and continentwide depression. The vainglorious pursuit of invincibility and indestructible armies that could contain peace forever after centuries of bloodshed was finally seen as all for naught. Totalitarian, maniacs, post-WWI, believed anything was possible after the French army was destroyed. Great Britain was still reeling from the disastrous consequences of the Pals battalions, comprised of friends, neighbors, and colleagues all recruited together, which saw entire English neighborhoods wiped out during fighting like the Battle of the Somme.[102]

WWII, in scale, magnitude, horrors, and casualties, easily overtook WWI. An incredible amount of energy was consumed and unleashed the worst human catastrophe in recorded history. One thing the Allies definitely had over the Axis Powers of Germany, Italy, and Japan was a gargantuan amount of oil. The Allies consumed over 7 billion gallons of oil prosecuting the war.[103] They had more access to and use of oil to power their war machines.

In fact, the fossil fuel-driven economies of the Axis and Allies had vastly different capabilities. German, Italian, and Japanese war industries were disjointed, and few complementary economic relationships existed. Each Axis country's industrial expertise rarely led to integrated material sharing with one another. On the other hand, the Allies produced superb weaponry, but what made the final, victorious difference was:

> "Critical areas such as transport, planes, merchant ships, locomotives, food supplies, medicines, <u>oil production</u>, and metals production, the Allies not only outproduced the Axis powers but indeed swamped them."[104]

Figure 3-3

HOW ENERGY WON BOTH WARS

World War I type-of-energy shown by the EIA[105], illustrating how oil, natural gas, and coal exploded before, during, and after WWI:

Link with quote explaining the above EIA graph: *"World War One was the first conflict to be fueled by oil. For the first time in warfare, petroleum possession became the lifeblood of armies and it entered into the strategic machinations of military planners from all nations involved."*[106]

Figure 3-4

Poster depicting need to conserve energy in World War II[107]:

What we saw from both wars was the beginning of the modern, energy-industrial-complex. We saw how the quest for deep-earth minerals and the use of energy led to today's world order, a global arrangement that has been in place under U.S. leadership for more than seventy years. Both world conflicts began for all the same age-old reasons, which range from conquest and ruling over others to the pursuit of resources (fossil fuels being the modern goal), with the military technology used for victory a given. War plus energy always produces the same results: battles fought, lives shattered, and human nature unchanged since the beginning of time.

The mechanized, industrialized warfare of WWII still affects people-groups, countries, and entire regions of the world. The Chinese, for instance, still hate the Japanese over the butchery inflicted upon China by invading Japanese forces from 1931 to 1946. It should surprise no one when the Chinese consistently break environmental treaties and treat energy as the pillar of their economy and existential survival after the Japanese raped, pillaged, and plundered China for over a decade. The Chinese are militarizing the South China Sea and Asia into the Indian Ocean so they can have land and sea buffers to keep them protected against future invasions.[108]

Figure 3-5

Map of China's recent incursions into the South China Sea[109]:

Certainly it is understandable that, after suffering the slaughter of more than fifteen to sixteen million of their soldiers and citizens (this is a conservative estimate) by the Japanese Imperial Army, the Chinese would regard abundant energy in whatever form (coal-fired power plants, nuclear power plants, imported natural gas) as an essential source of deterrence against real and perceived foes, right after their nuclear weapons and growing army.[110] Like the Chinese, Vladimir Putin's Russia also suffered disastrous losses from an invading army in World War II—in their case Nazi Germany, from 1941 until 1945 when the Germans were ultimately defeated. Under the circumstances, Putin and the Russian people's ambition for a land buffer between Western and Eastern Europe can hardly be dismissed as irrational.

This understandable paranoia has guided Putin to weaponize his country's vast oil and natural gas resources to ensure that an outside force never again invades Russia. The death toll inflicted on both China and Russia by invading armies ensures that they will always maintain large, aggressive armies, which will always need enormous amounts of fossil fuels to deter any future aggressors.[111]

Figure 3-6

Map of former Soviet Union[112]:

Figure 3-7

Map of Soviet Union after it was broken up[113]:

Current world governing systems, regimes, and ideologies all emerged from the chaotic aftermath of WWII, as did the need for a stable, prosperous peace that will not lead to another global war. This isn't an attempt to redefine, litigate, or explain either war; instead the focus here is on what type of energy won and defined those great wars, and led to our current systems.

It wasn't renewable electricity or nuclear, but oil, coal, natural gas, and aviation fuel. Especially oil and coal. When future wars, conflicts, or annexations take place, leaders and militaries will never rely on solar panels, windmills, biomass, or hydroelectric dams. They will want fossil fuels for their militaries, and 100 percent secure energy and electricity that come from fossil fuels. Nuclear power is the fuel of choice for any modern, blue-water navy in the 21st century.

Today's peace, which has prevailed since WWII, will endure only if the West, led by the U.S., continues fossil-fuel domination. Otherwise another Axis-type power may well arise, using oil, natural gas, coal, and nuclear to conquer and enslave mankind. Hitler, Stalin, Tojo, Churchill, and Roosevelt all understood that abundant, reliable, scalable, affordable, flexible, and safe energy would win WWII, and would decide if democracy or dictators would rule the world.[114]

How Oil in 1942 Changed the War and World

President Woodrow Wilson called World War I "the war to end all wars," but unfortunately, as the world has seen, nothing could have been farther from the truth.[115] WWI did not solve the problem of German militarism that had started in the late 1800s. This, in turn, allowed Italy and Japan to feel emboldened and undeterred by the Allies who should have allowed General John "Blackjack" Pershing to march into Berlin and occupy the city, arrest both the German high command and its leading political leaders while taking over their oil-and-coal-driven economy.

The most important year of WWII was 1942. Mid-1942 saw the Axis enjoying advantages by having France out of the war while suffering under German occupation. The German U-boat campaign made passage across the Atlantic for the Americans and Canadians deadly and treacherous for transporting troops and supplies. The British Empire was crippled, which, in turn, restricted the British economy in the amount of imports, exports, and commerce that could be conducted. Germany occupied not only most of "Fortress Europe" but Asian landmasses from the Volga River to the Atlantic Ocean, plus large swaths of North Africa. And what wasn't under Axis control in these continents and landmasses had Axis sympathies.

Japan obliterated eastern Asia and most of the Western Pacific before and after Pearl Harbor. All European colonial powers had been defeated, and their resources under the so-called Greater East Asia Co-Prosperity Sphere were under Japanese control. China and Korea were being raped physically, mentally, and emotionally, and stripped of resources by the Japanese Imperial Army and government. Russia was still weakened from the Bolshevik Revolution, Stalin's murderous purges, and U.S. military reductions post-WWI. Neutral countries such as "Portugal, Spain, Sweden, Switzerland, Turkey, Sweden, and

Switzerland," were all Axis-friendly or made "a great deal of money from favorable trade and commerce with the Third Reich." So, then, what changed the outcome of the war and, later, the brutal totalitarian nature of the world that prevailed from the end of WWI until late 1943. One thing: OIL.[116]

Figure 3-8

Map of German U-Boat campaign in the Atlantic[117]:

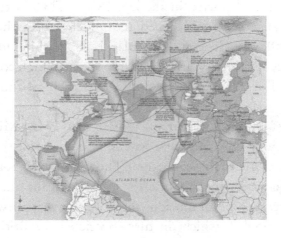

Figure 3-9

Map of JAPANESE GREATER EAST ASIA Co-PROSPERITY SPHERE[118]:

In 1942, with the Soviet Union mobilizing and the U.S. joining the British in the war effort, a new alliance suddenly had control over most of the world's oil supplies, which allowed greater mobility and range of naval operations.[119]

Germany, Japan, and Italy were no match for the combined navies of the Americans and British. Even though the British Empire was no longer what it had been before WWII, it still had access to natural resources (oil, coal, and natural gas) in Australia, Canada, Africa, and, thanks to its new ally, America.

The Third Reich under Hitler, by contrast, produced enough coal annually for its large electrical plants, steel production, and coal liquefaction efforts to power their military-industrial-complex war efforts, but lacked the availability of an abundant and reliable supply of oil and natural gas.

One advantage that the Allies began exploiting in 1942 was that the Germans, Italians, and Japanese had limited experience in producing oil as well as limited engineering experience in building and maintaining oil fields that produced refined products. The three Axis powers did not understand domestic output and the need for a skilled labor force to fuel their war machines that were in desperate need of oil, natural gas, and coal. To solve their oil issue the Nazis attempted large-scale production of coal into synthetic oil. This effort was never successful on a big enough scale to overcome Allied fossil fuel production.[120]

The Allies successfully coordinated their economic and energy efforts versus the Axis. But the Axis failed to coordinate their macroeconomic energy policies, which led to lower production figures of oil, coal, and aviation fuel. These critical energy imbalances only grew as the war continued. As a result, defeat for the Axis Powers soon became only a matter of time.

Energy created a strategic anomaly that Germany and Japan could never overcome. The U.S. was basically "immune from enemy attack of any sort" and allowed their energy production to exceed "three times as much fuel of all sorts, as all the other Allied and Axis nations *combined*." Moreover, the U.S. provided "90 percent of the Allies' aviation fuel requirements." The energy advantages, which the Allies enjoyed and exploited, allowed them to fly more sorties, attack more countries using thousands of tanks and armor, trucks, troop carriers, weaponry, and anything else needed to assault and occupy nations (starting in North Africa in November, 1942) while destroying enemy militaries.[121]

The Japanese attempted to exploit the Dutch East Indies via Royal Dutch Shell oil, and began refining products, but these efforts were stymied through oil-fueled U.S. submarine and aircraft blockades.

Eventually it was the combined might of Britain, America, Canada, Australia and the Soviet Union, backstopped by enormous amounts of shippable oil, natural gas, gasoline, diesel, aviation fuels, and coal, that obliterated the Nazi war machine, and did the same to Italian efforts at recreating the Roman Empire and the totalitarian nightmare for Asia that was Imperial Japan.

None of this, however, was possible until the Allies controlled the world's oil and coal supply.[122] The tides of war only began turning inexorably the Allies way once their fossil fuel supplies overpowered the Axis powers, which began taking shape in 1942.[123]

WWII's Energy Turning Point

The North African campaign of WWII that was being fought over Middle Eastern oil resources occurred from June 10, 1940, to May 13, 1943. These battles were fought in the Libyan and Egyptian deserts, and in Morocco, Algeria, and Tunisia. The turning point of the North African campaign, and possibly the entire war, is that German General Rommel was never able to persuade Hitler and Generals Franz Halder and Friedrich Paulus of the German General Staff to seize and hold the Suez Canal in Egypt.

If Rommel marches forward and captures Alexandria, Egypt, and the Suez Canal in tandem with German Army groups linking up in the oil-rich Caucasus, the result is not only an Axis-controlled Mediterranean, but the Eastern Front in Russia is suddenly within strategic grasp. WWII then takes on a different strategic and tactical direction. With defeat of Russia and the seizing of its supplies, along with increased amounts of Middle Eastern oil thanks to their capture of Suez, Germany would have access to abundant supplies of oil, diesel, gasoline, aviation fuels, and coal.

This bold move would have cut off the British from their oil supplies around the Eastern Mediterranean and would have left the entire region, which was considered one of the war's most strategic bodies of water, firmly under Hitler's control.

Figure 3-10

MAP OF NORTH AFRICA CAMPAIGN FIGHTING[124]:

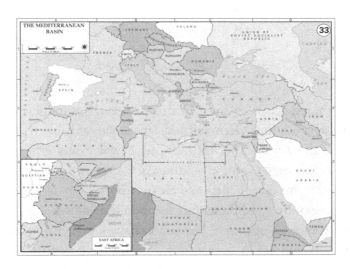

Figure 3-11

MAP OF MIDDLE EAST OIL SUPPLIES[125]:

PROVEN OIL RESERVES (BILLION BARRELS)							OIL PRODUCTION (1,000 BARRELS/DAY)					
	BP (2013)	OGJ (2013)	EIA (2013)	OPEC (2013)	% of World	R/P ratio		BP (2013)	OGJ (2013)	EIA (2013)	OPEC (2013)	Oil Wells
BAHRAIN	-	0.12	0.12	-	-	-	BAHRAIN		41	55	168	496
IRAN	157.0	157.3	154.6	157.3	9.4	-	IRAN	3,680	3,000	3,589	3,740	2,074
IRAQ	150.0	140.3	141.4	140.3	9.0	-	IRAQ	3,115	2,918	2,987	2,942	1,526
KUWAIT	101.5	101.5	104.0	101.5	6.1	89	KUWAIT	3,127	2,454	2,797	2,978	1,286
OMAN	5.5	5.5	5.5	5.5	0.3	16	OMAN	922	919	924	814	4,918
QATAR	23.9	25.2	25.4	25.2	1.4	33	QATAR	1,966	741	1,579	734	513
SAUDI ARABIA	265.9	265.9	267.9	265.9	15.9	63	SAUDI ARABIA	11,530	9,513	11,726	9,763	2,895
SYRIA	2.5	2.5	2.5	2.5	0.1	41.7	SYRIA	164	168	176	182	146
UAE	97.8	97.8	97.8	97.8	5.9	79	UAE	3,380	2,651	3,213	2,653	1,458
YEMEN	3.0	3.0	3.0	-	0.2	45	YEMEN	180	184	171	161	2,578
WORLD	1669	1645	1526	1478	100	53	WORLD	86,152	74,680	89,344	72,859	893,249

Sources: BP Statistical Review of World Energy (2003); Oil & Gas Journal (Dec. 2, 2013); Energy Information Administration (EIA, DOE/USA) website; OPEC Annual Statistical Bulletin (2013)
Notes: The data are for proven, recoverable, conventional oil reserves. Data on Share (%) of world and Reserves/Production (R/P ratio in years) come from BP (2013).

Sources: BP Statistical Review of World Energy (2003); Oil & Gas Journal (Dec. 2, 2013); Energy Information Administration (EIA, DOE/USA) website; OPEC Annual Statistical Bulletin (2013)
Notes: Number of producing oil wells from OGJ (2003).

Figure 3-12

Oil in decisive battles in World War II in or near Soviet Union[126]:

With shared access to some of this oil, coal, natural gas, gasoline, diesel, and aviation fuel, German's ally, Japan, suddenly has the resources to take on the American Marines and Naval assets while possibly solidifying their own Chinese holdings. Oil is thus the key to the war, powering all forms of vehicular and air transport. From aviation fuel for air forces to gasoline and diesel fuel for mobile armies and mechanized fighting forces, and, of course, blue-water navies, everything starts with oil. Rommel's success in Suez could have meant an entirely different world than the one we've all enjoyed for the last seventy-plus years.

What Have We Learned From WWI & II?

The absolute primacy of fossil fuels for the survival of our modern societies is one obvious lesson not learned from our two world wars, or from the Cold War, or more recent geopolitical nightmares. At least not learned by those of today's generation of voters and citizens who believe in the feasibility of a "Green New Deal," or think that global warming is the number-one issue for nations and societies. Assuming that we've not seen the end of armed conflict (an extremely safe bet), there will be more wars and militaries to fight them. Obviously, then, the "Green New Deal" as currently envisioned will never work.[127] No military on earth can function on intermittent electricity to move its ships, planes, tanks and armor, trucks, troop carriers, weaponry and anything else needed to defend its own territory or assault and occupy other nations.

The U.S., and any nation that goes down the primrose path of believing in climate change, global warming, or the "Green New Deal," faces an existential threat that will bankrupt their countries and set themselves up to be conquered and enslaved.[128] If the "Green New Deal" is actually implemented by weak-willed leaders and political parties, then expect another Hitler, Stalin, Tojo, or Mussolini to rise from the proverbial ashes and make deadly use of oil, natural gas, coal, and nuclear energy to crush all the postwar affluence that our grandparents and great-grandparents gave their lives and ruined their generational-selves to make possible.

In last century's global conflicts, as we've tried to show, civilization and freedom-loving countries were saved by oil. The lesson should be clear: Either take an all-of-the-above approach to energy, one that involves fossil fuels, nuclear and renewables, or be prepared to be subjugated again by countries (such as China, Russia, Iran, and North Korea) that want to set the world on fire the way the Axis attempted to do in WWII, and the Central Powers in WWI. Oil was the lifeblood that stopped them then, and it will be the essential resource we will need to check, deter and defeat tomorrow's enemies as well.

Meanwhile, oil will continue winning the peace that has served the world better than at any point in recorded history. Unless, that is, we in the West are too weak to resist the environmental movement's totalitarian nature. Unless, in a misguided quest to stop global warming, we do away with fossil fuels, thereby pulling the plug on our own world-leading economic power and undermining our own national security as well as the world's precarious balance of power.

It is no exaggeration to say that the safety and security of the world come from fracking in U.S. shale fields in states like Texas and Pennsylvania. With the U.S. now the leader in controlling the world's oil and natural gas supplies, world wars no longer threaten at this time. Oil carried the day in WWII, and it will ultimately defeat China, North Korea, Iran and Russia today. As long as Russia pursues this same geopolitical strategy of controlling oil, it will continue confrontation with the West. The Kremlin-owned and Putin-controlled oil and natural gas energy firm, Gazprom, "reported $15 billion in profits in the first nine months of 2018." So, it seems that there will be an ongoing struggle over which governing ideology controls oil, and thus rules the world. Will it be with an even hand or an iron fist? Either way, make no mistake; oil and now natural gas will remain the most important factors for winning wars, just as in 1942.

These two deep-earth minerals will also decide if we continue our post-WWII and U.S.-led, liberal-ordered peace and prosperity.[129] Or descend into socialism, which always leads to less freedom and chaos.[130]

Let's never forget that both world wars were won with oil and, of course, the "blood, sweat, and tears" of millions of brave men and woman of the various branches of the military, too many of whom made the ultimate sacrifice so that we can enjoy the freedom of our current lifestyles and government.

Chapter Four

Paris Accord Plans to Reduce Greenhouse Gases Miss the Mark
By Ronald Stein

Summary

The 184 countries that have ratified the Paris Accord seem to relate energy only to electricity.

Electricity alone is unable to support the energy demands of the military, airlines, cruise ships, supertankers, container shipping, and trucking infrastructures; nor can they support all the non-electric energy needs of infrastructures and supply all the products from the deep-earth minerals/fuels that are the basis of today's civilization and lifestyles. Intermittent electricity alone, from wind and solar renewables, has not, and will not, run the world's economies.

Paris Accord Plans to Reduce Greenhouse Gases Miss the Mark

There are numerous forecasts about climate change, but it's time to do more than perpetuate efforts for conservation and improvements in efficiencies, but to begin focusing on the specific plans as to how, when, and at what cost we can change everyone's lifestyle demands and dependency on the energy and the thousands of products from fossil fuels and achieve the sought-after 40 percent reduction in greenhouse gases (GHGs) that everyone attributes to fossil fuels.

Just like the TV commercial from decades that questioned "Where's the beef," it's time to focus on "how do we reduce our demands and dependency on fossil fuels", i.e., where's the plan to reduce GHGs?

All the nations that are party to the Paris Accord seem to relate energy merely to electricity generation, but not to providing fuels to the two prime movers that have done more for the cause of globalization than any other: the diesel engine and the jet turbine, both of which get their energy manufactured from crude oil. As mentioned earlier, without transportation, there can be no commerce. Nor does the Paris Accord acknowledge that renewables are incapable of manufacturing the chemicals that are the basis of the thousands of products we get from fossil fuels, products that are the basis of our standard of living in the modern world.

The 184 countries that have ratified the Paris Accord,[131] with the exception of Russia, Turkey and Iran,[132] are following the leadership of Al Gore, California Governor Brown, the former leader of the fifth-largest economy in the world, Arnold Schwarzenegger, and billionaire activist Tom Steyer to pursue intermittent renewable electricity from wind and solar to "save the world." Those "leaders" of the get-off-fossil-fuels campaign seem oblivious to the fact that 100 percent of the industries that use fossil fuels to "make thousands of products and move things" to support the economies around the world are increasing their usage or demand of those fossil-fuel energy sources each year, not decreasing it.

The world has become accustomed to the lifestyles provided by elaborate infrastructures, the military, medications the airline and cruise liner industries as well as the leisure and entertainment industries, and continuous technological advances that support the prosperity of growing populations that are all based on fossil fuels.

As above noted, however, Russia is *not* oblivious to the fact that whoever controls oil and natural gas controls the world.

It appears that the "leaders" of the get-off-fossil fuels are indirectly supporting Russia's efforts to have all the ratifying countries delay or stop any further exploration of fossil fuels by diverting those countries' efforts toward intermittent renewables of wind and solar for electricity.

The Kremlin's motive is to disrupt U.S. energy markets and influence domestic energy policy, since American energy represents a direct threat to Russian energy interests. Russia's efforts to influence U.S. energy policy are well documented in the public domain. U.S. presidential candidates, European officials, and the U.S. intelligence community have all publicly noted that Russia and its government corporations are funding a covert anti-fracking campaign to suppress the widespread adoption of fracking in Europe and the U.S., all in an effort to protect the influence of the Russian oil and gas sector.[133]

Russia, but not the 184 countries that have ratified the Paris Accord, is well aware that electricity alone, especially intermittent electricity from renewables, has not, and will not, run the economies in the world, as electricity alone is incapable of supporting the energy demands of the military, airlines, cruise ships, supertankers, container shipping, and trucking infrastructures. Nor can intermittent electricity from wind and solar provide the thousands of products from petroleum that are part of every transportation infrastructure, electricity generation, cooling, heating, manufacturing, agriculture, and virtually every product used in our daily and leisure lifestyles.

As we know, forecasts need to be based on assumptions, good or bad, valid or invalid, in order to arrive at the forecasted conclusions. The problem with the Paris Accord and the National Climate Assessment report, and other similar forecasts, is that most of the nations of the world seem to have bought into the "forecasted conclusions" regardless of the validity of those assumptions or conflicting forecasts on the existence of global warming or its probable causes or even the efficacy of various drastic remedies, such as the necessity of reducing GHG emissions by reducing our "lifestyle dependency" on fossil fuels.

The term "renewables" in these cases rarely refers to energy in its totality, but rather just to "electricity." Wind and solar farms can produce only electricity, and even that is intermittent, as we need the wind to blow or the sun to shin —continually—as far north as Oslo and as far south as Christchurch. It is a given that this is not going to happen. Electricity alone has its limitations in being able to energize the societies around the world.

Until we find that alternate energy, the magical elixir that replaces current reliable energy sources, we will have to concede that <u>every</u> indispensable industry and infrastructure that currently relies on energy from the deep-earth minerals/fuels to "move things and make thousands of products" in support of global economies is <u>increasing</u> its annual usage of those energy sources, not <u>decreasing</u> it. The longer it takes to "discover" this new alternate energy source, the harder it will be to wean the world off what has become the standard bearer.

The constant drive for more fuel efficiencies and conservation has slowed the use of energy, as reflected in just a slight uptick of the EIA curves for those deep-earth mineral/fuels even with the billions of people from India and China beginning to enjoy the lifestyles like those in developed countries.

The automobiles of today are much more efficient that the clunkers from the early 1900s and the gas guzzlers from the late 1980s. That's the good news. The bad news is that we now have many more cars and trucks on the road moving many more people and products. Today, there are 1.2 billion vehicles on the world's roads with projections of 2 billion by 2035. By some estimates, the total number of vehicles worldwide could double to 2.5 billion by 2050.

Electric vehicles (EVs) are being hyped as "green" because they have no tailpipes. It is common knowledge they use electricity to charge the batteries that make them run. What isn't common knowledge is that products and chemicals manufactured from deep-earth minerals/fuels are used to make those vehicles. And, by the way, the tailpipe that is not on the EV is actually located at the power plant that makes the electricity to charge the car, and at the refinery facilities manufacturing the materials needed to build the cars in the first place.

Electricity can charge my iPhone, light up my TV, and turn on my computer, but cannot manufacture the products and chemicals required to make those phones, TVs, and computers.

Electricity allows us to watch on our iPhones, TV's, and iPads the progress being made in the space program and our military operations, but electricity doesn't launch spacecraft nor move the planes, tanks, and vehicles of the military.

Any "super grid" of electricity will be unable to support the two prime movers that have done more for the cause of globalization than any other: the diesel engine and the jet turbine. Both get their fuels from oil. Without these modern workhorses, transportation as we know it comes to a grinding halt. And without transportation, as mentioned, there is no commerce. Wind and solar farms will not be coming to the rescue, not now, not ever. And, not incidentally, proposed locations for those farms that require vast acreage are being rejected by local citizens with a profound statement: not-in-my-back-yard!

But if renewals aren't capable of providing the answers to all our urgent energy needs, what can we do about the impact of emissions from our current primary energy source on climate changes? The answer is that, until electricity storage technology can support intermittent electricity from wind and solar, the world will continue to need redundant fossil-fuel backups for those windless and cloudy days to provide continuously uninterruptable electricity to the economy.

Interestingly, the primary economic reasons refineries even exist is to manufacture the aviation, diesel, and gasoline fuels for our military and transportation industries worldwide. From one 42-gallon barrel of oil about 19.4 gallons of gasoline are manufactured. The rest (over half) is used to manufacture the chemicals and by-products to make the things that are part of our daily lifestyles.

It may be shocking to most, but there are no economic reasons just to manufacture all the other chemicals and by-products from crude oil that have become part of our daily lives and essential infrastructures.

The signatories to the Paris Accord who are placing their bets on electricity generation by renewables are doing so in apparent ignorance of the U.S. Energy Industry Administration (EIA) projections that world energy consumption demands for fossil fuels (coal, oil, and gas) will continue to grow with most electricity in the world projected to be generated by nuclear, natural gas, and coal, with minimal reliance on intermittent electricity from renewables such as wind and solar.

Wind turbines cannot produce electricity when the wind is not blowing, and solar panels cannot produce electricity when the sun is not shinning. Consequently, wind power and solar power routinely need to be backed up by reliable and immediately available energy sources, which are often fossil fuels-based (gas, oil, coal). So, as wind and solar power installations expand across the world, more fossil fuel plants will need to be built to back them up to provide continuously uninterruptable electricity.[134]

Figure 4-1

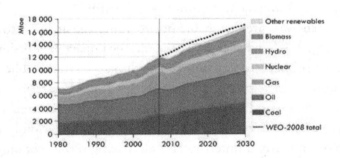

Global demand grows by 40% between 2007 and 2030, with coal use rising most in absolute terms

Observations of Figure 4-1

> As the population grows and the billions in developing countries like China and India join the energy society, we see the predominance of reliable, scalable, abundant, and affordable coal, oil, and natural gas meeting their energy needs.

There is another (and seldom-mentioned) drawback to seeking more and more intermittent electricity from the renewables of wind and solar. Astoundingly, in view of the environmental movement's well-publicized efforts to protect animal life, U.S. wind farms are "legally" killing hundreds of thousands of birds, eagles, hawks, and bats every year. And not only is this slaughter being ignored, but society has actually given the wind-farm industry a free get-out-of-jail card!

In December, 2016, the administration of then-President Obama finalized a rule that lets wind-energy companies operate high-speed turbines for up to 30 years, even if means killing or injuring thousands of species that are protected under the Bald and Golden Eagle Protection Act and the Migratory Bird Treaty Act. Under that rule, wind farms may acquire an eagle "take" permit from the U.S. Fish and Wildlife Service (USFWS) that allows the site to participate in nationwide "incidental" killing of up to 4,200 bald eagles annually without compensatory mitigation. It's shocking that wind farms can obtain legal permits from the USFWS to kill those majestic bald eagles.

The Paris Accord also missed the mark recommended by the U.S. EIA's *International Energy Outlook 2018*,[135] which focused on how different drivers of macroeconomic growth may affect international energy markets in three heavily populated and high economic growth regions: China, India, and Africa.

Figure 4-2

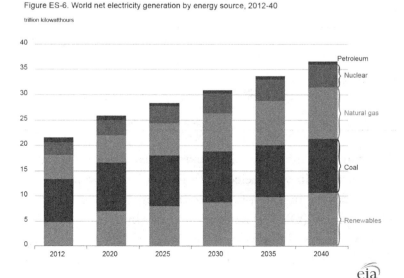

Observations of Figure 4-2

Petroleum	Continued minimal use of petroleum directly for electricity generation.
Nuclear	Slight gain in quantity of continuously uninterruptible electrical generation from now to 2040 as more nuclear power generating plants come online worldwide.
Natural Gas	Slight gain in quantity of continuously uninterruptible electrical generation in the world from now to 2040 as natural gas is an abundant and reliable source of energy.
Coal	Slight gain in quantity of electrical generation from now to 2040 as developing nations worldwide seek the most abundant and reliable source of energy.
Renewables	Gains in quantity of _intermittent_ electrical generation from now to 2040 as more countries seek electrical power generation from wind and solar.

According to the U.S. EIA *International Energy Outlook*,[136] the strongest growth in world electricity generation is projected to occur among the developing, non-Organization for Economic Co-operation and Development (OECD) nations. Increases in non-OECD electricity generation average 2.5%/year from 2012 to 2040, as rising living standards increase demand for home appliances and electronic devices, as well as for commercial services, including hospitals, schools, office buildings, and shopping malls.

The time has come to stop the pointless rhetoric about which forecast is more valid than the other, but to focus on the plans, schedules, and costs to implement the world's desire to reduce greenhouse gases (GHGs) by 40 percent.

It's a great idea to reduce our usage of fossil fuels through conservation and efficiency improvements, as that would extend the availability of fossil fuels for thousands of years. Since most nations seem to agree that a 40 percent reduction in our dependency on fossil fuels is imminently required to stop destruction of the earth, it's time also to stop tweaking the forecasts, so those nations can agree on the plans, timetable, and costs to alter current lifestyles and improve conservation efforts and efficiencies in order to reduce our fossil fuel consumption by 40 percent in the coming years.

In addition to reducing the fossil fuel reliance of our lifestyles, we need to focus on those industries that cannot function on electricity alone but depend heavily on fossil fuels and the chemicals from crude oil, all of which are made with the chemicals and by-products of oil.

There are 16 of these critical infrastructure sectors (as delineated by the Cybersecurity and Infrastructure Security Agency, or CISA) whose assets, systems, and networks, whether physical or virtual, are considered to be so vital to the U.S. that their incapacitation or destruction would have a debilitating effect on security, national economic security, national public health or safety, or any combination thereof. Here is a summary of these critical industries, all of which depend heavily on fossil fuels:[137]

Chemical Sector: This sector is composed of several hundred-thousand U.S. chemical facilities in a complex, global supply chain and converts various raw materials into more than 70,000 diverse products essential to modern life.

Commercial Facilities Sector: This includes a diverse range of sites that draw large crowds of people for shopping, business, entertainment, or lodging. Facilities within the sector operate on the principle of open public access, meaning that the general public can move freely without the deterrent of highly visible security barriers.

Most of the following are privately owned and operated, with minimal interaction with the federal government and other regulatory entities: entertainment and media, gaming, lodging, public assembly, real estate, retail, and sports leagues.

Communications Sector: The private sector, as owners and operators of the majority of communications infrastructure, is the primary entity responsible for protecting sector infrastructure and assets. Working with the federal government, the private sector is able to predict, anticipate, and respond to sector outages and understand how they might affect the ability of the national leadership to communicate during times of crisis, impact the operations of other sectors, and affect response and recovery efforts.

Critical Manufacturing Sector: This includes several core industries:

- Primary Metals Manufacturing
    - ✓ Iron and Steel Mills and Ferro Alloy Manufacturing
    - ✓ Alumina and Aluminum Production and Processing
    - ✓ Nonferrous Metal Production and Processing
- Machinery Manufacturing
    - ✓ Engine and Turbine Manufacturing
    - ✓ Power Transmission Equipment Manufacturing
    - ✓ Earth Moving, Mining, Agricultural, and Construction Equipment Manufacturing
- Electrical Equipment, Appliance, and Component Manufacturing
    - ✓ Electric Motor Manufacturing
    - ✓ Transformer Manufacturing
    - ✓ Generator Manufacturing
- Transportation Equipment Manufacturing
    - ✓ Vehicles and Commercial Ships Manufacturing
    - ✓ Aerospace Products and Parts Manufacturing

✓ Locomotives, Railroad and Transit Cars, and Rail Track Equipment Manufacturing

Dams Sector: There are more than 90,000 dams in the United States; approximately 65 percent are privately owned and approximately 80 percent are regulated by state dams' safety offices. The Dams Sector has interdependencies with a wide range of other sectors, including: Communication, Energy, Food and Agriculture, Transportation Systems, and Water.

Defense Industrial Base Sector: This is the worldwide industrial complex that enables research and development, as well as design, production, delivery, and maintenance of military weapons systems, subsystems, and components or parts, to meet U.S. military requirements. The Defense Industrial Base partnership consists of Department of Defense components, more than 100,000 Defense Industrial Base companies and their subcontractors, companies providing incidental materials and services to the Department of Defense. Defense Industrial Base companies include domestic and foreign entities, with production assets located in many countries.

Emergency Services Sector: The mission of this sector is to save lives, protect property and the environment, assist communities impacted by disasters, and aid recovery during emergencies. Five distinct disciplines compose the ESS, encompassing a wide range of emergency response functions and roles:

- Law Enforcement
- Fire and Rescue Services
- Emergency Medical Services
- Emergency Management
- Public Works

The ESS also provides specialized emergency services through individual personnel and teams. These specialized capabilities may be found in one or more various disciplines, depending on the jurisdiction, such as Tactical Teams (i.e., SWAT), Hazardous Devices Teams/Public

Safety Bomb Disposal, Public Safety Dive Teams/Maritime Units, Canine Units, Aviation Units (i.e., police and medevac helicopters), Hazardous Materials (i.e., HAZMAT), Search and Rescue Teams, Public Safety Answering Points (i.e., 9-1-1 call centers), Fusion Centers, Private Security Guard Forces, and National Guard Civil Support.

Energy Sector: The energy infrastructure is divided into three interrelated segments: electricity, oil, and natural gas. The U.S. electricity segment contains more than 6,413 power plants (this includes 3,273 traditional electric utilities and 1,738 nonutility power producers) with approximately 1,075 gigawatts of installed generation. Approximately 48 percent of electricity is produced by combusting coal (primarily transported by rail), 20 percent in nuclear power plants, and 22 percent by combusting natural gas. The remaining generation is provided by hydroelectric plants (6 percent), oil (1 percent), and renewable sources (solar, wind, and geothermal) (3 percent). The heavy reliance on pipelines to distribute products across the nation highlights the interdependencies between the Energy and Transportation Systems Sector.

Financial Services Sector: This includes thousands of depository institutions, providers of investment products, insurance companies, other credit and financing organizations, and the providers of the critical financial utilities and services that support these functions. Financial institutions range from some of the world's largest global companies with thousands of employees and many billions of dollars in assets to community banks and credit unions with a small number of employees serving individual communities.

Food and Agriculture Sector: This sector, almost entirely under private ownership, is composed of an estimated 2.1 million farms, 935,000 restaurants, and more than 200,000 registered food manufacturing, processing, and storage facilities. This sector accounts for roughly one-fifth of the nation's economic activity. The sector has critical dependencies with many sectors, but particularly with the following: Water and Wastewater Systems, Transportation Systems, Energy, and Chemical.

Government Facilities Sector: These facilities include general-use office buildings and special-use military installations, embassies, courthouses, national laboratories, and structures that may house critical equipment, systems, networks, and functions. In addition to physical structures, the sector includes cyber elements that contribute to the protection of sector assets (e.g., access control systems and closed-circuit television systems) as well as individuals who perform essential functions or possess tactical, operational or strategic knowledge.

The Healthcare and Public Health Sector: This sector protects all sectors of the economy from hazards such as terrorism, infectious disease outbreaks, and natural disasters. Operating in all U.S. states, territories, and tribal areas, the sector plays a significant role in response and recovery in the event of a natural or man-made disaster. While healthcare tends to be delivered and managed locally, the public health component, focused primarily on population health, is managed across all levels of government: national, state, regional, local, tribal, and territorial.

The Healthcare and Public Health Sector is highly dependent on other sectors for continuity of operations and service delivery, including Communications, Emergency Services, Energy, Food and Agriculture, Information Technology, Transportation Systems, and Water and Wastewater Systems.

Information Technology Sector: This sector is central to the nation's security, economy, and public health and safety as businesses, governments, academia, and private citizens are increasingly dependent upon IT sector functions. These virtual and distributed functions produce and provide hardware, software, and information technology systems and services, and—in collaboration with the Communications Sector—the Internet.

Nuclear Reactors, Materials, and Waste Sector: From the power reactors that provide electricity to millions of Americans, to the medical isotopes used to treat cancer patients, this sector covers most aspects of America's civilian nuclear infrastructure. The Nuclear Sector-Specific Agency within the Department of Homeland Security is responsible for coordinating the security and resilience of the Nuclear Sector. The sector is interdependent with other critical infrastructure sectors such as Chemical, Emergency Services, Energy, Healthcare and Public Health, and Water and Wastewater Systems.

Transportation Systems Sector: This sector consists of seven key subsectors:

- Aviation includes aircraft, air traffic control systems, and about 19,700 airports, heliports, and landing strips. Approximately 500 provide commercial aviation services at civil and joint-use military airports, heliports, and sea plane bases. In addition, the aviation mode includes commercial and recreational aircraft (manned and unmanned) and a wide variety of support services, such as aircraft repair stations, fueling facilities, navigation aids, and flight schools.
- Highway and Motor Carrier encompasses more than 4 million miles of roadway, more than 600,000 bridges, and more than 350 tunnels. Vehicles include trucks, including those carrying hazardous materials; other commercial vehicles, including commercial motor coaches and school buses; vehicle and driver licensing systems; traffic management systems; and cyber systems used for operational management.
- Maritime Transportation System consists of about 95,000 miles of coastline, 361 ports, more than 25,000 miles of waterways, and intermodal land-side connections that allow the various modes of transportation to move people and goods to, from, and on the water.
- Mass Transit and Passenger Rail includes terminals, operational systems, and supporting infrastructure for passenger services by transit buses, trolleybuses, monorail, heavy rail—also known as subways or metros—light rail, passenger rail, and vanpool/rideshare. Public transportation and passenger rail operations provided an estimated 10.8 billion passenger trips in 2014.
- Pipeline Systems consist of more than 2.5 million miles of pipelines spanning the country and carrying nearly all the nation's natural gas and about 65 percent of hazardous liquids,

as well as various chemicals. Above-ground assets, such as compressor stations and pumping stations, are also included.
- Freight Rail consists of seven major carriers, hundreds of smaller railroads, over 138,000 miles of active railroad, over 1.33 million freight cars, and approximately 20,000 locomotives. An estimated 12,000 trains operate daily. The Department of Defense has designated 30,000 miles of track and structure as critical to mobilization and resupply of U.S. forces.
- Postal and Shipping moves about 720 million letters and packages each day and includes large integrated carriers, regional and local courier services, mail services, mail management firms, and chartered and delivery services.

Water and Wastewater Systems Sector: There are approximately 153,000 public drinking water systems and more than 16,000 publicly owned wastewater treatment systems in the United States. More than 80 percent of the U.S. population receives their potable water from these drinking water systems, and about 75 percent of the U.S. population has its sanitary sewerage treated by these wastewater systems.

Critical services, such as firefighting and healthcare (hospitals), and other dependent and interdependent sectors, such as Energy, Food and Agriculture, and Transportation Systems, would suffer negative impacts from a denial of service in the Water and Wastewater Systems Sector.

If you study the following chart, you will find one glaring statistic that stands out. The country that reduced its greenhouse gas emissions the most was the United States.[138] The British Petroleum (BP) Statistical Review of World Energy:

"Finds that in 2017, America reduced its carbon emissions by 0.5 percent, the most of all major countries. That's especially impressive given that the United States' economy grew by nearly 3 percent – so the US had more growth and less pollution – the best of all worlds."[139]

Figure 4-3

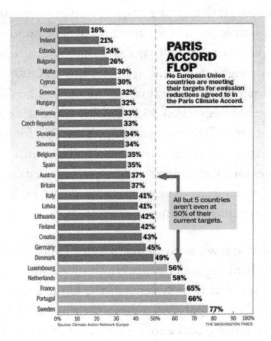

Observations of Figure 4-3

> No European Union countries are meeting their targets for emission reductions agreed to in the Paris Accord.

The largest reason for this counterintuitive occurrence—and why the U.S. was the only country to meet the Kyoto Protocols for emissions reduction—is the fracking revolution of shale oil and natural gas. This has led to the world, and particularly the U.S., transitioning to clean, flexible, scalable, affordable, and abundant natural gas over coal-fired power plants for energy and electrical power generation.

As will be discussed in our chapter on "How China and India View Energy," the world's largest emitters of greenhouse gases and CO2 are India and China. The Institute for Energy Research analyzed the data and concurred:

"That China produces 28 percent of the world's carbon dioxide emissions. India is the world's third largest emitter of carbon dioxide and had the second largest increment (93 million metric tons) of carbon dioxide emissions in 2017, <u>more than twice as much an increase as the U.S. reduction</u>."[140]

Truly, the Paris Accord means nothing when it comes to a cleaner environment. Only U.S. fracking of natural gas has produced lower emissions coupled with economic growth. Since the developed nations have become addicted to the lifestyle prosperity provided by fossil fuels (and to meet the demands of the 20 industries noted above), it's time to <u>stop</u> tweaking the forecasts about the demise of the world from GHGs and focus instead on serious efforts for conservation and improvements in efficiencies; and to start developing plans to change lifestyles in order to reduce GHGs, and thereby extend the availability of fossil fuels for thousands of years.

Chapter Five

How China and India View Energy
By Todd Royal

Summary

Billions of people in India and China are beginning to prosper because, for the first time in their long histories, these ancient countries are gaining access to energy and electricity.

Both countries overwhelmingly use coal, nuclear, and natural gas to power and develop their industries and commerce. Chinese and Indian citizens alike are starving for more energy—not less—the energy that is provided by fossil fuel, nuclear and renewables.

How these two countries use energy is obviously of great importance to world emissions levels, since coal is the dirtiest form of scalable, reliable, affordable, and abundant energy currently available to the billions in the developing world.

Introduction

China and India are the two most populous countries in the world. As of 2018, China had almost 1.4 billion people, a figure that is projected to grow to 1.5 billion by 2045.[141] India accounted for approximately 1.3 billion people in 2018 and is expected to grow to almost 1.7 billion by

2045.¹⁴² Currently, 2 out of every 7 people on our planet are Chinese or Indian. Both countries are desperate for energy.

There is a famous tale about an incredible, fifteen-day Christmas feast at Camelot for King Arthur in *Sir Gawain and the Green Knight*.¹⁴³ Before the knights can celebrate, Arthur insists that he first be told "the tallest of tales, yet one ringing with truth." The tallest energy tale being told in our day is doubtless the one about China and India leading the world in renewable electricity. What does have the ring of truth is the proposition that, for the rest of this century, China and India will play a decisive role in global health and prosperity by determining how energy is extracted, produced, and used.

As the U.S. shale revolution continues gaining strength, it is playing an expanding role in deciding how China and India view their own energy futures.¹⁴⁴ Our increased petroleum exports exert downward pressure on market prices, which, in turn, puts a strain on countries such as Venezuela, whose existence as a viable country relies on oil prices being high, or at least stable, to maintain its government budget. Increased shale oil exports are also a strong factor in the Organization of Oil Exporting Countries (OPEC) making peace and finding a common purpose to combat U.S. shale oil with Russia. All these interwoven international threats affect how and where China and India will have their own energy needs met.

International climate conferences like the COP24 in Katowice, Poland, in December 2018 have been rendered basically irrelevant due to the overwhelming abundance of U.S. shale oil and natural gas, both of which China and India crave. China and India now use these international conferences mainly for public relations, and the way they respond to someone like Wells Griffith, the U.S. administration's adviser on energy and climate, hailing the "energy renaissance" caused by U.S. shale and how the U.S. "is now the number-one combined oil and gas producer in the world," is by importing more oil and natural gas.¹⁴⁵

Both countries understand energy's primary position in their development. U.S. energy policies—and how China and India view energy—would have been different today if oil and natural gas exploration and production (E&P) were still stuck in the technology of the mid-2000s before the U.S. shale revolution. Under President George W. Bush's administration, imports of oil and natural gas were growing at unprecedented levels.[146] That is no longer the case, which has a deep impact on how China and India view and use energy to their benefit. Let's begin with China.

How China Views Energy

In 2019 the new leader of the U.S. Democratic Party seems, by popular consensus, to be socialist Congresswoman Alexandria Ocasio-Cortez (D-NY). "AOC," as she's been nicknamed, is calling for a "Green New Deal" that relies on intermittent renewables, electric vehicles, and heavy government taxes, mandates, and handouts to citizens and illegal aliens who will not work.[147]

China isn't embracing this "Green New Deal." Chinese President Xi Jingping has touted his country's transition to clean, carbon-free energy and electricity from renewables, but the facts show a much different energy reality.[148] China accounts for roughly half the world's coal consumption. China's coal demand peaked in 2013; and dropped "about 4 per cent between then and 2016, as the government pushed to cut local air pollution."[149] These regulations have since been scaled back in winter months to meet rising demands for heat in colder, northern Chinese regions. Renewable electricity and natural gas imports have been unable to meet energy and electrical consumption needs. This caused coal consumption to begin rising again in 2017.[150] Abundant U.S. exports of natural gas to Chinese ports on a daily basis cannot meet heating oil demands for Chinese citizens, their economy, and military.[151]

Figure 5-1[152]

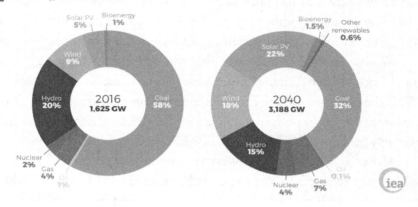

The Brookings Institution in 2018 claimed Chinese coal consumption had peaked.[153] To the contrary, China's coal use will only grow. CoalSwarm, a nonprofit that monitors, researches, and tracks investment in coal-fired power stations and plants worldwide, has "warned about the prospect of a 'massive surge' of new plants in China caused by a rush of permit awards by provincial authorities back in 2014-16."[154]

The International Energy Agency (IEA), in its *Coal 2018* report, stated:

> "Global coal use had grown again this year (2018), as it did in 2017, driven by strong demand from power plants in China and India."[155]

The IEA then proclaimed: "Coal's fate largely rests on the Chinese power sector."[156]

China's July 2018, three-year air pollution plan titled, *Three-Year Action Plan for Winning the Blue Sky War,* and its follow-up, the *2020 Action Plan for Air Pollution,* "is less demanding" than previous plans and was possibly causing air quality in the Beijing area to begin deteriorating back to previous levels before the Chinese government began tackling crippling air pollution countrywide.[157]

Recent air emission records have shown that "cities in northern China were covered by blankets of smog in November 2018."[158] China's global economic ambitions are making it difficult to improve air quality and lower emissions while sustaining growth in manufacturing and jobs.

Reuters reported in late 2018 that the coal city of Jincheng's "clean air drive had been 'sending shockwaves through the local economy.'"[159] With the explosion of new coal-fired power plant construction in China, emissions from poisonous coal smoke will likely increase respiratory illnesses not only for China, but also for all of Asia and Central Asian countries.

Most environmental and Western economic experts seem to believe China has reduced its domestic coal consumption. Instead, Chinese companies have shifted their dirtiest coal-fired power plants onto overseas customers. Regrettably, these countries are opening Pandora's energy box when they allow China into their economy. Once China has their hooks into a country, they attempt to suck them dry through too-good-to-be-true infrastructure loans and grants.

China knows underdeveloped countries desperate for energy will take loans to aid development of energy and infrastructure. Chinese banks demand the loans be paid back immediately, and when they can't, the asset(s)—such as light railways, bridges, highways, coal fired-power plants—are seized or acquired to pay back the loan(s). Through such arrangements, China is now in virtual charge of the domestic and foreign affairs of many poor countries, unbeknownst to their citizens and future governments.[160] In early January 2018, The *Wall Street Journal* reported on one such occurrence: "Secret discussions for years between China and Malaysia show how China uses its political and financial clout to bolster its position overseas," as an example.[161]

Energy, and particularly coal, is a foreign policy weapon for China. At the time of this writing (January, 2019), Chinese firms are building six new coal-fired power plants in Vietnam and Bangladesh and "11 new coal plants" in other regions as well.[162] China has also exported to Pakistan its dirtiest and least-expensive-to-build coal-fired power plants.[163]

Pakistan, The Chinese & Energy-Hungry Nations

Pakistan has an energy crisis. The current government has responded by having China build coal-fired power plants via the China Pakistan Economic Corridor (CPEC).[164] Nine coal power plants worth nearly $35 billion in new loans will be used to address Pakistan's "energy paralysis."[165] What will be the negative impact on Pakistan's health, considering that coal is the dirtiest form of scalable, reliable, abundant, and flexible energy currently available?

Some believe that coal can be clean, affordable, and emissions-free in the near future. "Clean coal" is a political buzzword for some sort of undiscovered technology, but what are the facts? Here are the basics of clean coal and clean coal technology:

> "Clean coal technologies range from wet scrubbers, which remove sulfur dioxide from coal-generated gas, to coal washing, which removes soil and rock from coal before it's sent to the factory. Hypothetically, the term is applied to anything that makes coal plants cleaner and more efficient. Typically, clean coal is talking about carbon capture and storage (CCS), a technology around since the 1980s that tries to cut down on sulfur dioxide and coal ash, and the heat trapping gas (CO_2)."[166]

Crucial to achieving cleaner coal are the newly termed high-efficiency low-emissions (HELE) coal technologies being developed by Benjamin Sporton, former chief executive of the World Coal Association. "This technology provides significant immediate CO_2 reduction and is a key step on the pathway to better CCS."[167]

The countries using HELE technology—besides China and Japan (which uses HELE as their default energy technology)—are "Germany, Italy, India, South Korea, Poland, Malaysia, Indonesia, the Czech Republic, the Netherlands, Slovenia, the United States, Australia, and South Africa."[168]

Germany is building and using coal-fired power plants at a record pace after the implementation of *Energiewende*, Germany's plan to transition to 100 percent renewables.[169] Germany, like China, realizes that coal currently provides 40% of the world's electricity. The October 2017 IEA report, *WEO-2017 Special Report: Energy Access Outlook*, highlighted the massive role coal has for energy access in China, India, Germany and for worldwide, on-demand energy access.[170] According to the IEA report, in the last 16 years "Nearly all of the countries who gained access to electricity worldwide did so through new grid connections, mostly from fossil fuels—45% of which came from coal."[171]

Along with most of the rest of the world, the Chinese will keep using coal for energy and electricity, but also as a way to give loans to vulnerable energy-hungry countries. Coal isn't leaving China's economy anytime soon. As an alternative, the Chinese should begin working with American natural gas firms to bring cleaner-burning natural gas to China, Pakistan, Vietnam, Bangladesh, and every country under China's sway in their multi-trillion dollar "debt diplomacy,"[172] which is known as the Belt and Road Initiative (BRI).[173] China has also invested more than $34 billion in vulnerable, energy-starved Africa.[174]

Air conditioning, as odd as that may sound, will also become a global issue for China. The International Energy Agency (IEA) has studied how China's energy use will expand with more air conditioning use.[175] Faitih Birol, Executive Director, IEA, has stated: "Growing demand for air conditioners is one of the most critical blind spots in today's energy debate."[176]

The IEA study revealed that China is now the largest air-conditioning market in the world.[177] India intersects with China when it comes to air-conditioning use, for the subcontinent's tropical climate along with the summertime heat of Beijing will radically affect how much coal, natural gas, and petroleum these two countries use in the coming decades.[178] But there is another critical aspect of energy use that China understands far better than India does.

Greenhouse Gases

The 2018 Intergovernmental Panel on Climate Change (IPCC) asserts that the world must cut or even eliminate greenhouse gas emissions 50% below 2010 levels by 2030 and be at net zero by 2050 to "avert climate disaster."[179] Greenhouse gas emissions are defined as:

> "A gas that absorbs and emits radiant energy within the thermal infrared range and causes the greenhouse effect. Primary greenhouse gases in the Earth's atmosphere are <u>water vapor, carbon dioxide, methane, nitrous oxide, fluorinated gases and ozone</u>."[180]

The Chinese will expand fossil fuel use and never impose any restrictions that would hinder Chinese growth. That is a fact. As President Xi, the Politburo ruling committee, the Chinese Communist Party (CCP), Chinese businesses, and average citizens all realize, "Such a wrenching energy transformation is unrealistic, undesirable in the extreme and thankfully unnecessary."[181]

Instead, China will embrace organizations such as the Non-governmental International Panel on Climate Change (NIPCC) that have produced reports debunking man-made global warming, and the 2018 IPCC report.

The NIPCC researches and produces reports contributed to by hundreds of scientists, citing thousands of peer-reviewed, scientific reports discrediting the IPCC's claims that human greenhouse gas emissions are the main cause of climate change.[182] The NIPCC asserts:

> "Historically there is no correlation between the amount of carbon dioxide in the atmosphere and the earth's temperature. NIPCC shows that claims of increasingly extreme weather related to anthropogenic climate change are verifiably false."[183]

Whether we believe in global warming and climate change isn't the issue. Realize this: China will never reveal its true energy intentions. We must look at their actions to figure out how they view energy. They will keep building coal-fired and nuclear power plants while importing oil, coal, petroleum, aviation fuel, and natural gas from the U.S., Russia, OPEC, or anyone else who can help bring energy to a billion-plus people.

The Chinese will also embrace the NIPCC's 2019 report, *Climate Change Reconsidered II: Fossil Fuels* (CCRIIFF), showing overwhelming harm coming to China, or any society or economy, if they stop using oil, natural, coal, and nuclear and move to renewables.[184] Over 6,000 essential products have their origins in a barrel of crude oil.

There isn't a hospital, ambulance, or grocery store that could stay open without coal, natural gas, and oil. The Chinese realize this, and the fact that fossil fuels supply over 81 percent of today's primary energy; which is actually a conservative number when you consider that renewable electricity needs constant backup from coal-fired, nuclear, or natural gas power plants throughout its entire usage 24/7/365.[185] The CCRIFF research confirms that access to fossil fuels allows agriculture and medicine to flourish. Modern health care in China depends on obtaining and utilizing fossil fuels for "IV drip bags, tubing, medical machinery, electronic casings and syringes."[186]

Plummeting Chinese Birth Rates & Energy

China's birth rates have plummeted. They need more, not fewer, healthy Chinese citizens for their economic miracle to continue.[187] Chinese birth rates have been devastated from decades of its one-child policy.[188] China has killed baby girls the way the United States has killed over 19 million black babies since 1973 when abortion became legal.[189]

China, like the United States, has drastically diminished birthrates that will cripple its economy and society if government, non-governmental organizations, and a new social consensus don't combine to encourage larger families and having children in general.

But, ultimately, only by burning more fossil fuels can China (and other demographically challenged nations) overcome the lowered birthrates that invariably lead to unproductive economies and will have severe consequences for global health.

What's the alternative for China in the short and long term? Do we expect them to return to the kind of lives that English philosopher Thomas Hobbes famously described "as poor, nasty, brutish and short," without reliable, scalable, flexible, and affordable energy?[190] The U.S Census Bureau in 2016 calculated a worldwide increase of 35 years in the average age of death since 1970, and declines in death rates for all age groups, even those 60 years and older.[191] What countries would seek to reverse such encouraging trends?

The United Nations defines poverty as living on and/or being paid $1 a day, and on that basis calculates an 80 percent decline in poverty rates during the years 1970-2006.[192] The CCRIFF states, "The corresponding total number of poor has fallen from 403 million in 1970 to 152 million in 2006."[193] The IPCC reductions, on the other hand, would "reduce the world's GDP by 96 percent."[194] The IPCC's plan, and the Paris Climate Agreement, would plummet per capital global income and growth in just the United States and Europe all the way back to 1820-1830 levels.

With the greatest global decreases in poverty occurring in China, that vast nation has become a tonic and toxin for world markets through its sheer size and economic growth patterns. China doesn't care about pollution, nonbinding environmental treaties like the Paris Climate Agreement, or Western environmental good will if any of these inhibit their country from leaving crushing poverty for the first time in their 5,000-year history. Emissions from China will rise, damn the consequences to the environment, unless it can be convinced by global leaders to use natural gas-fired power plants over coal-fired power plants. China will say they are using renewables to satisfy naïve, Western environmentalists more concerned about green "virtue-signaling" than what actually lowers emissions for a billion people.[195]

China Views Energy Geopolitically

China wants to rule the world and displace the U.S. world order. China wants to remake the world, but the U.S. stands in the way because of its abundant oil and natural gas.[196] Energy has thus become the objective in the new, geopolitical Cold War between China and the U.S.[197]

For more than seven decades since WWII, the United States has been overly engaged in the Middle East. While Middle Eastern oil remains important to the U.S., it now means more to China. The reason is simple: the shale oil revolution taking place in Texas, Oklahoma, South Dakota, Pennsylvania, Colorado, New Mexico, and other U.S. states that, in addition to drilling, are now using hydraulic fracturing (fracking) to extract their oil and natural gas resources.

Abundant U.S. oil and natural gas deposits mean the Middle East is now a less centralized global energy market and one "less able to control prices." The U.S. can now pick and choose how it remains involved in the entire region. Abundant oil gave President Obama the ability to leave Iraq and President Trump to try to exit Syria.[198] It also allows the U.S. under the Trump administration (and will allow future administrations) the ability to block China's rise as an ascendant power.

China takes a clear-eyed approach to U.S. involvement in the Middle East. With the region in a perpetual state of war, China will assuredly ramp up its own engagement to ensure that oil and natural gas are still delivered to Chinese ports. The U.S. pullback from the Middle East means China will have to use military resources they would otherwise use against Asia and India.

China won't go for regional hegemony (defined as leadership or dominance by one social group or country over another) status. They will instead step through the minefields of civil-war-torn Yemen, unstable Syria, brutish Saudi Arabia, and the never-ending Israeli-Palestinian fight to "seek friendships and trade relationships (think oil and natural gas imports) while carefully avoiding taking sides in any rivalries."[199]

China doesn't care about lives, refugees, or returning millions of displaced, former Syrian citizens to their rightful homes. They only care, deeply, about oil and natural gas imports that come their way from the Middle East. Chinese decisions are not based on Western environmentalists or media reports about pain, suffering, or achieving political democracy in countries like Saudi Arabia or Iran. China's focus is locked on its need for fossil fuels.

So not only will China never acquiesce to the drastic, energy-restrictive proposals for fighting global warming and climate change being put forward by the Western environmental movement, they will watch drilling reports in Texas just as much as they will scrutinize the U.S. Navy's Seventh-Fleet movements in Southeast Asia, the Taiwan Straits, and the Indian Ocean.[200, 201, 202]

India

Never before in human history have we seen two countries (China and India), each with over a billion people, in need of such gargantuan amounts of energy to keep their economies accelerating and their citizens alive. Moreover, with China currently undergoing an economic slump, it will likely be overtaken by India both demographically and economically in approximately ten years.[203] India is poorer than China, and its GDP is less than China's, yet, on balance, India's positives will overtake its negatives.

Capital Economics forecasts 5-7 percent annual growth until 2040 for India.[204] India's need for energy began after its "foreign currency crisis of 1991."[205] The foreign currency crisis jump-started the process of opening India up economically, politically, and culturally for the first time since its independence from the British. Gross domestic product (GDP) rose to:

> "Close to 5 per cent a year between 199-2017. Five-year moving average of growth of GDP per head reached 7.2 per cent in the years to and including 2007. If maintained GDP per head would double every 12 years. That would be transformative – and not just for

India, since its population is forecast by the United Nations to reach 1.6bn (17 per cent of the world's total) by 2040."[206]

India's economy faces massive challenges in overcoming pollution problems. India is "among the top five greenhouse-gas (GHG) emitters globally."

More than 592 million Indian citizens use firewood for cooking, worsening pollution. Rural-living Indians use crop residue and animal waste for energy needs; and roughly 80 percent of the population "still relies on biomass fuels for cooking activities," which increases dirty air.[207]

Biomass cooking is dangerous because it "contributes to the indoor air pollution phenomenon, which caused 488,200 Indian deaths in 2004 alone and is growing yearly."[208] India is moving toward commercial fuels over wood, crop waste, animal feces, human power, and strong animals, but it is a slow process taking rural citizens away from what they know and have used for centuries.

Electricity access in India has improved. Generating capacity is growing, but electricity shortages and power outages are still persistent.[209] According to the country's 2011 census, 396 million Indian citizens do not have access to electricity.[210] That means that "approximately 30 percent of India's generated power is lost in transmission." This causes weak distribution, electrical grid overload, commercial losses of power, poor billing and collection, and electrical theft.[211] Having poor electricity access also has heavy implications for India's battle with China.

A Great Power struggle has broken out between India and China. Whoever controls the most energy will win this ongoing conflict and become the dominant power in Asia for the rest of the century. India achieved its independence more than 70 years ago. India has charted its own course during that period, but times have changed. China's dominant rise in Asia, economically and militarily, has caused India to move into closer partnership with the U.S. India will depend on U.S. security guarantees for its own military buildup and for its ever-increasing need to secure oil, natural gas, coal, and nuclear for its energy and electrical demands and the continuing modernization of its economy.

In 2017 there was a military standoff with China in the "disputed Doklam area." This land mass lies between the countries of Bhutan and Pakistan. India and Pakistan hate each other, and China aligning with Pakistan has raised the stakes for India.[212] The Indian Ocean is now in play. This is India's traditional sphere of influence the way the Atlantic and Pacific Oceans are for the United States and the Arctic Ocean for Russia.[213]

We can see the importance India places on its energy future by its efforts to block China's rise in the Indian Ocean, and in both Central and Southeast Asia. As for countering its existential enemies, the Pakistanis, India's obvious strategy to achieve this goal is by acquiring energy at all costs.

India and China alike pay lip service to the Western environmental movement and to the use of renewables by the U.S., the European Union (EU), and the North Atlantic Treaty Organization (NATO), while utterly rejecting the premise that they cannot use fossil fuels and nuclear energy. The use of nuclear by both India and China is quickly growing. While Western countries continue to reject nuclear energy over safety concerns, India and China are currently building hundreds of nuclear reactors.[214]

According to the International Energy Agency (IEA), "nuclear power production will grow by 46 percent by 2040 – more than 90 percent of the net increase will come from China and India."[215] Both countries will "drive the world's nuclear power production growth."[216] Agneta Rising, the director general of the World Nuclear Association, told CNBC:

> "Asia, for its part, saw 8 to 9 percent growth in nuclear capacity (2017-2018) and the largest growth in nuclear energy is in the Asia region, especially in China and India, adding that nuclear power is 'absolutely compatible,' and 'necessary,' for a low carbon future."[217]

Michael Shellenberger, a *Time Magazine* "Hero of the Environment" recipient, wrote in early 2019 that the only way to achieve zero carbon electricity and lower pollution levels that China and India both struggle with is by using nuclear energy.[218] Nuclear energy use will grow, because China added three new nuclear reactors in 2017, bringing its total number of operating reactors to 41.[219] Only the U.S. and France have more. India also knows that China's *13th Five Year Plan* outlined the use of more nuclear energy to clean their air and diversify from heavy imports of fossil fuels.[220] This increased China's nuclear capacity more than 18 percent in 2018. India is doing the same thing.

India will not sit back idly and be overtaken by China. India's view of nuclear energy changed when China allied with Pakistan through the Chinese-Pakistan Economic Corridor (CPEC). The IEA reported India has the seventh-largest nuclear production fleet in the world, with 22 working nuclear reactors that produce total net electrical capacity of 6,255 megawatts (MW) of power; but this amount still leaves them significantly behind China's 42,800 MW power capacities.[221]

Megawatts (one megawatt is equivalent to a million watts) "are used to measure the output of a power plant or the amount of electricity required by an entire city."[222] The net growth in nuclear generation from 2016 to 2040 for China and India will account for 91 percent of the world increase in nuclear output, according to the IEA's World Energy Outlook 2017.[223]

India has eased rules on foreign firms operating nuclear facilities as a way to spark the country's indigenous nuclear program, since its economy is having problems importing and/or producing enough fossil fuels to meet its needs. Nuclear is helping India counter China's rise. Does India take the same aggressive stance as China when it comes to using coal? The answer is yes.

Global coal demand rose in 2017, because China accounts for roughly half the world's coal consumption. India rushed into using renewables, causing coal-fired power plant investments to crater. But India's demand for energy didn't diminish, and they have now reversed course by joining China in upping their use of coal. Nearby Asian countries Indonesia, Pakistan, Bangladesh, and the Philippines are also using more coal.

This use of coal by India, China and other Asian nations offsets emission declines in the U.S. when they substituted natural gas for coal. Global oil and gas consumption are growing in 2019. Coal use is declining in Western countries, but vast areas of India, Africa, and Asia will see increased emissions through increased use of coal.[224] More than half the world's population resides in these regions.

Figure 5-2[225]

Coal Plants by Country: Annual CO2 (Million Tonnes)								
CoalSwarm Global Coal Plant Tracker, January 2019 *(Units 30 MW and larger)*								
Country	Announced	Pre-permit	Permitted	Announced + Pre-permit + Permitted	Construction	Shelved	Operating	Cancelled 2010-2018
Total	509	550	342	1,401	960	1,944	9,574	5,128

India now has fourteen of the world's most polluted cities. New Delhi, the capital, is the sixth worst-polluted city in the world as measured by the World Health Organization (WHO).[226] Years of growth in their auto and coal-fired generation industry have caused these problems.

India cannot fight environmental devastation as long as they are also fighting China and Pakistan. The West is mostly safe, secure, and prosperous. The EU and U.S. can care deeply about environmental standards and cleanliness, but India doesn't have that luxury.[227] To push back against the country's declining environment, Prime Minister Narendra Modi has unveiled the National Clear Air Programme (NCAP):

> "That aims for 20-30 percent reduction of particulate matter (PM) concentration over the next five years, with an overall goal of mitigating air pollution and improving air quality in the country. But [it] has no clear targets and targets are not legally binding in the current NCAP plan."[228]

Newly built coal-fired power plants will make cleaning up India's polluted cities difficult to achieve. Ideological antagonism to coal by Western environmentalists won't keep India or China from using more coal. Recent (2018 and 2019) aerial photography has shown construction under way of Chinese coal-fired power plants; India, meanwhile, is the world's second-largest coal consumer and is escalating the burning of coal at an annual growth rate of six percent.[229]

The Indian and Chinese governments may say they want clean air, and to comply with the Paris Climate Agreement, but nothing will stop each country from striving to conquer the other—and all of Asia and Central Asia—this century.

The Great Power Competition Between China & India

Both countries will allow the Western nations to continue their get-off-fossil-fuel movements and their dysfunctional politics, both domestic and international.[230] For China and India, the issue of national energy imperatives has nothing to do with Trump or the EU. Indeed, these nations have only the vaguest comprehension of the kind of society capable of electing an energy, economic, and societal illiterate like Socialist Alexandria Ocasio-Cortez.

China and India will never follow the "Green New Deal." Frankly, the first New Deal didn't work.[231] (Those interested should read *FDR's Folly: How the New Deal Prolonged the Great Depression* by Jim Powell to verify this assertion.) China and India—within their Great Power Competition over the Indian Ocean, Central Asia, and Asia—will sit back and watch Western-aligned Asian allies, the EU, and U.S. as they "muddle through endemic crises menacing to [their] very existence (e.g., economic stagnation, demographic decline, rising unassimilated Islamic populations in many EU democracies, high taxes, mounting debt and the fiscal unsustainability of Western European social democracy)."[232]

Western environmentalist and political parties in the EU and U.S. believe fossil fuels are evil. China and India, locked within their life-and-death rivalry, seek energy, not the moral high ground. Whoever controls energy—particularly, coal, oil, petroleum, aviation fuel, natural gas, and nuclear—controls the world.

China and India will place themselves on the opposite end of the energy spectrum by continuing year after year to import and burn tankers full of coal, oil, and natural gas from countries that are authoritarian, human rights abusers, and that couldn't care less about carbon emissions, countries like Saudi Arabia, Russia, Iran, Venezuela, Iraq, Nigeria, Angola, and Algeria.

In this power struggle for Asia, China and India will never allow lack of pipelines, domestic politics, or sensitivity to Western environmentalists to keep them from besting their rival or attaining the First World status enjoyed by the U.S., the EU, and their Western-aligned Asian allies.

Simply put, China and India will never stop using coal, oil, natural gas, or nuclear, no matter the cost to the environment. If China builds coal-fired power plants, so will India. Hence, both countries are furiously building, and using, coal-fired power plants.

China and India realize coal is plentiful ("estimated 1.1 trillion tons of proven coal reserves worldwide that at current rates of production will last 150 years"), and it is abundant and cost effective to the end-user of the product.[233] The biggest coal reserves are in the U.S., Russia, China, and India. China and India will continue using record amounts of coal in their life-and-death struggle against each other since they view energy through a geopolitical, survival-of-the-fittest perspective.[234]

This has severe environmental consequences. But how can the West, the UN, or leading environmental organizations tell more than 2 billion people they cannot have access to the same energy opportunities and growth the West has enjoyed for more than seventy years? It simply won't happen. Instead, world health organizations, research universities, think tanks, and multinational corporations interested in global health and clean air should begin working toward clean coal technology.

What we are seeing with how China and India view energy is no different than the way all great nations seek a domain of power and area of influence.[235] For China it is global, extending from their country up to the Arctic and down to the tip of South America. India is seeking regional primacy to keep unfriendly or hostile nations out of their backyard, which is the threat that China represents to them. India wants a ring of security all around the Indian Ocean up to Pakistan and into Central Asia.

Figure 5-3[236]

China has been successful in accomplishing this task; India has not. This is why China is currently threatening them. Historically, in its quest for regional dominance, India doesn't seek out or even like alliances, but with the threat of China ever-looming, they have become friendlier with the U.S., Australia, the EU, Japan, South Korea, and other nations in an attempt to block China's ascendant rise in their backyard.[237]

> "Smaller nations such as Sri Lanka, Bangladesh, Bhutan, Nepal, Maldives, Mauritius, and Seychelles fall under India's shadow, but with Pakistan now aligned with China, accessible, abundant, and reliable energy becomes more important than ever before for India's

military and economy. The example of how China has encroached on India's traditional sphere of influence is Nepal's attempt to become friends and trading partners with China and India the last few years. But now Nepal has allied with Maldives since that island nation in the Indian Ocean veered towards the Chinese influence and money that China's Belt and Road initiative provides."[238]

This type of behavior from traditional Indian allies that were peaceful, quiet neighbors shows the unsettling regional effect of Chinese money and military power. The competition between China and India won't stop anytime soon, or even in the distant future, unless something drastically changes.

Conclusion

The quest for energy is how China and India will struggle for power in the 21st century. Both countries will not accept the threat of global warming stopping or even deterring their growth. Both governments and their economies have militaries and billions of people who are energy hungry.

This chapter asked the question: How do China and India view energy? The answer is an insatiable demand for whatever source of energy is available no matter the consequences. And, unarguably, coal is leading the way, with the promise of renewables being a ruse to soothe Western feelings about clean air and emissions. Whatever environmental treaties or protocols the West cooks up will be annihilated by sheer survival imperatives when it comes to China and India. Heavy concern for economic growth and fossil fuel use extends into the foreseeable future; so, the world better start planning for a way to mitigate even heavier coal use.

Nations and citizens affected by China and India's global jet streams can only hope nuclear plants under construction are as highly scrutinized, planned, and built as carefully as their Western counterparts. Currently, the same rigorous standards and procedures are not in place. The world could be looking at a nuclear disaster on the horizon. Both China and India view energy as an amoral source of power that is to be used for survival and advancement during this century.[239] The rest of the world should take careful note.

Chapter Six

Renewable Electricity
By Todd Royal

Summary

There is a deep-rooted fallacy that wind and solar farms produce clean energy and electricity.

The truth is that renewable electricity is intermittent, dilute, and needs constant backup from coal, natural gas, or nuclear energy power plants to provide continuously uninterruptible electricity.

In order to generate "renewable electricity," wind and solar farms require land-devouring sites that, by any aesthetic evaluation, turn into unsightly monstrosities that destroy trees (along with other vegetation), wildlife, and ecosystems. Among the unpublicized results of such "green farming" are higher electricity prices, increased emissions, and lower property values.

Introduction

Renewable energy is hardly new. It has been used since man discovered fire and wood for cooking and heat. Wind power propelled ships for thousands of years, and waterpower was used for turning grinding mills in ancient farms. Windmills still dot modern landscapes, and the Romans "even used geothermal water for heating."[240] Until the Industrial Revolution arrived in the middle of the 18th century, renewable sources were the only type of energy available. Wood, fire, water, biomass, cow dung, horse manure, and animals were the energy sources that were used by homes, businesses, and governments. It was the discovery of fossil fuels and their vast energy potentials that made possible the Industrial Revolution, economic prosperity, and technological advancements in everything from medicine to global travel.

Ever since that time, historically speaking, oil, natural gas, and coal have reigned supreme. Now, over concerns of pollution and rising emissions, global citizens, companies, and entire governments are embracing solar panels and wind turbines. Since renewables are, by definition, any type of electricity obtained from a natural resource (sun, wind, water, tides, rain, geothermal heat, biomass), their demand is growing. Thus far, however, fossil fuels—oil, petroleum, coal, and natural gas—have kept renewables from increasing further.[241]

What renewables have accomplished, all the same, is truly mesmerizing. Harnessing solar power coming from the Sahara Desert, hydroelectric power out of the Hoover Dam, and wind power off the coast of England are wonderful achievements. This ability to energize limitless sun, wind, and waterpower is why people and nations hope that one day earth can be powered by these free, zero-carbon, natural resources. What was once disparaged as a "niche" electricity sector is not only making a comeback but may even be destined for greatness. In 2016 "renewable electricity received 94 times more in U.S. federal subsidies than nuclear and 46 times more than fossil fuels per unit of energy generated."[242] Wood, wind, and cow manure, once used by small farms and unsanitary cities in the pre-Industrial Revolution era, have now been replaced by solar and wind farms on a global basis.[243]

Media, government, academia, and environmentally concerned citizens all seem to have accepted as fact that renewable electricity derived from solar panels and wind turbines will eliminate our reliance on fossil fuels (oil, coal, and natural gas) along with nuclear electricity, and usher in a new age of global prosperity. Headlines like this are common: "Renewables are on track to replace fossil fuels and move the world toward a low-carbon future."²⁴⁴

But are fossil fuels really about to go the way of the horse and buggy in favor of the zero-carbon future promised by renewable energy? Solar and wind power are popular forms of electricity that both authors of this book—*Energy Made Easy*—hope fulfill all these grandiose expectations at some future point. But we also dare to offer realistic, contrarian views of the current state of on-demand energy and electricity.

First, it needs to be said that China will be the biggest factor in whether or not renewables overtake fossil fuels as a primary source for reliable electricity. China, the world's second-largest economy, is in its "drill, baby, drill" phase. Only when it emerges from its current obsession with fossil fuels and begins to consider energy alternatives will we be able to make reasonable projections as to whether renewable electricity will ever become scalable, reliable, affordable, flexible, and abundant.²⁴⁵ The United States is just as shortsighted when it comes to limited use of renewables in favor of the abundance of oil, natural gas, coal, and nuclear to power its economy and military. Significantly, China has the same global ambitions for power and prosperity as the U.S., the North Atlantic Treaty Organization (NATO), the European Union (EU), and the entire Asian hemisphere (including India).²⁴⁶

Why <u>not</u> get electricity from the sun, wind, and water? Surely global health, innovative new electricity sources, and doing away with fossil fuel extraction and production (E&P) are all excellent reasons to embrace renewable electricity? The problem, unfortunately, is that we can't simply switch to electricity from wind, sun, and water at this time. Germany, for example, now realizes that its transition to solar and wind farms for electricity has been a failure.²⁴⁷ There are issues regarding the amount of land required for wind and solar farms, how steeply emissions rise when these renewals are widely used for electricity, and the problem of replacing all the parts that make up wind turbines, solar panels, and hydroelectric dams without continuing reliance on all the essential products that derive from crude oil.²⁴⁸

This chapter will tackle seven basic questions regarding renewable electricity: <u>What is it</u>? <u>How long has it existed</u>? <u>What is the future of</u>

renewables? <u>What are the results from renewables now being widely deployed as a main electricity source</u>? <u>Why do they not currently work</u>? <u>What needs to happen for renewables to displace fossil fuels and the thousands of products that come from crude oil</u>? Lastly, <u>what are the geopolitical implications of renewables at this time</u>? Let's get started.

What Is Renewable Electricity (RE)?

The United States Energy Information Administration (EIA) definition is:

> "Energy from sources that are naturally replenishing (sun, wind, hydroelectric, wood are examples) but flow-limited (intermittent – the sun doesn't always shine, and wind doesn't always blow is how to explain intermittent). Renewable electricity is virtually inexhaustible in duration but limited in the amount of electricity that is available per unit of time."[249]

Figure 6-1

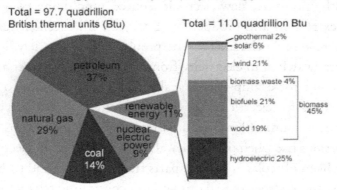

Figure 6-2

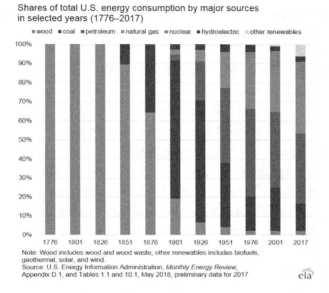

Per Figure 6-1, in 2017 the U.S. received 11% of its electricity from renewables. As Figure 6-2 shows, U.S. electricity consumption from renewables mainly comes from biofuels, solar and wind. In 2017 RE provided the U.S. roughly:

> "11 quadrillion British thermal units (Btu) – 1 quadrillion is the number 1 followed by 15 zeros – equal to 11% of total U.S. electricity consumption. About 57% of U.S. renewable electricity consumption was by the electrical power sector, and about <u>17% of U.S. electricity generation was from renewable electricity sources</u>."[250]

While strictly looking at RE in possibly reducing greenhouse gas emissions:

> "RE energy sources more than doubled from 2000 to 2017, <u>mainly because of state and federal government</u>

<u>requirements and incentives to use renewable electricity</u>. The U.S. Energy Information Administration projects that U.S. renewable electricity consumption will continue to increase through 2050."[251]

If global tax incentives were cut, renewables would have a hard time surviving. Unfortunately, renewables still need taxpayer money and incentives to thrive and not lose money.

Until the start of the Industrial Revolution in the mid-1800s, the U.S. and all other major countries received their energy from wood. This included heating, cooking, and light. Hydropower and solid biomass "were the most used renewable electricity resources until the 1990s."[252] Not until the late 1800s did the U.S. and other industrialized countries begin using coal, oil, petroleum, and natural gas.

The EIA's *International Energy Outlook 2017* contains the same projections used for the EIA's *International Energy Outlook 2018* showing the amount of renewables used by nations for electricity.[253] The 2018 IEA report focuses on reporting macroeconomic developments for Africa, China, and India, since these three are becoming the highest pollution-emitters and users of electricity. As these three economies and populations grow—particularly Africa and India—their respective energy needs are expected to quadruple.[254]

The chart below (Figure 6-3) indicates world reliance on renewables will grow to 25% of energy consumption by 2050:

Figure 6-3[255]

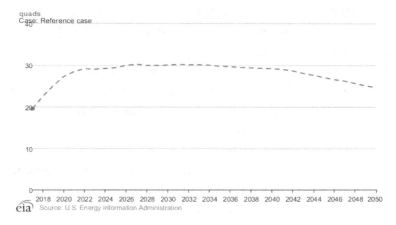

Figure 6-4

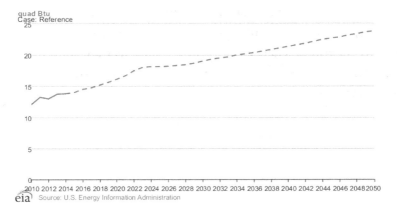

Link for above-graph source will also take you to renewable energy use broken down by regions in the world: https://www.eia.gov/outlooks/aeo/data/browser/#/?id=9-IEO2017)

Both studies show the viability of renewables becoming the world's number-one energy-to-electricity source, a giant step toward minimizing fossil fuel use and achieving a low-carbon or even a zero-carbon world. But what needs to be explained is that carbon-free electrical generation will not—indeed, cannot—replace all other forms of energy in totality. Energy is more than just electricity!

Electricity will not run the economies of the world at this time, nor by 2050, according to the EIA's *International Energy Outlook for 2017* or *2018*. Electricity alone is incapable of supporting the energy demands of the military, airlines, cruise ships, supertankers, container shipping, trucking/trucking infrastructures, medications, vaccines and space programs. No individual, entity, organization, or government has described a plan for how this will happen on a scalable, reliable, affordable, flexible, or abundant basis such as fossil fuels now provide. It can only be hoped that that will change.

What Is the Future of Renewable Electricity?

Renewables still need better energy density, which leaves us with a great many unanswerable questions as to how the modern world is going to do without energy from crude oil and its thousands of essential products.[256] Here is a link to a partial list of the products that come from a barrel of oil.[257]

Figure 6-5[258]

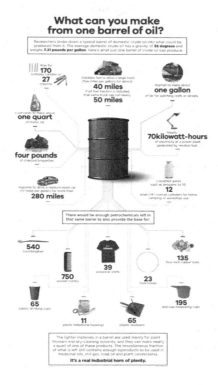

The U.S. oil and natural shale boom is another harsh reality that solar and wind are also competing against. For decades ahead, we can expect billions of barrels of oil and trillions of cubic feet of natural gas to be coming from America.[259] As an example, the U.S. is the largest exporter of oil to the United Kingdom (UK) for the first time since the mid-1950s Suez Canal Crisis under the Eisenhower administration. The U.S. shale bounty has not only supplanted the dwindling UK North Sea supply of oil and natural gas, but has overtaken major UK suppliers like Norway, Russia, Nigeria, and Algeria.[260] U.S. shale oil and natural gas dominance is remaking the global energy landscape and causing nations to buy and use more fossil fuel than ever before.

Some additional focus on geopolitical realities can help shed light on the future of fossil fuels versus renewables. Let us examine the case of Sri Lanka and China. Sri Lanka is a tiny, heavily indebted island nation in the middle of strategically important shipping lanes just south of India. Sri Lanka owes billions to China, a debt that falls due in the first half of 2019 (this chapter was written in February 2019) in exchange for being a large beneficiary of China's Belt and Road Initiative (BRI) "to build ports, roads, railways, pipelines across Asia."[261] In fact, the Hambantota Port in southern Sri Lanka, built primarily by the Chinese, is so heavily indebted and unable to repay Chinese-backed loans that the Sri Lankan government has leased most of the port facility back to China to assist in settling these debts. Many influential officials believe the BRI is actually a "program to trap countries in debt to give it (China) greater sway and advance its military aims" of greater control over Asia, the Indian Ocean and South China Sea.[262] The Hambantota Port was granted a 99-year lease on the facility for use as debt repayments. The example of China and Sri Lanka is particularly illustrative because militaries—particularly blue-water navies—use nuclear generators. Armies and air forces use oil, petroleum, natural gas, and coal.

Renewables are having a hard time lowering overall energy costs and emissions and overcoming the challenges of the sun not shining or the wind not blowing. Currently, we are told that solar panels and wind turbines are cheap to build and easy to deploy, while costing no more than fossil fuels; yet they cause electricity prices to rise. Why?[263] Alex Epstein's book, *The Moral Case for Fossil Fuels*, and Vaclav Smil's book, *Energy and Civilization*, go deeper into the sun-not-shining and wind-not-blowing examples of why renewables remain a tough sell for cheap electricity.

For the purposes of this chapter, here is a simplified explanation: Renewable electricity causes all forms of energy and electricity to be more expensive because the sun, wind, and water are unreliable, intermittent, dilute, and have low energy density, unlike fossil fuels, which are reliable, scalable, abundant, affordable, efficient, and flexible. Renewables also require smart electrical grids that can move electricity simultaneously among cities, counties, states and even countries and continents. Unfortunately, that form of electrical grid hasn't yet been invented. Renewables cannot handle the job of powering millions of electric vehicles from an electrical grid that itself relies only on solar, wind, and hydroelectric.[264] Renewables from solar and wind electrical plants require backup at all times from coal-fired, natural gas, or nuclear power plants, or some type of industrial batteries. In addition, new transmission lines need to be installed, lines capable of handling sun, wind- and water-powered electricity; otherwise prices skyrocket.[265]

There is no shortage of examples to help us understand the limitations of renewables. In January-February of 2019, the U.S. experienced a brutal cold wave that blanketed large portions of the country with ice, snowfalls, and sub-zero temperatures. Over U.S. skies there was no sun shining or wind blowing. The coldest temperatures were reported at night or in early morning hours. Temperatures dropped as low as minus 16 degrees Fahrenheit during this brutal winter cold spell and storm.

The Mid-Atlantic Region of the U.S. is overseen by the PJM (originally Pennsylvania, New Jersey, and Maryland) regional transmission organization whose task it is to "coordinate the movement of wholesale electricity in all or parts of Delaware, Illinois, Indiana, Kentucky, Maryland, Michigan, New Jersey, North Carolina, Ohio, Pennsylvania, Tennessee, Virginia, West Virginia and the District of Columbia."[266] PJM's job is also to monitor electrical reliability, deliverability of electricity, and the best possible way for heat and air conditioning to reach consumers and businesses.

On January 31, 2019 at 8 a.m., PJM's electricity was in a deep freeze. Demand, however, began to peak. PJM had total electrical power usage at 140,000 megawatts (MW), a gargantuan number. Wind power was providing just 1,000 MW of electricity and solar provided zero electricity to counter the sub-zero temperatures."[267]

To help keep the heat running, PJM turned to coal, natural gas, and nuclear.

Corporations seriously concerned about climate change are understandably attracted by the growth in renewables that reached 13 percent in 2018 and was projected to double in 2019.[268] Baker Hughes, one of the world's largest oil services company, "is considering a pivot towards good and services for the wind and solar industries, eying the long-term transition to cleaner electricity."[269] Naturally enough, a company like Baker Hughes is attracted by the 94 percent increase in taxpayer subsidies to solar and wind farms. But they don't want themselves or their customers freezing to death in a crisis. Which explains why not one of these corporations in the U.S. affected by this winter storm relied on wind and solar to keep their manufacturing plants and offices from being ruined. Neither was one dollar of sales and revenue lost by overreliance on wind and solar. Until renewables can overcome uncooperative weather patterns of this magnitude, they will remain an unreliable, overly expensive niche form of electricity.

Since solar was a non-factor in the PJM example above, with wind the main focus, perhaps solar would prove a more reliable and efficient energy source than wind? Unfortunately, solar also has provided many examples of being unreliable, high-priced and requiring even more land than wind farms and fossil fuels. My home state of California has the well-known, taxpayer- subsidized, and Google-funded Ivanpah solar farm and electrical generating station.[270] Michael Shellenberger, who has received *Time Magazine's* "Hero of the Environment" award, points out the following unfortunate facts about Ivanpah solar: "To produce the same amount of electricity that comes from California's Diablo Canyon nuclear plant it would take 18 Ivanpah solar farms."[271] Further, to then bring that power to ratepayers, it would require 18 separate transmission lines, whereas a coal- or natural gas-fired power plant or nuclear electricity requires only one set of transmission lines. Concerning this, Shellenberger adds:

> "New transmission lines can make electricity cheaper, but not when they are used only part of the time (intermittent nature of renewables) and duplicate rather than replace current equipment; and by contrast nuclear plants like Diablo Canyon and San Onofre nuclear plants in California are on the coast near where most Californians live versus solar farms [being] far away in the desert."[272]

So, back to wind farms and the manifold problems that limit their future. Wide-open green spaces are needed for wind farms in contrast to the single-family neighborhoods, suburbs and cities where most people live. The resulting connection costs are astronomical. What about materials used? If the future is to be bright for renewables, shouldn't they have a smaller carbon footprint and contribute to the new green economy? They should, but unfortunately, they don't. Solar and wind both require more steel, fuel, glass, concrete, and cement. Indeed, all the materials that renewables require throughout the entire value and supply-chain process— "from mining to processing to installing to disposing of the materials later as waste"—have their chemical origins in barrels of crude oil.[273]

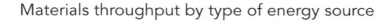

Figure 6-6[274]

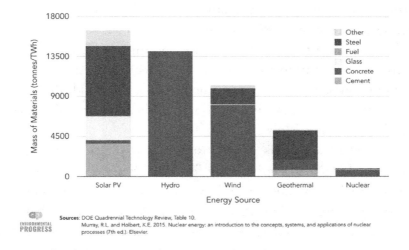

Land-use requirements for renewables are also much greater than for traditional electricity sources. California's Ivanpah solar farm, despite being a technological marvel, "produces 18 times less electricity on more than 290 times more land than [the] Diablo Canyon nuclear plant." Add in new transmission lines for the plant plus the amount of land needed and costs jump significantly. But what, it may be asked, if you took out the cost of land and of new transmissions lines, as California has done by mandating that all new homes have solar on their roof? Doesn't that eliminate higher costs?[275] Exactly the opposite. Costs increase at least $10,000 per new home and for all existing homes that install solar. The higher installation costs add undue cost burdens in comparison with comparable homes being powered by coal or natural gas-powered plants or nuclear electricity.[276]

Nor is this a blue-state-versus-red-state comparison. Arkansas, a solidly Republican red state, has embraced both solar and wind but has run into the same land issues. Arkansas found that <u>for 18,000 megawatts of nuclear electricity, it takes 1,100 acres of land, which equals 1.7 square miles; while for 1,800 megawatts of wind power it takes 108,000 acres of land, which equals 169 square miles; and for 1,800 megawatts of solar power it takes 13,320 acres of land equaling 21 square miles</u>.[277] The amount of land required to provide coverage to mature, advanced economies equal to their current electrical use would be staggering. You can do the math for yourself. Just for the U.S., take total electrical use and the above numbers to find out what the land use would be for each state. That is roughly the amount of land plus solar panels plus wind turbines (on and offshore) required even to approach the output levels of fossil fuels on the U.S. electrical grid. Remember, that all solar and wind farms need continuously uninterruptible backup from fossil fuel or nuclear!

Now take California's newly installed law—Senate Bill 100 (SB 100), passed in 2018— mandating fossil fuel-free electricity and zero carbon electricity by 2045. California is the fifth-largest economy in the world and home to Silicon Valley. I've made the point that land-use issues are hard to overcome. According to Robert Bryce, senior fellow at the Manhattan Institute, the land-use math for all renewables in California (or frankly elsewhere) clearly shows that, due to economic and technological constraints, sole reliance on renewables is simply not feasible at this time, or in the near future.[278] In a *Los Angeles Times* article, Mr. Bryce cites a study done by Stanford University civil and environmental engineering professor Mark Z. Jacobson, in which Jacobson and other experts added up the numbers of what it would take for California (or anywhere in the world considering a shift to large-scale or 100% renewables) to achieve 100% renewable electricity.²⁷⁹ Professor Jacobson reasonably estimates:

> "It would require 124,608 megawatts of onshore wind-power capacity, 32,869 megawatts of offshore wind capacity, and 236,243 megawatts of solar-electricity capacity."²⁸⁰

In 2017 "global solar capacity totaled about 219,000 megawatts." California would thus need more solar capacity than currently exists globally; and Jacobson's math revealed that "33,000 megawatts of concentrated solar plants, or roughly 87 facilities as large as the 377-megawatt Ivanpah solar complex," would be needed throughout California.²⁸¹ Ivanpah is located in the Mojave Desert and covers 5.4 square miles. Environmentalists waged a fierce fight to stop or limit Ivanpah over concerns for the endangered desert tortoise.

Wind electricity also brings a large onshore or offshore footprint.²⁸² This land-and-sea footprint breaks down "to about 3 watts per square meter," according to the Department of Energy.²⁸³ Professor Jacobson postulates that California would need 124.6 billion watts of onshore wind capacity, which means state officials would need to set aside "41.5 billion square meters or about 16,023 square miles of turbines." Los Angeles is a little more than 4,000 square miles, so California would need to cover a land area four times larger than Los Angeles County (the largest county in the U.S.) with nothing but windmills.

Political issues can also affect wind power. In 2015 the Los County Board of Supervisors voted unanimously to ban large wind turbines in unincorporated areas of L.A. County. San Diego, Solano, and Inyo counties also passed restrictions on turbines. The head of the California Wind Energy Association told the *San Diego Union-Tribune* in 2017, "We're facing restrictions like that all around the state… It's pretty bleak in terms of the potential for new development."²⁸⁴ California currently has 5,632 megawatts of installed wind capacity, 153 megawatts <u>less</u> than in 2013.

The math is even bleaker when you calculate the amount of land needed for wind and solar in order to achieve electricity parity when California's San Onofre Nuclear plant (SONGS) is closed. San Francisco (SF) is about 46.89 square miles (121.4 km). For wind power to replace San Onofre would take land six times the size of SF, and for solar it would require land 12 times the area of SF. Furthermore, it would take 84 acres to produce 2,200 megawatts of power, whereas SONGS only require 0.13 square miles.[285] To replace Diablo Canyon's 2,160 megawatts will also require enormous land sprawl from wind and solar to achieve one-for-one megawatt replacement.

This isn't a problem specific only to California. The once popular 468-megawatt Massachusetts Cape Wind Project was ultimately scuttled over fierce opposition to locating dozens of turbines offshore. Would Californians, and the citizens of other U.S. states and countries across the world, accept onshore or offshore wind projects many times larger than what was proposed in Massachusetts? What will stakeholders think when these huge land-mass footprints begin lowering home values, eliminating pristine, environmentally sensitive areas and scenic coastline, and destroying land-use policies in order to keep our economies functioning? These same rationales and land-use numbers for electricity replacement can be applied to any city or country (from Georgetown, Texas, to Germany) and to its citizens, affected stakeholders, and governments. Renowned land-use expert Joel Kotkin of Chapman University calls this type of rush into renewable electricity "green-virtue signaling."[286] He believes it makes people feel good without requiring them to learn the facts about land being destroyed, lives never reaching their potential over a lack of electricity, and death being a very real possibility during crippling cold and blistering heat waves.[287]

The two figures below show the amount of land needed for a hydraulic fracturing (fracking) site. Less than 2 acres.

Figure 6-7[288]

Renewables require "vastly more land, longer and less-utilized transmission lines and large amounts of storage whether from lithium batteries, new dams, or compressed air caverns."[289] The future is still great for renewables—mainly solar and wind farms—but the constraints and limitations that both sources of electrical power impose mean prosperity will be less wherever they are widely deployed. That is catastrophic news for the more than 2 billion people on our planet currently without access to "reliable" electricity.[290]

Why Don't Renewables Currently Work?

Proponents of renewables argue that they lower costs for electricity. If this is the case, then wide-scale renewable use should lower electricity costs along with emissions to provide cleaner air over natural gas. Instead, it is U.S. government entities like the EPA that "polluted with impunity in Colorado in 2015, and New York city still pollutes Newtown Creek whenever there's heavy rainfall," whereas ExxonMobil "has spent millions cleaning up Newton Creek, which happens to run through Congresswoman Alexandria Ocasio-Cortez's native Brooklyn."[291] Meanwhile, natural gas being implemented over coal in the U.S. has resulted in the "largest reduction of CO_2 emissions in the world for the ninth time this century."[292]

The heart of the natural gas fracking revolution is in the Marcellus Shale in Pennsylvania. John Hanger, a former Secretary of Planning and Policy for the State of Pennsylvania, "has pointed to the states of South Dakota, North Dakota, Oklahoma, Kansas, Texas, and Iowa" as places where heavy solar and wind farm utilization has worked. According to Mr. Hanger, these U.S. states are "examples of high wind/solar use (up to 30% or more usage and deployment) and these states have average/below average prices."[293] However, Madison Czerwinski and Mark Nelson of Environmental Progress researched the data and found Mr. Hanger was incorrect.

Using data from 2009-2017, Czerwinski and Nelson found that U.S. electricity prices rose 7 percent, which coincided with solar and wind growing from 2 to 8 percent during the same time period.[294] Mr. Hanger might say that doesn't mean that the increase in solar and wind use caused electricity prices to rise; and that is a valid point. So, here are the results from 2009-2017 from the states Mr. Hanger listed, starting with South Dakota. That state's electricity prices rose 34 percent when electricity from solar and wind grew from 5 to 30 percent.[295] North Dakota electricity prices rose 40 percent when electricity from solar and wind grew from 9 to 27 percent.[296] This is very problematic, since North Dakota has one of the largest oil and natural gas deposits in the world – the Bakken formation.[297] Oklahoma electricity prices rose 18 percent when solar and wind use grew from 4 to 32 percent in the oil-rich state.²⁹⁸ Kansas' electricity prices rose 33 percent as solar and wind grew from 6 to 36 percent.²⁹⁹ Kansas is seen as a fossil fuel-friendly state. Iowa electricity prices rose 21 percent when solar and wind grew from 14 to 37 percent of electrical generation.³⁰⁰

What about Texas, the home of the U.S. shale revolution, and third-largest oil producer in the world after Saudi Arabia and Russia?³⁰¹ Texas electricity retail prices fell 14 percent even though solar and wind use grew from 5 to 15 percent, which seems to prove that solar and wind can indeed lower electricity prices.³⁰² Nevada also had a similar result as electricity prices fell 15 percent when solar and wind grew from 1 to 12 percent in one of the sunniest and hottest states in the U.S.³⁰³ The real question is why are these two states energy and electricity outliers? The answer is that both use more natural gas than do other U.S. states. Natural gas is abundant and inexpensive. That's why Texas and Nevada's electrical prices decreased.

Texas' natural gas prices during 2009-2017 (the time period cited in the examples for other states) fell 21 percent.³⁰⁴ Not coincidentally, wholesale electricity prices also fell 21 percent in Texas.³⁰⁵ Lower natural gas prices led to lower electricity prices, which led to solar and wind installations being supposedly cheaper when they really weren't. The natural gas power plants that were backing up renewables is what led to those lower electricity prices.

While Texas is the epicenter of the fracking-shale-revolution, it also allows failures of its natural gas power plants, which occurred with "high-profile bankruptcies" to the natural gas electrical power sector in 2017.³⁰⁶ Since Texas has a gunslinger mentality when it comes to its natural gas-powered electrical generation plants, this means supply will tighten. The likely scenario moving forward for Texas is that prices will explode in 2019 and beyond until the Texas Legislature, governor and the state's main energy regulatory body, the Texas Railroad Commission, make up their minds to intervene in electrical markets in order to keep supply flowing and prices lower.³⁰⁷

Nevada is also interesting for understanding the dilemma posed by solar energy. Like Texas, Nevada had its electricity prices fall 15 percent. As mentioned above, the state's use of electricity from solar and wind also grew from 1 to 12 percent between 2009-2017. Solar plants in Nevada are some of the most efficient in the U.S., producing electricity at "30 percent of its rated capacity."[308] New Jersey is the opposite of Nevada with its long winters and scant sunshine for months on end. Consequently, New Jersey's renewables have only a "capacity factor" of 12 percent.[309] Nevada's wholehearted embrace of natural gas for electricity is the real reason solar is working there, and not Nevada's piercing sunlight that is uninterrupted most of the year.

Natural gas plants are flexible—meaning they can be turned on and off quicker—to accommodate the up-and-down nature of solar and wind electrical generation plants. This lowers Texans and Nevadans' electrical bills and allows easier integration of renewables into their states' electrical grids.

Sadly, other problems arise when solar grows to over 15 percent of the electrical generation and grid mix. According to energy scholar Lion Hirth, "Solar's value drops by 50 when it arrives at 15 percent of the electrical mix." [310] The build-out of solar and wind farms in the U.S. would result in extremely high price increases in electricity if it wasn't for natural gas. Three U.S. states meet the criteria of low amounts of natural gas usage with large electrical price and increased emissions.

California is the U.S. leader in renewable use, and California electricity prices rose 22 percent when their solar and wind mix grew from 3 to 23 percent.[311] The co-author of this book, Ronald Stein, makes a persuasive case that California is a national security threat over the amount of crude oil imported as a result of overreliance on solar and wind while severely limiting oil and natural gas E&P.[312] Hawaii's electricity prices also rose 23 percent, and they have abundant, year-round sunshine. However, their percentage of solar and wind grew from 3 to 18 percent.[313]

Minnesota is another state to uses heavy government involvement to force renewables usage over oil, natural gas, coal, or nuclear. Minnesota wants 15 percent of renewables to come from wind electrical generation farms to meet this quota. The results have been disastrous. A 2017 paper by the Center of the American Experiment, *Energy Policy in Minnesota:*

the High Cost of Failure, chronicles that Minnesota spent $15 billion on wind electricity over fossil fuels. This extravagant outlay did not lower state CO2 emissions, however, but it did cause Minnesota's electricity prices to rise above the national average for the first time on record.[314] The CO2 emission issue is particularly troubling when you consider:

> "Between 2005 and 2014, Minnesota's CO2 emissions fell 6.6 percent (off greater use of natural gas), while the US reduced CO2 emissions by 9.4 percent. From 2015-2017 greenhouse gas emissions from electricity in Minnesota have risen (lower natural gas use), even as more wind power was installed."[315]

Minnesota's electrical prices have also risen, even as:

> "Wind generators receive a production tax credit of 2.3 cents per kilowatt hour (compared with an average consumer price currently of 13 cents per kilowatt hour), <u>which means wind power producers can underbid other sources of electricity and still make lots of money</u>."[316]

We are told that the cost of renewables is the same as, or less than, oil, natural gas, coal, and nuclear. This isn't true. So far, not one U.S. state or country that has used solar and wind power has reported a one-to-one cost. Costs are without exception higher, and so are the taxes to pay for electricity sources that do not work as advertised. The case could be made that economically advanced U.S. cities should have been able to switch to renewables as their primary source of electricity. Al Gore praised the city of Georgetown, Texas, for making the switch to 100% green electricity in his 2017 film, *An Inconvenient Sequel*. However, exactly the opposite occurred; and, historically, all of Al Gore's predictions have been proven false.[317] Georgetown, Texas, budgeted $45 million to fund its renewable electricity portfolio, but ended up paying $53.6 million according to City Manager David Morgan. Mr. Morgan also reported that, at the end of 2018, the City of Georgetown "had to sell its surplus renewable power for less than forecast."[318]

The Future of the World Is the Green New Deal

The "Green New Deal" (GND) that U.S. Congresswoman Alexandria Ocasio-Cortez unveiled in February 2019 had actually been tried before via a group of Democratic labor-environmental activists who called theirs a "new Apollo project."[319] This group sought $300 billion for electricity efficiency and renewable electricity. In 2007, then presidential candidate Barack Obama made their project a part of his electricity platform—and, eventually, part of his administration's energy policy and law. Between 2009-2015, the U.S. government spent $150 billion on this earlier GND, with roughly half going to renewables.[320] Twenty-four billion of these dollars were wasted on biofuels. It is now known that biofuels pollute more than fossil fuels.[321] Biofuels also destroy rainforests.[322] The U.S. government thus helped destroy forests, ruin people's lives, and cause widespread emission increases all through the mandated use of renewables.

Germany and California have both become "poster children for how not to deal with climate change."[323] Germany has spent $580 billion on renewables since Angela Merkel's energy policy *(Energiewende)* made green electricity a hallmark of her governance. "Emboldened by its prowess in engineering and a consensus across all political parties in favoring green electricity, Germany was the first major economy to make a big shift in its electricity mix toward low-carbon sources."[324]

Merkel's *Energiewende* policy has failed spectacularly.[325] If the nation had spent that money on nuclear electricity, or natural gas-powered electrical generation plants, Germany would have a significantly lower carbon footprint, and would not have the second-highest electricity bills in Europe.[326] The other failings of Merkel's policy are sad and maddening all at the same time: Germany produces enough electricity from solar and wind to power all German households.[327] Yet all this renewable electrical generation makes no progress toward the nation's climate policy goals because emissions are rising due to increased use of the coal-fired power plants needed to back up intermittent and unreliable renewable electricity.[328]

Germany's military is also in shambles after having spent more than $560 billion on renewables. Merkel and the Germans who voted for her have put NATO in a bind, reaching out for cheap Russian natural gas via the Nord Stream 2 pipeline project for their renewable electricity projects. Germany is also not meeting NATO's 2 percent standard of GDP spending on the military as another consequence of their renewable electricity laws.[329]

Other European countries' energy policies are just as bad as Germany's. Denmark has the highest electricity prices in Europe as a result of its 100 percent embrace of renewables and attempting to become carbon-free.[330] Spain's electricity prices in 2009 were below the European average, but today are among the highest in the EU, which has caused the Spanish government to cut solar and wind subsidies.[331]

Nor are Europe and the U.S. the only advanced countries to make foolish electrical choices. Australia, particularly South Australia, saw dangerously high electricity prices accompanied by a political crisis after it began using renewable electricity and battery storage technology that don't work in tandem, or even as standalone technologies.[332] Electricity prices in South Australia are now the highest in the country.[333] Australia and South Australia have also incorporated Tesla's electricity battery storage technology into their renewable electricity mix.

Electricity storage for wide-scale, societal deployment that is scalable, affordable, and reliable needs to include <u>electricity security, renewable power production, and cyber security</u>. It was reported in November 2017 that Tesla's lithium-ion battery storage system deployed in South Australia was successful.[334] In December 2017 it was further written that Tesla's battery was:

> "Smoothing out at least two major electricity outages, responding more quickly than coal-fired backups, and Tesla's battery system at the Hornsdale Power Reserve (<u>www.hornsdalepowerreserve.com.au</u>)

kicked in, in just 0.14 seconds throughout December 2017 after one of Australia's biggest plants, the Loy Yang facility, suffered a sudden, unexplained drop in output."335

If Tesla's battery storage system is that effective, why did the *Financial Times* declare in August 2018, "Energy Is at the Roots of Australia's Political Crisis"?336 Countries, states, counties, cities, towns, and villages that deploy battery electricity storage systems are doomed to higher rates and unreliable electricity of the kind that Australia, Germany, Denmark, Spain, and California are all experiencing.

There are battery electricity-storage-system advocates who contend that the technology is available, scalable, affordable, and offers flexibility comparable to that provided by natural gas and nuclear electricity for low- to zero-carbon electricity resources. However, a 2016 Massachusetts Institute of Technology (MIT) study rebuked such claims and concluded: "Commercial large-scale batteries available today are rated to deliver stored electricity for only two hour or ten hours duration."337

The U.S. Department of Energy's (DOE) *Quadrennial Energy Review (QER) Part 1 (2015)* has also weighed in on electricity storage needs:

> "To establish a framework and strategy for storage and flexibility: Electricity storage is a key functionality that can provide flexibility, but there is little information on benefits and costs of storage deployment at the state and regional levels, and there is no broadly accepted framework for evaluation of benefits below the bulk system level."338

For electricity storage systems to work will require a strategy and technology that include flexibility, commonly accepted planning methods, on-demand consumer use, national and international connected transmission lines and the ability to handle the variable, dilute, intermittent nature of renewable electricity generation. Part 2 of the DOE's *QER* in 2017 also stated that electricity storage systems will need to handle <u>increased cyber-security concerns and electrical grid modernization for it to be a factor in renewable electricity and a carbon-free society becoming a reality</u>.[339] No one can definitively state when electricity storage technology will be available that can offer the hundreds of hours of storage necessary if solar and wind farms are ever to replace fossil fuels and lead to a carbon-free society.[340]

Physics and engineering offer their own cautionary advice regarding the unquestioning use of renewable electricity. For instance, shouldn't <u>newer</u> solar and wind farms offer declining costs through heavier penetration in the future? And yet, economically speaking, "The value of solar and wind decline in value as they become larger shares of the electricity grid for physical reasons."[341] This may explain why California and Germany both pay some of the world's highest prices for their electricity. German ratepayers in 2017 had to subsidize their government spending to the tune of 24.3 billion euros "above market electricity prices in 2017 for its renewable electricity feed-in tariffs."[342]

What I hope this section has demonstrated is that moving toward 100 percent renewable electricity (mainly from solar and wind farms) within 10, 20, or even 30 years would require trillions in taxpayer subsidies. Since globally we are only at 1 to 8 percent of renewable electricity penetration—and anything beyond 1 percent normally means large quantities of wood and cow dung being burned (biomass)—the 100 percent goal doesn't seem realistic. Which means fossil-fuel use will continue to grow, not decline. Even $150 billion in U.S. taxpayer subsidies over the last decade haven't lowered electrical costs, replaced the 6,000 products that we derive from crude oil or begun to fuel the entire global and U.S. transportation industry. It is no exaggeration to say that achieving anything close to 100 percent renewable penetration by 2050 would cripple economic growth and human progress, thereby leading to global anarchy.

No commodity is more macro-economically important than electricity and the prosperity that a barrel of crude oil produces. We are understandably addicted to prosperity. Make-work government programs simply don't work, and that's what renewables end up being—another

FDR-like Works Progress Administration (WPA), which failed miserably during the Great Depression and will fail miserably now.[343]

My true desire is for renewable electricity to be made workable, and for all nations to achieve full functionality using low-carbon grids, off-grid, or micro-grids. What is needed, and with increasing urgency, is an all-of-the-above policy for energy (oil, natural gas, coal, nuclear, and all forms of renewable electricity) until renewables can overcome their dilute, energy-dense, and intermittent nature.

Can Renewable Electricity Ever Replace Fossil Fuels?

At this time the answer is no, as the world needs energy that electricity alone cannot provide. The International Energy Agency (IEA), the U.S. Energy Information Administration, and OPEC have all arrived at the same conclusion: fossil fuels are completely interwoven into our global economic systems. Political headwinds and citizen revolts will become a stumbling block in the path of renewables ever overtaking fossil fuels when people begin to realize the substantial negatives associated with renewables. Germany, for example, has enough solar panels and wind turbines theoretically to eliminate all fossil-fueled and nuclear power-generated electricity; and yet Germany still has higher emissions and electricity prices. But crude oil remains embedded in every step of the renewable electricity process.[344] The considerable negatives associated with voracious land use for renewables are another negative factor that cannot be overstated, since the media along with government entities and citizens having a vested stake in renewables never seem to mention it.

For the U.S. to achieve clean, renewable and zero-emission electricity sources by 2030 as outlined, there is an actual plan in place from Stanford Engineers led by Professor Mark Jacobson, a plan that I discussed earlier in a California-only context.[345] This 2015 plan for the entire U.S. would:

> "Involve installing 335,000 onshore wind turbines; 154,000 offshore wind turbines; 75 million residential

photovoltaic systems; 2.75 million commercial photovoltaic systems; 46,000 utility-scale photovoltaic facilities; 3,600 concentrated solar power facilities with onsite heat storage; and an extensive array of underground thermal storage facilities."[346]

To achieve those numbers would take an area <u>roughly 500,000 kilometers larger than California</u>.[347] And bear in mind, Los Angeles County and Massachusetts—two very liberal blue U.S. states whose governing elites deeply believe that global warming is man-made—still encounter huge problems gaining approval to build wind and solar farms over stiff environmental resistance.[348]

Environmentalist activist Bill McKibben, along with Al Gore and Naomi Klein, enthusiastically endorsed Professor Jacobson's belief that the whole world—obviously including the U.S.—could be powered electrically by renewables.[349] Alas for this grandiose plan, the computer modeling Jacobson used has been shown to be based on false assumptions.[350] For instance, Jacobson's study asserted that "<u>the U.S. could increase power from its hydroelectric dams ten-fold. Their real potential turned out to be just one percent of that</u>."[351] The Jacobson study is now generally considered irrelevant.

What has been revealed by this study, and others similarly endorsed by the Al Gore club of environmentalists, is that too many duplicitous individuals and organizations are invested in and receiving money directly from oil, natural gas, and renewable electricity interests. They are being paid to defame nuclear electricity, raking in billions while feigning environmental care and stewardship.[352] Frankly, it's despicable, especially when nuclear-generated electricity is still the only 100 percent carbon-free source.

Environmental degradation, as I've attempted to show, is an integral part of the renewables process. Bear in mind, the underlying motive of this survey is a profound wish for renewables to work. But without examining the negatives associated with renewables and the need to rid the sector of predatory faux-environmentalists and opportunistic investors, this form of clean electricity will never become a dominant force globally. The materials needed for renewables are not unlike those needed for electric vehicles (EVs), namely cobalt and lithium, which come from the Democratic Republic of Congo where child slave labor and poor working conditions are the norm.[353]

The magnitude of materials needed for renewables (steel, glass, concrete, cement) dwarfs those for nuclear or fossil fuels while not producing the same amount of electricity.[354]

Land Use by Electricity Source in Acres/MW Produced[355]

Source	Acres per Megawatt Produced	Electricity generation reliability
Natural Gas	12.41	availability is continuous and uninterruptible
Nuclear	12.71	availability is continuous and uninterruptible
Wind	43.50	available when the wind blows, thus intermittent
Solar	70.64	available when the sun shines, thus intermittent
Hydro	315.22	

Figure 6-8[356]

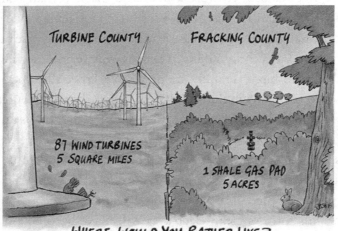

WHERE WOULD YOU RATHER LIVE?

Figure 6-9[357]

Figure 6-10[358]

The amount of waste for the voltage of electricity that solar farms offer also poses daunting challenges, to say the least. A senior Chinese solar official had this to say about solar electricity's incredible waste problem:

> "The problem of solar panel disposal will explode with full force in two or three decades and wreck the environment since it is a huge amount of waste and they are not easy to recycle."[359]

Wind turbines are giant, loud, inefficient, and destructive of the environment. Wind farms kill endangered birds like the American bald eagle. And there is accumulating evidence that wind turbines connected to electrical wind farms kill more human beings than nuclear electricity does.[360] But the truly surprising part about solar and wind farms is how little electricity each contributes—"just 1.3 and 6.3 percent of electricity in the U.S. and 1.3 and 3.9 percent of electricity globally."[361]

The unquestioning acceptance of renewables, without understanding their limitations, has now infected *Foreign Affairs,* the leading publication of the Council on Foreign Relations. The globally respected magazine stated unwisely in its March-April 2019 edition:

> "The market now favors clean electricity: in many U.S. states, it is cheaper to build new renewable electricity plants than to run existing coal-fired power plants. By combining solar power with new, efficient batteries, Arizona and other sunny states will soon be able to provide electricity at a lower cost per megawatt-hour than new, efficient natural gas plants."[362]

These assertions are false, misleading, and unfortunately typical of the green electricity narrative that continues blithely to ignore facts, common sense, physics, knowledge of how weather behaves, and basic economics. Of course, we can all hope for a future in which renewables overcome the many formidable barriers thus far detailed. But the clear and present geopolitical dangers posed by renewables must concern us, and these dangers are rarely discussed.

The Geopolitical Dangers of Renewable Electricity (RE)

Whoever rules over energy and electricity controls the world. Dictators in China, Russia, and Iran (CRI) understand that power comes from the fossil fuel resources that power their armies, navies, and missile systems.[363] The world is under threat from these three countries.

Renewables also pose a danger to the world, as unlikely as that may seem, because they are so unstable yet popular to masses of people. There is a great power competition taking place between the U.S., the EU and NATO on one side and CRI on the other.[364]

Why, it may be wondered, do renewables constitute a geopolitical liability, compared to fossil fuels and nuclear? Countries will say "we are green," "we are moving toward solar and wind farms for electricity," or "we are moving toward being carbon-free or toward low-carbon electrical sources," when none of those things is true. The West, led by the U.S. and Europe, has completely embraced renewables, and those who lead this charge, like Bill Gates and Al Gore, do not understand how this embrace can actually damage world peace and prosperity. If the U.S., the EU, NATO, and Asian allies were to use only renewables, their militaries, economies, and transportation systems would revert back to horse-and-buggy days. This would allow our three-headed adversarial alliance, the CRI, to take over and rule the world. The last time these types of dictatorial governments, militaries, and regimes exercised such power, it led to the deadliest war in history, WWII.

The *British Petroleum (BP) Statistical Review of World Energy* (using population data from the World Bank) shows how renewables will never come close to displacing oil, natural gas, coal, and nuclear in coming decades. If Western nations ignore such chilling and persuasive warnings, and all the other cautionary signs on the road to our energy future, we can realistically expect World War III to occur. This isn't hyperbole to sell a book, but a cold, hard fact that needs to be confronted.[365]

Figure 6-11

Population and Energy Consumption - 2017
USA compared to rest-of-world (ROW)
MTO = million tons of oil equiv., KGO = kilograms oil equiv.

	USA	ROW	World
population (millions)	324	7,226	7,550
energy use (MTO)	2,235	11,276	13,511
per capita energy use (KGO)	6,898	1,561	1,790

The chart above (Figure 6-11) shows the U.S. population in 2017 at 324 million (from U.S. Census data), which is only 4.3 percent of the world total, whereas there are roughly 7.2 billion people in the rest of the world (ROW). Row 2 (from the *BP Statistical Review*) reveals that in 2017 the ROW used 11.276 billion metric tons of oil equivalents (MTOE). The U.S. used 2.2 billion MTOE, and this came out to roughly 17 percent of all energy consumed worldwide. The average American used and consumed almost 4.5 as much energy as the average ROW person. In kilograms of oil equivalents (KGOE), row three of the chart shows that in 2017 the average American burned 6,898 KGOE while the average ROW person burned 1,561.

The next chart (Figure 6-12, two paragraphs down) shows the amount of energy that will be needed by 2035 for the world to achieve human longevity, upward-surging economic results, and the likely avoidance of wars over resources. Edward Ring of the California Policy Center makes some interesting assumptions about trends in the charted figures.

> "A primary assumption is that Americans become somewhat more efficient with using electricity, with their per capita KGOE/year consumption declining from the 2017 average of 6,898 to 5,000 by 2035. Other assumption is that people living in the ROW increase their electricity consumption from the 2017 average of 1,561/year up to 2,500/year by 2035."[366]

Mr. Ring's quoted assumptions are reasonable given the population and economic growth projected for China, India, and the continent of Africa.

Figure 6-12

Population and Energy Consumption - 2035
USA compared to rest-of-world (ROW)
MTO = million tons oil equiv., KGO = kilograms oil equiv.

	USA	ROW	World
population (millions)	355	8,538	8,893
energy use (MTO)	1,775	21,345	23,120
per capita energy use (KGO)	5,000	2,500	2,600

Based on the above chart, total global energy production (before accounting for electrical use) "Will need to increase by 71 percent, from 13.5 billion metric tons of oil equivalent in 2017, to 23.1 per year in 2035." These are based on World Bank projections for 2035 that have U.S. population estimates growing to 355 million and "total world population increasing to 8.9 billion."

The real question to be asked is whether solar and wind farms can supply and sustain these drastic electrical increases.

The answer, according to the *BP Statistical Review of World Energy*, is a <u>resounding no</u>. The chart below (Figure 6-13) reveals that the electricity share of renewables (the orange slice) is a negligible non-factor compared to where the overwhelming majority of global energy comes from: coal, natural gas, and oil. Economic development, technological progress, and innovation will all decline, infant mortality will increase, and another world war will likely happen—and soon—if the West persists in this foolish march toward renewables.[367]

Energy Review shows the fuel mix of global energy production today.

Figure 6-13[368]

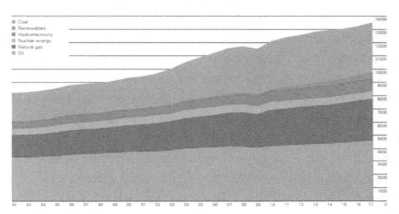

There are more than 2 billion people currently without electricity, with the continent of Africa alone having more than 635 million inhabitants without any form of modern energy or electricity.[369] This lack of scalable, affordable energy that fossil fuels and nuclear provide looks to be a direct correlation for the inherent instability of Africa with its lower economic growth, higher rates of overpopulation, and inability to combat radicalization by groups like ISIS. On other continents, there are another roughly 1.5 billion people who exist under Africa-like conditions, facing the same destabilizing and demoralizing troubles that renewables simply cannot eradicate at this time.

If the most advanced country in the world—the United States of America, with its access to thousands of world-class research facilities, Silicon Valley, and funding for research and development (R&D)—can't solve or even clearly discern the problems caused by renewables, it is doubtful that Africa or the other 1.5 billion energy-starved people can do so, now or in the decades ahead. But a blind global pursuit of renewables will lead to war, geopolitical nightmares, and doom billions to higher electrical costs, along with unreliable electricity and a likely reversion to dirty coal-fired power plants as their primary source of electricity backing up renewables. All of which is in line with <u>the U.S. Energy Information Administration's estimates that 77 percent of the world's electricity needs by 2040 will continue to be met by fossil fuels</u>.[370]

China, India, the U.K., France, Germany, and the State of California all talk of banning the combustible engine vehicles that run our militaries and most modern transportation systems. If the West truly believes that China and India will really follow through and ban combustible engine vehicles, then we will be committing societal suicide. Based on China and India's use of dirty coal-fired power plants, building of nuclear power plants, and their ever-growing economies and population, neither of these countries will stop anything that could slow its growth or impair its geopolitical rivalry against the other.[371]

To underline this point, China is building the dirtiest-emitting coal-fired power plants in Pakistan. In order to counter China geopolitically, India is also weaponizing energy, stabbing back at the China-Pakistan alliance by building the largest coal-fired power plant in recent memory on the Great Barrier Reef in Australia.[372] China, Pakistan, and India pursuing these three-sided energy wars is similar to how Russia's state-owned energy firm Rosneft is being used by the Kremlin to weaponize its foreign policy against the West. (See the Chapter on *The Weaponization of Energy* for additional information on this subject.)

Conclusion

Energy and electricity are the building blocks for human flourishing and human longevity. Stable, reliable, affordable, abundant, and flexible energy that oil, natural gas, coal, and nuclear provide can be used as a realist-balancing option against countries like China, Russia, Iran, North Korea, Syria, and Venezuela, and territories or nations that harbor terrorists. All these entities (and others) are on the march for additional energy resources to power their bombs, guns, and militaries, and that source certainly isn't renewable energy.

The geopolitical nightmare-in-the-making that renewables present can be stopped if all nations will embrace the abundance of fossil fuels and make them available for people across the world who lack access to energy and electricity. Fossil fuels and nuclear offer real hope to bring these billions out of energy poverty and never-ending wars. Yes, certainly, renewables will one day be used on a wide-scale basis, leading to a world of low-carbon electricity. But an all-of-the-above approach to energy is the best decision moving forward, a clear-eyed approach that uses coal, oil, natural gas, and nuclear to bring prosperity and a cleaner environment to all nations.

This policy will give renewables the opportunity, with proper research and development, to overcome their intermittent, dilute, non-energy-dense nature. When that happens, then they will be ready for wide-scale use and deployment. I hope, in my lifetime, that my home and family will be using micro-grids powered by solar panels and wind turbines that are backed up by clean, hydroelectric dams. But until that hoped-for day becomes reality, let's use carbon-free nuclear and low-emitting natural gas for our homes, businesses, and transportation options. Together let's take a sober-minded approach to renewables.

Chapter Seven

Electrical Grid
By Todd Royal

Summary

The electrical grid has many deficiencies that are strangely overlooked in most current discussions of energy and electrical policy and deliverability to ratepayers and consumers.

For example, solar panels on residential homes reduce revenue to utility companies, revenue that is needed for critical grid maintenance and electrical infrastructure improvements. At the same time, there are increasing charging demands being placed on the grid from electrical vehicles (EVs), resulting in harsh electrical load demands that utility companies will have difficulty maintaining with reduced revenue from the solar panel movement.

The term "electrical grid" refers to all the networks through which electricity is generated, transmitted, and distributed to the end user. A "smart grid" is one that includes a variety of operational and energy measures, including smart meters, smart appliances, renewable electricity resources, and energy-efficient resources.

Introduction

Most of us simply turn on the lights or push buttons to make our air conditioning and heating unit work. We are too busy to think about how this happens or where this takes place. But our prosperous, luxurious lifestyles can be traced back to the electrical grid. Much attention of late has been focused on our electrical grid and the need for this essential and almost unimaginably expensive piece of infrastructure to evolve—so that:

> "100 percent of the nation's (can be any nation, not just the United States) electric power [can be obtained] from renewable sources, be 'smart,' allow for every residential and industrial building to have great energy (and electricity) efficiency and minimize greenhouse-gas emissions."[373]

This chapter will attempt to look into these various issues and address them without bias. How much will this updated, technologically sound and flexible electrical grid cost? Researching this book for over six years and working for the American Society of Civil Engineer's report for six months in 2018-19 on California energy and electricity, I discovered that <u>no one had any reasonable idea how to fulfill the objectives listed in the quote above</u>.

Further, no one knew what it would cost to achieve the goals that a new, advanced smart electrical grid would supposedly accomplish. In fact, there are no plans anywhere in the world for how long it will take to plan, build, and perfect on-demand, 24/7/365 electrical delivery to consumers and ratepayers.

The best we know of any cost estimates for a new grid for just the United States came from a 2011 independent nonprofit firm that was primarily funded by utility companies. The firm was the Electric Power Research Institute (EPRI), which estimated that the cost of a national smart grid, including electricity storage systems, would be $338 billion to $476 billion.[374] Utility companies would need to invest between

$17-24 billion per year to replace, build, and put into use a brand-new smart grid system in the U.S. with all costs passed onto consumers. Other estimates have the cost of a new grid starting around $5 trillion plus and climbing, since planning, land-use issues, and building a new smart grid would take decades.[375]

The most recent costs related to grids by a modern country came from China in 2018-19. The Chinese government through its Belt and Road Initiative (BRI) spent $180.9 million to connect 224,000 people from the capital of Maldives to a Maldivian island.[376] From that, we can try to estimate what it would cost for a new, modern smart grid built for billions of people in India, China—or, say, 350 million Americans—and the cost is surely greater than the EPRI estimates. The $180.9 million was simply to connect one island to another using the existing Maldivian grid.

And there are other factors that need to be taken into account. First, there is the American fracking revolution (since the early 2000s) that will put pressure on the cost and maintenance of the existing grid and smart grid(s). Then there is European Union (EU) instability. There is the Italian economy, shrinking at an average rate of 0.5% per year, and the French economy, only growing at an average of 0.8% a year. Both would be in worse shape if oil prices per barrel were in the $125 range. That was the price in 2013-14 before the oil price crash. The U.S. shale phenomenon "keep[s] these fragile economies afloat; at an oil price of $125 a barrel, the Eurozone—and its banking system—might well face another economic crisis."[377]

If a multi-trillion-dollar smart grid is needed for advanced and emerging economies, where do cheap American oil and natural gas fit into the equation? According to Walter Russell Mead, foreign policy and natural security specialist at *The Wall Street Journal*, U.S. shale now has to be accounted for in all energy, electricity, national security, economic, and foreign policy decisions. Without U.S. shale, there can be no new electrical grid or a carbon-free, low-carbon, or clean, green economic transition.[378]

These issues will need to be resolved before new grids can start being built on a global basis, because renewable energy for electricity needs continuous and uninterruptable backup. U.S. shale currently provides the natural gas for natural gas-power plants to accomplish that goal. Without this uninterruptable backup, electrical grids are overwhelmed with fluctuating solar and wind farm electricity, as California was when it led the U.S. in electricity imports between 2013-2017 according to the Energy Information Administration (EIA).[379]

But let's step back from these issues of geopolitical tensions and affordability of smart grids to ask a more fundamental question:

What Is An Electrical Grid?

Electricity that comes from an electrical grid is more than standalone structures, entities. and wires strung together for miles and miles. A grid is an inanimate object the same way a home is empty unless filled with people. Electricity from a grid comes from energy. This energy comes from fossil fuels, nuclear power plants, hydroelectric dams or renewable energy. Energy and electricity are interchangeable and interdependent.

There is a gross misunderstanding that electricity can be a cure-all for everything wrong with the environment and modern economies. Electricity does not power modern economies, militaries, or all forms of transportation without major behind-the-scenes support from energy that is scalable, reliable, functional, affordable, flexible, and abundant. These essential variables are not characteristic of electricity, but they are present in nuclear, fossil fuels and renewables. Energy and electricity must work together for prosperous economies, human longevity and technological advancement to continue.

The electrical grid's official definition is multifaceted since:

> "An electrical grid or electric grid is an interconnected network for delivering electricity from producers to consumers. It consists of generating stations that produce electrical power, high-voltage transmission lines that carry electricity from distant sources to demand

centers, and distribution lines that connect individual customers."[380]

Simply put, for the purposes of making energy and electricity easier to understand, "<u>The Electrical Grid is the means through which electricity is generated, transmitted, and distributed to the end user</u>."[381]

"End user" is defined as any person(s) who needs, expects, and pays for continuous and uninterruptible on-demand energy and electricity. Meaning, you flick on the light switch, and the lights automatically turn on without delay or excuses. That is on-demand energy and electricity. Electrical grids are engineering marvels, though many are now outdated like those in the U.S. and in many Western-aligned nations.[382] The extent of the electrical grid's complexity can be seen in the US electrical grid:

> "Where more than 9,200 electric generating units having more than 1 million megawatts of generating capacity [are] connected to more than 600,000 miles of transmission lines."[383]

The same scale of complexity and amount of materials and engineering needed for the U.S. grid can be found in grids used in China, India, the EU, and large swaths of South America, the Middle East, and Africa.

The grid also includes asset owners (utility entities/companies), manufacturers of materials needed for the grid to exist and deliver electricity, and government and private officials at all levels of the grid. An example of the extent of government involvement and complexity in the grid is the Office of Electricity (OE) within the U.S. Department of Energy. The OE works with the government, business, and individual sectors of the U.S. economy to "strengthen, transform, and improve electricity infrastructure to ensure access to reliable, secure, and clean sources of electricity."[384]

The Electrical Grid Debate and Issues to Understand

Any discussion over the grid is further heightened over the issue of clean sources of electricity. Some of the ways and means being used to incorporate these green technologies into the grid are generating their own energy and electrical dismay. A case in point is the State of Vermont, where emissions have risen over 16.3% since 2005 (a problem being encountered by many states and countries). This was not the outcome anticipated by the Vermont Legislature when it pledged to:

> "Reduce emissions 25% below 1990 levels by 2012, and 50% below 1990 levels by 2028, through the use of renewables and energy (electricity) efficiency, via the electrical grid."[385]

These same kinds of emission-level problems are happening in Germany, Denmark, Spain, Australia, and in U.S. states, counties, and cities (including California, Arkansas, San Bernardino County, California, Henry County, Indiana, and the City of Georgetown, Texas). There has been an apparent lack of research in these localities as to how the grid affects the environment. For example, when the Vermont Legislature decided to use mainly renewables over nuclear or natural gas, that actually made the grid dirtier and less efficient, resulting in higher emissions.[386] Vermont's rising emissions caused by the state's reliance on renewables have consequences for the health, longevity, and efficiency of grids in the U.S. and in other countries.[387] Current grid technology cannot handle the intermittent electricity that results from renewable energy (mainly solar and wind electrical generating power). During the same 2005-2015-time span, U.S. per capita emissions declined 17% while Vermont's per capita emissions rose 5%.[388]

The next-to-last section in this chapter will delve further into the severity of Vermont's actions on the electrical grid and on global health, while attempting to show how an all-of-the-above approach (fossil fuels, nuclear, hydroelectric, and renewables all working in concert) is the best approach when it comes to energy and electricity.

But religion and birthrates also affect the grid, and in interesting and unexpected ways. U.S. states that have rising birth rates are usually religious and, by having larger families, should have higher emissions, yet the opposite occurs. U.S. states and other regions of the world that have embraced renewable energy for generating electricity are typically less religious, or non-religious, often tending to embrace abortion, yet these regions are seeing rising emissions and higher electrical rates.[389] Clearly many factors other than energy sources can affect grid and global health.

Deep, probing questions about grids need to start being asked.[390] Proponents of electrical grid modernization should advocate for consumers to be given better access to critical information on electricity use during peak days, times, hours, and seasons. This could possibly help utilities manage electrical grids when they are overwhelmed during cold winters or hot summers.[391] Or when renewables produce too much electricity from solar power.[392] Problems associated with battery storage systems integrating with the grid are another issue to understand, since currently these systems aren't working as advertised.[393]

Transforming any electrical grid will come up against the dilemmas of what are the best ways to deliver electricity, strategic research, and a coordinated effort between government and the private sector for effective research and development (R&D).

Technology-constraints from renewables are the biggest issues electrical grids will face moving forward. There isn't one electrical grid on the planet that can handle large-scale deployment of renewable energy onto its network. Energy battery storage systems currently available do not have enough capacity to store energy from the sun and wind for the days, weeks or months typically required by intermittent electricity.[394]

Intermittent electricity is defined:

> "As any source of electricity that is not continuously available for conversion into electricity (on the electrical

grid) and outside direct control since the primary electricity cannot be stored. Intermittent electricity sources may be predictable but cannot be dispatched to meet the demand of an electric system (an electrical grid)."[395]

Electrical grids need highly trained and technically proficient civil and electrical engineers demonstrating perfection in analytical capabilities and in knowing how energy and electrical infrastructures work together to deliver on-demand electricity. The reason energy and electricity must work in unison is the need for energy, electricity and the electrical grid to be scalable (in how much energy it uses), reliable (in keeping with its mission of delivering continuous and uninterruptible on-demand electricity), and affordable (so that ratepayers aren't price-gouged).

An electrical grid, according to the U.S. Office of Electricity, needs to accomplish: "Resiliency, reliable and affordable delivery of electricity while modernizing grid scale electricity storage; smart grid research and advanced technologies."[396] Electrical grids need R&D for upgrades to next-generation smart grids (which will be discussed in the next section), grid-scale electricity storage (which, according to the U.S. Department of Energy's Quadrennial Energy Review, or QER, is not yet in existence), and a host of complex engineering, electronic, math, regression analysis, econometrics, physics, chemistry, construction and management techniques that include:

> "Advanced technologies such as solid-state transformers and power flow controllers that can optimize power delivery and enhance resilient power electronics, complex interactive capabilities that can allow the system (electrical grid) to respond to change (adaptive networks); intelligent communications and control systems; and new measurements, data analytics, and models that leverage the latest scientific advancements in mathematics and computation."[397]

Today's electrical grid is one of the most complex, incredible, and yet outdated breakthroughs. Grids need to become smarter through "enhanced information technology, which turns the electrical grid into an intelligent network."[398] This is accomplished by increasing the durability and resiliency of the grid using state-of-the-art technologies, equipment, networks, and control systems that can deliver electricity in faster frequencies.

One thing should be made clear: <u>At this time there is no such thing as a smart grid currently in use</u>. An entire smart electrical grid that can move electricity throughout parts of the grid to meet high or low demand is <u>not yet technologically feasible</u>. On a positive note, however, there are many countries, governments, private organizations, nongovernmental organizations (NGOs) like the United Nations (UN), and wealthy individuals all attempting to master the technology and build a smart electrical grid.

Now let's move on to one of the major debates within the energy and electrical sector—the not-yet-invented but explainable smart electrical grid.

Electrical Grid Economics

Solar at home, perhaps paired with an electric car in the garage or an energy battery storage system in the basement to store electricity generated from sunshine for use at night or on a cloudy day, could reduce the profits of the companies that operate the electrical grid.

With homeowners making their own electricity, utilities will lose many lucrative customers and confront a dwindling base of ratepayers to help offset big electrical infrastructure costs such as building new power plants or maintaining the grid. When too many Americans get off the grid, it may put utilities into a death spiral of fewer electricity sales to cover maintenance costs. Thus, solar power may pose an existential threat to the future viability of the entire electrical utility industry.

Although solar installations now account for less than one-quarter of one percent of U.S. electricity supply, if rooftop arrays became as ubiquitous as chimneys, the utilities fear that they could go out of business or exist merely to maintain the grid. Germany and Spain are considering imposing fees on solar power for access to the grid to ensure maintenance of this critical infrastructure, while other areas are attempting more aggressive tactics, seeking to deter or even block further solar power development.[399]

Smart Grids

The International Energy Agency (IEA) "is an autonomous organization, which works to ensure reliable, affordable and clean energy (electricity) for its 30 member countries and beyond to help government, industry and citizens make good energy (electricity) choices."[400] The IEA is a Paris-based research-and-predictive-analysis firm that was formed a year after the 1973 Arab oil embargo crisis. The IEA has tracked the development of smart grids since their inception. The IEA shows that investments in smart grid technologies "grew by 12% between 2014-2016, but key areas such as smart distribution networks are lagging behind." (see Figure 7-1 immediately below)[401]

Figure 7-1

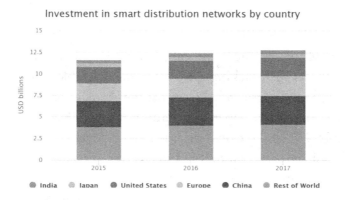

Currently, smart meter deployment has to be part of smart grids for them to succeed. Other shortcomings include a lack of set standards and conditions and uneven use in countries where smart grids have been installed.[402] Even more serious problems may arise from smart meters' intrusiveness into personal information and lack of cyber security. Another major shortcoming is in the general understanding of how electronic meters distribute electricity throughout the grid. For instance, many electricity consumers worry that smart meters will shut off their air conditioners during hot summer months and fluctuate heat during winter storms and colder temperatures. When the end user needs electricity the most, in other words, the installed smart meter in a home or business may sense electrical grid overload and shut off the power. While the smart meter may be smart enough to sense grid overload, the electrical grids they interface with may lack the flexibility to send excess electricity into a battery storage system, or simultaneously to other parts of the grid where ratepayers and consumers could use the excess electricity at a lower cost. Investments in smart meters grew 3% in 2017. But clearly these highly touted devices will need a framework and a new business model for them to play a leading role in clean energy to electricity.

The U.S. is still the leader in smart meter technology, but a May 2015 U.S. Department of Energy (DOE) analysis of smart meter investments, deployment, and use from the 2009 American Recovery and Reinvestment Act found that considerable work still needs to be done:

> "The business case for the smart grid based on results to the value proposition for many of the projects [is] lacking. Without considerable capital costs (taxpayer funded from the government or private corporations), operation and maintenance costs (O&M), and the quantification of all benefits, it is not possible to determine the value of the projects from a cost versus benefit perspective. In most cases, it is not possible from the results to determine if these projects are cost competitive with other solutions from a least cost perspective. Furthermore, as most of the projects were first-of-a-kind or pioneer DEMONSTRATIONS,

the capital and O&M costs associated with these technologies are most likely higher than their value once these technologies mature. A definitive cost-benefit analysis cannot be undertaken at this time."[403]

What this long quote explains is that a technological breakthrough is needed for smart meters and a smart grid to transition us to a "Green New Deal," or the "promises of greater energy (electricity) efficiency and reduced greenhouse gas emissions."[404] The smart grid has taken off mostly in the public imagination without sufficient understanding of the costs, the implications for civil liberties, or how long it will take to build that type of grid from either the ground-up or by adding on to existing electrical grids.

The smart grid has the potential to bring stability and reliability, but the belief that a grid will solve every environmental ill is misguided. At the current state of development, smart grids actually cause more problems than they alleviate. Until a sweeping new smart electrical grid becomes feasible both technologically and financially (that is, without burdening taxpayers and government budgets with enormous costs), smart grids will likely continue to be more promise than reality. At the very least, before rushing ahead with further smart-grid implementation, we need more information about, and a fuller explanation of, this particular energy-to-electricity issue.

A better solution, while we're figuring out smart electrical grids, is to update existing grids with state-of-the-art technology and to use coal-fired power plants for emerging economies and low-emission-burning natural gas-power plants in advanced and wealthier countries. And while we're at it, we also need to invent the technology that fully and simultaneously implements energy to electricity that can be stored in energy battery storage systems and moved across the grid at on-demand, continuous and uninterruptible speeds.

A first step in planning this next generation electrical grid is analyzing who are its stakeholders. The likely order of who benefits starts with the on-demand user, the ratepayer, individual and business. Next comes the infrastructure builder who has to construct this complex, computerized electrical grid capable of whipping electricity across network providers, system operators, and utilities in different states, regions, countries, and ultimately across oceans and continents. When the requirements for all those stakeholders are met, then a smart electrical grid may indeed become a reality—a grid that is both efficient and cyber-secure that experts can troubleshoot immediately, and that can gain wide acceptance and buy-in from all parties involved. Of course, this new grid will continue facing challenges until all regulatory issues are resolved and "the various (global) partners together negotiate technology standards."[405]

Back in 2010 at the height of the smart grid allure, *The Atlantic* magazine made an astute observation:

> "The biggest problems with the $1.5 trillion installation of the Smart Grid (possible cost for a new US grid) are not the dicey technological, financial and regulatory riddles that currently obsess bureaucrats, but chewy philosophical ones. The Smart Grid is rolling out because all the right interest groups love it."[406]

Environmentalists want renewables. Corporate interests want to sell appliances. Utilities want to manage electricity with less people, which increases their profitability. And regulators want to lessen electrical outages "that already cost the U.S. economy $119 billion a year." But just as troubling, perhaps, as having corporate greed play a role in making vital energy and electrical policy decisions, is having those decisions made for political or ideological reasons, such as the current enthusiasm over green ideals whose appeal is often more emotional than factual.

There are so many factors involved in delivering electricity, but one factor too often overlooked is that of cyber security. Smart grids use the power of information technology to intelligently deliver energy, and this entails giving those grids access to massive amounts of consumer data. Organizations like the American Civil Liberties Union (ACLU) should definitely be concerned:

"To enable households and small businesses to make sensible and comprehensible choices about their own electricity consumption [and] to avert the backlash that is likely to come if the public sees the smart grid as a means of manipulating behavior and forcing people to do things they do not wish to do."[407]

Electric grids, whether smart or antiquated (as most grids are globally), need stable energy from fossil fuels, nuclear or intermittent renewables rather than feel-good sentiments and technologies not even close to being scalable, reliable, flexible, abundant, or affordable.

Why Grids Need Stable Electricity

E.F. Schumacher was a former German coal executive whose midlife conversion to the gospel of alternative energies anticipated (by about four decades) that of Tom Steyer. Steyer (as mentioned in earlier chapters) made billions off coal-fired power plant investments while becoming an ardent environmentalist. But Schumacher not only turned into a New Age environmental guru, but in 1973 published a book titled *Small Is Beautiful*. Schumacher's book extolled the virtues of the destitute lifestyles of dying Indian farmers while demonizing energy and electricity. Schumacher especially hated nuclear electricity, calling it "the most serious agent of pollution of the environment and greatest threat to man's survival on earth."[408] All the facts so far, however, prove Mr. Schumacher completely wrong. Nuclear energy remains the world's only zero-carbon, reliable, stable, and abundant electricity generation source.[409]

Let's look at Vermont again as an example of why electrical grids need stable and reliable power for converting into electricity. The National Resources Defense Council (NRDC) claims that the electrical grid, through its electricity efficiency, will reduce emissions and alleviate the needs for fossil fuels and nuclear power.[410] Electricity efficiency is important, and using resources wisely makes good sense for consumers, business and government. The question then arises, where did Vermont go wrong with its energy and electricity efficiency? In fact, they didn't, since Vermont was ranked a top-five state for both energy and electricity efficiency by the American Council for an Energy-Efficient Economy in 2018, and the previous four years also won this honor.[411]

The problems happened when Vermont's top electric utility provider and grid manager began distributing solar panels and aggressively helping customers go "off-grid" with solar and batteries, thus ensuring the increased need for continuous and uninterruptible backup from fossil fuel or nuclear power resources.[412] The problems can be traced back to Vermont's single functioning nuclear plant, Vermont Yankee, and specifically to misguided climate activist and radical-environmentalist Bill McKibben who led a successful effort to shut the Vermont Yankee nuclear power plant down. McKibben stated:

> "I believe Vermont is completely capable of replacing (and far more) its power output (electricity from the electrical grid) with renewables, which is why my roof is covered with solar panels."[413]

The point isn't whether you agree or disagree with nuclear energy and electricity but understanding the fact that current grids simply cannot handle renewables in large doses.

Pro-nuclear environmentalists tried to warn McKibben, Senator Bernie Sanders, and other Vermonters in favor of shutting down Vermont Yankee in a 2010 thorough analysis of the consequence of these actions:

"Vermont's rising emissions (occurred because) Vermont's utilities couldn't replace electricity with in-state generation they lost from Vermont Yankee, instead turning to electricity imports from the New England power pool, primarily from natural gas."[414]

Currently, the Vermont electrical grid is experiencing widespread instability.[415] Additional data highlights that "Vermont's emissions from transportation were higher in 2005 than in 2015."[416] Which raises another question. Vermont is considered "environmentally sound" in transportation, so what gives?[417]

It comes back again to the grid, and environmentalists like Senator Bernie Sanders (who wants to deny all new nuclear plant licenses), Bill McKibben, the Sierra Club, NRDC, and the Environmental Defense Fund who only put their stamp of approval on renewables. A threat-matrix is developing for fossil fuel firms to the extent "that without continued investment in new supplies [of oil and gas], the global economy could be threatened by shortages" in the near and long-term future.[418] As an example, two U.S. pipelines in the crucial Texas Permian Basin are having difficulty attaining regulatory approval from the U.S. Federal Energy Regulatory Commission because of environmentalists.[419]

Every one of these environmental organizations and individuals has global reach that will greatly impact the electrical grids of the U.S. and Western-aligned nations. Maybe it's time for the environmental movement's global reach to look instead at bringing zero-emission nuclear power to underdeveloped countries. Such an initiative could save millions of lives and start these impoverished countries on the road to prosperity. Unfortunately, so far none of these pro-renewable leaders seems to realize that grids in Vermont and elsewhere cannot handle unstable energy to electricity.[420] Nor do they seem to care that more and more people simply do not want land- and ocean-consuming solar and wind farms.[421]

But others might argue that it is anti-environmentalists and climate-deniers who are refusing to accept the benefits of solar and wind farms. That the anti-environmentalists are the ones actually harming the grid and the environment, while progressive citizens are ready to welcome clean, renewable electricity that comes from industrial-sized solar and wind farms—yes, even in their backyards and communities. This sounds like a plausible argument. However, the exact opposite took place in Vermont, and McKibben blamed Vermont's governor and energy regulator when he said: "They bowed to opponents of wind power and imposed a *de facto* moratorium on new wind turbines. I thought that was a mistake."[422]

Grids cannot handle fluctuating wind electrical generation farms. The late Professor David J.C. MacKay at the University of Cambridge "calculated that wind electricity requires about 700 times more land to produce the same amount of electricity (for the electrical grid) as a fracking site."[423] This explains why California's largest county by land mass, San Bernardino County, through its elected County Board of Supervisors, decided to:

> "Ban construction of large solar and wind farms on more than 1 million acres of private land. This vote highlighted a challenge California could face as it seeks to eliminate the burning of planet-warming fossil fuels."[424]

In place of large solar and wind farms, San Bernardino County has decided to build coal plants to support its electrical grid.

In a concluding statement on Vermont's electric grid instability (caused by the Green Mountain State's adamant support for renewables over fossil fuels and/or nuclear power), Michael Shellenberger, a former *Time Magazine* "Hero of the Environment," has written:

> "Consider Vermont. The only wind farm to be built in the entire state over the last 10 years was the Deerfield Wind Project. According to Lisa Linowes of Wind Action, it took from 2009 to 2017 for the project to be completed, because of litigation that the giant wind farm is sited in the middle of a critical black bear habitat. <u>Can you guess how many wind farms the size of Deerfield would be needed in order to replace the annual quantity of electricity from Vermont Yankee, one of the smallest nuclear plants remaining in the U.S. when it was closed? The answer is 59</u>. At the Deerfield rate of deployment, Vermont will make up for the clean energy and (electricity) lost from the closure of Vermont Yankee sometime around the year 2491."

Anti-nuclear campaigners and the get-off-deep-earth minerals/fuels crowd have caused Vermont's emissions to rise, its citizens' health to worsen, and inflicted strains on the state's electrical grid that will cost taxpayers considerably.

The grid is then forced to comply with a source of electricity that it is not designed to handle and that needs hours of battery storage that hasn't yet been invented. Current electricity battery storage systems can store only between 8-12 hours of electricity.[425] What needs to be understood about batteries is that they wear out over time, require continual maintenance and eventually require disposal, including disposal of highly toxic chemicals.

The integration of batteries and intermittent renewables onto electrical grids raises questions about the actual validity of calling solar and wind industrial-sized farms "green," considering the fact that electricity should do no harm to the on-demand, end user. The time is ripe for a new, smart electrical grid that can address these critical issues. But, for now, let's take a detailed look at how the grid failed during an Arctic blast that hit the Midwest and Eastern parts of the U.S. in January-February 2019, a failure that, with fossil-fuel backup, could have resulted in people being frozen to death.

The 2019 U.S. Cold Front and the Electrical Grid

The U.S. energy consulting and analytical research firm, Wood Mackenzie (WM), used the 2019 "polar vortex" to measure demand and reliability of the electrical power grid. The report, titled *"Performance Review: Nuclear, Fossil Fuels and Renewables During the 2019 Polar Vortex,* was stunning in its findings.[426] It examined "how various forms of energy performed, including projections of how resources would fare in a 100 percent renewable electricity scenario."[427] The findings showed how one of the larger, more advanced U.S. electrical grids failed when it relied on renewable energy to electricity. The WM report revealed:

> "Any mix of wind and solar to serve load would require long-duration storage or optimization of multiple 'stages' of shorter duration."[428]

The report, like the 2015 and 2017 U.S. Department of Energy's *Quadrennial Energy Review (QER)*, notes that wind and solar could be built to scale where the electrical grid was supplied adequately. But people across the U.S. during brutal winter days would have been without heat and power for several hours each day since the electricity storage capacity for wind and solar to make economic and technological sense does not exist. During the 2019 Arctic-cold days, the sun wasn't shining bright enough, and the wind wasn't blowing consistently enough to supply heat to homes and businesses. The U.S. economy in the Midwest and Northeastern states during this polar vortex would have simply shut down due to lack of electricity because of overreliance on sun and wind power.

The WM study also noted "a lack of adequate transmission to exchange power between various grid operators, and even within grids."[429] The smart grid section of the study illuminated the fact that the "smart grid" exists only as a theoretical term, not in actual reality. The report goes to some length in order to prove that assertion as fact, not opinion. And that provable fact has far-reaching implications for the health of grids across the world that are being asked to integrate solar, wind, biomass, and hydroelectric when storage systems do not exist to the capacity that electrical grids require to keep the lights on, the heat circulating, and air conditioning cooling during hot summer months.

On two brutally cold days, January 30-31, Mid-continent System Operator (MISO) and Southwest Power Pool (SPP) grids reported that their wind generation power was fulfilling its electrical duties.[430] What was later found to be true, however, was that "coal, natural gas and nuclear power did the heavy lifting" of keeping the heat running and fulfilling the on-demand duties the grid is expected to accomplish.[431] The WM study also revealed:

> "Limited transmission capacity meant that MISO South power prices remained low and that as the cold let up in SPP it was unable

to provide support to MISO and PJM [this company was discussed in the renewable energy-to-electricity chapter] due to transmission limitations."[432]

The electrical grid suppliers still couldn't meet on-demand electrical needs when the polar vortex ended. WM found electrical "storage between 18 to 40 hours" was needed "to bridge the gaps in the first polar vortex of 2019, as long as there were no gaps in transmission."[433] <u>To use renewable electricity when it was most needed and to turn an outdated, though technologically advanced electric grid(s) into a smart grid, the entire electrical framework for the Midwest and Northeastern parts of the U.S. needs new transmission lines, new generation systems, storage systems that aren't in existence and a new multi-trillion dollar, yet-to-be-invented smart grid.</u>

WM's study falsely claimed that solar and wind were working in tandem to cover peak loads when the sun was setting or the wind wasn't blowing consistently enough, but there were large gaps that renewables couldn't handle during the coldest nights and days. Interestingly enough, even the 2019 polar vortex didn't equal in severity or length the one that hit the U.S. in 2014. Under these scenarios, the utilities managing and servicing the electric grids:

> "Drew 17 percent more natural gas per week than to meet demand, and the <u>renewable grid would need up to 40 hours' worth of energy (electricity) storage to make it through the worst of the cold weather. In a more widespread and longer chill, it would NEED EVEN MORE STORAGE.</u>"[434]

It should be noted that no power source (even coal) is 100 percent reliable during extreme weather events. The grid managers were the real heroes.

Conclusion

With a smart electrical grid employing smart meters, cutting-edge technology, and renewable electricity as the main electrical source for the on-demand user, then the electrical grid managers are the key to this endeavor. The key for electrical grid health and reliability is making sure the electricity sources called upon aren't prone to intermittent failure. Most grids in advanced nations and even in emerging markets have managers adept at integrating all forms of energy into electricity. As discussed in this chapter, the problems occur when grid managers are forced to rely on renewable energy and battery storage systems.

Obviously needed are more transmission lines, along with renewable electricity generating capacity that can handle these fluctuating needs. No country or continent has yet met these requirements for a smart electrical grid that has zero-carbon resources powered by renewable electricity. The closest any country, region, or continent has come to this goal are Denmark and France with their expanded use of nuclear electricity.[435]

Prospects for an electrical grid that is smart and carbon-free will remain bleak until massive technological breakthroughs materialize. New electrical grids need to be built globally (as much if not more than military modernization programs) since current electrical grids are old, unsound and unable to handle the strains they are now being tasked with. Moving forward, it will be fascinating to watch the three-way collisions that will take place among environmentalists, capitalists, and free-market thinkers who seem to have only one thing in common—they clearly don't understand what today and tomorrow's electrical grids can and cannot manage.

Chapter Eight

Electric Vehicles
By Ronald Stein

Summary

This chapter is not intended as a discussion of the pros and cons of electric vehicles (EVs), but rather as an introduction to some of the subject matter associated with, and issues arising from, the electric vehicle industry. Those issues, however, do include various challenges and problems confronting the industry, many of these based on future projections, but others already glaringly obvious.

Electric Vehicles

We'll discuss the subject matter of the electric vehicle industry in order: 1) transparency of the supply chain for lithium-ion batteries; 2) weight of the batteries; 3) CO_2 emissions from electric vehicles; 4) charging of the batteries; 5) recycling of used batteries; 6) electric vehicle sales; and 7) worldwide vehicle registration projections.

The Dark Side of Green Technology: No Transparency of the Supply Chain for the Lithium-Ion Batteries

The key minerals used in today's batteries are cobalt, of which 60% is sourced from one country, the Democratic Republic of the Congo[436] (DRC), and lithium, of which more than 50% is sourced from the Lithium Triangle in South America,[437] which covers parts of Argentina, Bolivia and Chile. Today 20% of cobalt is mined by hand. Amnesty International has documented children and adults mining cobalt[438] in narrow man-made tunnels, at risk of fatal accidents and serious lung disease.

The mere extraction of the exotic minerals cobalt and lithium[439] used in the batteries of EVs presents social challenges, human rights abuse challenges, and environmental challenges.[440] Not only are working conditions hazardous, but living conditions are abysmal, with workers making such meager wages that they are forced to live in abject poverty; and, whether on-duty or off, regularly exposed to out-of-control pollution and many other environmental issues that cannot be ignored.

The cobalt mined by children and adults in these horrendous conditions in the DRC in Africa then enters the supply chains of some of the world's biggest brands. There are no known "clean" supply chains for lithium and cobalt, yet the richest and most powerful companies in the world continue to offer up the most complex and implausible excuses for not investigating their own supply chains.

Tesla Motors' "dirty little secret" is turning into a major problem[441] for the EV industry—and perhaps mankind. If you think Tesla's Model S is the green car of the future, think again. Energy independence, a reduction in greenhouse gas emissions, lower fuel costs, these promises are all factors behind the rise in the popularity of electric vehicles. Unfortunately, under scrutiny, all these promises prove to be more fiction than fact.

Recently, the Environmental Protection Agency and the U.S. Department of Energy undertook a study to look at the environmental impact of lithium-ion batteries for EVs. The study showed that batteries that use cathodes with nickel and cobalt, as well as solvent-based electrode processing, have the highest potential for environmental impacts, including resource depletion, global warming, ecological toxicity, and adverse effects on human health. The largest contributing processes include those associated with the production, processing, and use of cobalt and nickel metal compounds, which may cause adverse respiratory, pulmonary, and neurological effects in those exposed.

Weight of the Electric Vehicle Battery

The "elephant in the room" of rechargeable batteries is the electric vehicle or EV. The Tesla battery pack weighs in excess of 1,200 pounds,[442][443] while the iPhone battery is only 0.026kg. California already has 50% of the EVs nationwide. To meet former California Gov. Jerry Brown's executive orders to push the state toward having 5 million electric cars on its roads by 2030 would mean 6 <u>billion</u> pounds of lithium-ion batteries just in California!

Figure 8-1

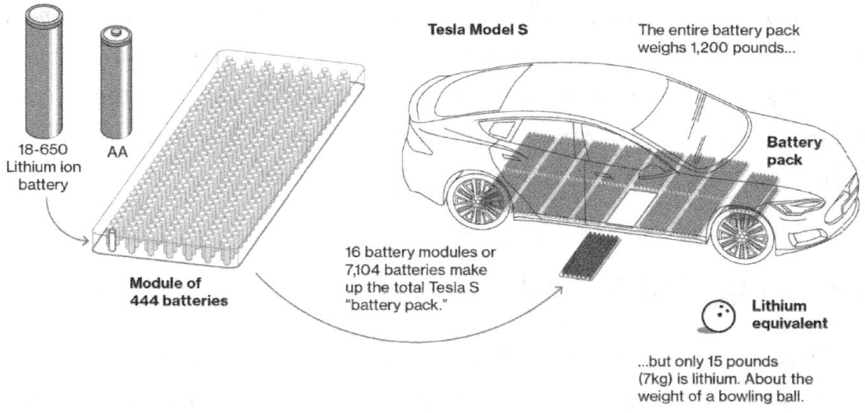

18-650 Lithium ion battery

AA

Module of 444 batteries

Tesla Model S

16 battery modules or 7,104 batteries make up the total Tesla S "battery pack."

The entire battery pack weighs 1,200 pounds...

Battery pack

Lithium equivalent

...but only 15 pounds (7kg) is lithium. About the weight of a bowling ball.

CO2 Emissions From Electric Vehicles

Electric vehicles in Germany account for more CO2 emissions than diesel ones,[444] according to a study by German scientists.

The mining and processing of the lithium, cobalt, and manganese used for batteries consume a great deal of energy. A Tesla Model 3 battery, for example, represents between 11 and 15 tons of CO2.

Given a battery lifetime of 10 years and an annual travel distance of 15,000 kilometers, the CO2 given off to produce the electricity that powers such vehicles also needs to be factored in, the scientists say.

When all these factors are considered, each Tesla emits 156 to 180 grams of CO2 per kilometer, which is more than a comparable diesel vehicle produced by the German company Mercedes.

Charging of Lithium-Ion Batteries

Fast-charging EV batteries can reach 70%-to-80% capacity in less than 40 minutes. But if you happen to be tenth in line at a Costco "recharging" station, that means you should probably count on a five-hour wait to get recharged!

The futuristic charging stations that may replace gas stations may need to provide some major amenities to help drivers fill all the idle hours they'll be at the station, awaiting their opportunity to get connected. For example:

- Restaurants
- Starbucks-type coffeehouses
- Theaters
- "WeWork" office space

The corresponding three curves for batteries sizes 75, 155, and 220 kWh for miles gained versus charging time using a Supercharger[445] are:

Figure 8-2

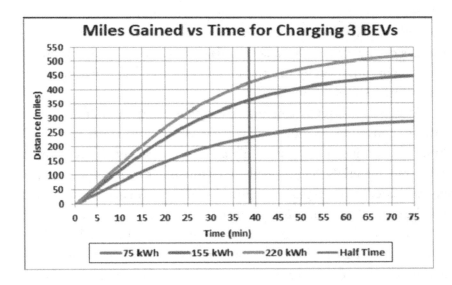

Recycling of Lithium-Ion Batteries

The lithium battery recycling challenge[446] is that increasing oil prices, demand for urban vehicles, megacities, and focus on sustainable transportation have kick-started a substantial trend toward automotive electrification such as hybrids and electric vehicles.

There are several challenges that are likely to impact lithium supply in the future. Although there are enough lithium resources available globally to meet current demand, almost 70% of global lithium deposits are concentrated in South America's ABC (Argentina, Bolivia, and Chile) region. There is an inherent risk when any industry's essential raw material is available only in a specific geography. Unrest or instability of the governments in these regions can greatly affect the supply and thus have impact on the battery price and, in turn, the vehicle cost.

The exotic minerals of lithium and cobalt are both extremely limited in their supply and available locations, compared to crude oil that can be found in almost every country and ocean and at various depths. The limitations of supply and the minable locations for these in-demand commodities present a very serious challenge as to how to continue the EV revolution when those supplies begin to diminish.

Lithium is also consumed by several other applications or sectors, such as construction, pharmaceuticals, ceramics, and glass; in fact, so far, the consumption by the automotive industry has represented only a small fraction of the total.

At present, batteries account for only about a quarter of the current lithium consumption, but that figure is expected to reach about 40% by 2020. Lithium constitutes only a small portion of the cost among other raw materials needed for battery manufacturing. However, with an estimated million-plus EVs already on the roads as of 2015, there will be a significant pressure on lithium suppliers to cater to demand.

To secure lithium resources, intergovernmental as well as OEM-governmental partnerships are being established. Vehicle manufacturers and national governments are treating lithium as a prime future energy source and, as a result, have started forging alliances to safeguard their needs.

Toyota and Magna International-Mitsubishi have both established partnerships with lithium exploration companies and have invested large sums to develop lithium deposits in Argentina in order to safeguard and secure the resources to meet their needs. Japan has forged a partnership with the Bolivian government, which binds the former to offer comprehensive economic aid in exchange for supplies of lithium and other rare-earth metals from the latter.

Lithium supply and its price in the future are expected to be impacted by several factors, such as additional demand from consumer electronics, geopolitical relationships, environmental impact of mining, and larger acceptance of new modes of "mobility solutions" such as electric two-wheelers.

While lithium is 100% recyclable, current economics do not make such recycling profitable or practical. Recycled lithium can cost five times as much as lithium produced from the least costly brine-based process.

The battery-recycling market is largely price-driven as technology is not a critical differentiating factor. All the key participants implement the same level of technology in their product offerings. Therefore, the key differentiating factor becomes price, which in a competitive environment reduces profitability for battery-recycling firms.

With lithium recycling in its infancy, there is currently no main recycling infrastructure in the world that treats only automotive Li-ion batteries.

Electric Vehicle Sales

Today, EV sales appear to be proportional to gas prices around the world, i.e., the higher the local gas price, the greater the EV sales. According to statistics for the fourth quarter of 2018, most prices worldwide are considerably higher than in the United States.

Possible restrictions on future EV sales may be attributable to "range anxiety," "charging anxiety," and the projected battery life span of 10 years, versus the lifespan of diesel and gasoline vehicles that can go well beyond 50 years.

Projected electric vehicle sales worldwide in 2025[447] (in 1,000 units)

- Europe   6,335
- China   4,846

- US   928
- Japan   638
- Rest of the world   1,484

Electric vehicles on the road are projected to grow from 3 million to 125 million by 2030, International Energy Agency (EIA) forecasts in their Annual Energy Outlook[448] (AEO).

However, as sales increase, the taxes collected at the fuel pump will diminish, reducing government revenues for road repairs and miscellaneous environmental projects, and for the general fund.

Since sales are directly related to the availability of the lithium-ion batteries, Tesla's long-term production pace can be threatened by mineral shortages.[449]

Figure 8-3

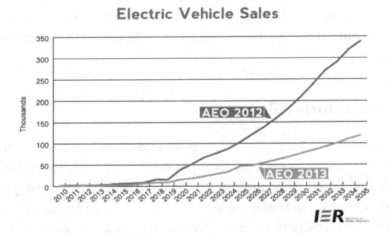

Worldwide Vehicle Registrations

Currently, there are 1.2 billion vehicles on the world's roads, with projections of 2 billion by 2035.[450] By some estimates, the total number of vehicles worldwide could double to 2.5 billion by 2050.

China still has far fewer vehicles per person than Western countries; it has 1.3 billion of the world's 7 billion residents, but only 100 million or so vehicles. If ownership in China were to equal the U.S. rate, the vast country would have a billion vehicles all by itself.

The U.S., by contrast, has maxed out at about 250 million vehicles for its population of 300 million, and that total is expected to grow only incrementally in the future.

Registration of electric vehicles is projected to be only in the single digits, around 5 to 7 percent. If current projections become reality by 2035, 5 to 7 percent of the 2 billion vehicles would equate to 125 million EVs on the world's roads and highways. Whatever positives would result, the negative impacts would be impossible to ignore: More than 125 <u>billion</u> pounds of lithium-ion batteries will need to be disposed of in the decades ahead.

With limited amounts of new roads being constructed to handle the increased number of vehicles, the doubling of vehicle registrations in the coming decades will result in doubling of the number of vehicles on existing roadways. So, another urgent topic of discussion in the decades ahead will be <u>congestion</u>. Creative minds will be tasked to come up with ideas on how to get all those vehicles <u>off</u> those roads in order to prevent global gridlock and at least keep congestion under control.

Chapter Nine

Requirements for a Carbon-Free Society
By Todd Royal

Summary

The benefits of a carbon-free society are often discussed, but rarely are the high costs of achieving this technological breakthrough or the financial impact that breakthrough would have on various economies.

Under current technologies, France has demonstrated that the only way to achieve scalable, reliable, flexible, abundant, and affordable carbon-free electricity capable of powering modern societies is through the use of nuclear power.

Meanwhile, the non-electrical energy that has empowered the military, transportation, infrastructures, and global travel has actually done more for globalization and human progress than anything in mankind's history. Those energy needs have been, and continue to be, met with deep-earth minerals/fuels.

Introduction

The Energy Information Administration (EIA) "expects renewable energy to be the fastest source of growing electricity generation for at least the next two years (2019-2020)." The report further states, "Utility-scale solar will expand by 10 percent in 2019 and 17 percent in

2020. Wind will grow by 12 percent and 14 percent in 2019, and 2020." The report goes on to say that total electricity generation will fall by 2 percent in 2019 and should be flat in 2020. This means renewables will grow 10 percent in 2018 to 13 percent in 2020.[451] The 2018 EIA *International Energy Outlook* has total renewable use at 18.0% and electricity generation at 29.8% by 2050.[452] While these are promising numbers, it is clear that coal, oil, and natural gas will remain the leading sources of energy for decades.

Figure 9-1

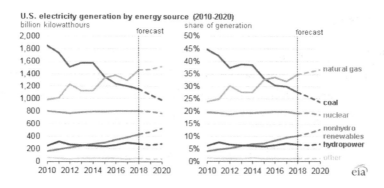

Becoming a carbon-free society will not happen from electricity alone. According to the 2017-2018 EIA *International Energy Outlook,* electricity is unable to support the energy demands of the military, airlines, cruise ships, supertankers, container shipping, trucking/trucking infrastructures, medications, vaccines, or the space program. Nor can intermittent, dilute energy-to-electricity from wind turbines, solar panels, or current batteries (with a shelf life of energy storage of no more than 8-12 hours) supply everything our society requires for us to maintain comfortable and healthful lifestyles. To meet our climate goals, according to the International Energy Agency (IEA), will require nuclear power.[453]

Clearly, for decades ahead, it will be difficult to achieve a carbon-free, or even a low-carbon society (though low-carbon electricity through advanced electrical grids is a distinct possibility). As mentioned in the chapter summary, the best-case scenario for a carbon-free society is to be found in France, which relies on nuclear energy to deliver most of its electricity. In fact, France derives approximately 75 percent of its electricity from nuclear. The French government believes that electricity should be clean, carbon-free, and abundant; and only nuclear energy currently meets those requirements. France is also the world's largest net exporter of electricity due to nuclear energy's low cost of generation. This nets the French economy, and its government treasury, more than €3 billion per year.

What *Is* Carbon?

Before proceeding further, let's take a closer look at this ubiquitous element that we are apparently determined to eliminate from modern energy generation. What is carbon? The dictionary informs us that the name comes from the Latin word "carbo," for "coal."

> [Carbon] "is a chemical element with the symbol C and atomic number 6 and is the 15th most abundant element in the earth's crust, and 4th most abundant element in the universe by mass after hydrogen, helium and oxygen. Carbon's abundance, its unique diversity of organic compounds, and its unusual ability to form polymers ('polymers are and form a large molecule or macromolecule, comprised of many repeated subunits. Both synthetic and natural polymers play essential and pervasive roles in everyday life') at the temperatures commonly encountered on Earth enables this element (Carbon) to serve as a common element of all known life. It is the 2nd most abundant element in the human body by mass (about 18.5% after oxygen)."[454]

We cannot have a carbon-free society until we figure out how to replace carbon in the body—and as the most common element in the world. If the advocates for a carbon-free world intend that economies and societies use carbon-free energy to generate electricity, then only nuclear meets that requirement, whether we like it or not over contrived safety concerns. The U.S. National Aeronautics and Space Administration (NASA) is on record as believing that a carbon-free society can be a reality within the coming decades. But NASA has yet to provide any specifics for how that will take place.

There are real-world factors and basic life necessities that stand in the way of our having a carbon-free world. And here we must acknowledge the more than 6,000 products, from plastics to makeup, all of which come, in one way or another, from a barrel of crude oil. Fossil fuels, as we have repeatedly pointed out, are the wellspring of the prosperous lifestyles that trace back more than 150 years to the start of the Industrial Revolution, the discovery of crude oil, and the development of the chemical engineering processes by which crude oil is refined into a myriad of useful products.

Crude oil is a mixture of hydrocarbons that came from plants and animals fossilized millions of years ago; it is these existing crude oil deposits that we can refine into petroleum products. Petroleum products also come from coal, natural gas, and biomass. After the crude oil is extracted, it is refined and separated into usable products. Prime examples are gasoline distillates, diesel fuel, jet fuel, heating oil, petrochemicals, feedstocks, waxes, lubricating oil, and asphalt. Everyday necessities that come from crude oil and can be bought at grocery and hardware stores include roofing materials, shoes, soap, detergents, vaporizers for respiratory illnesses, and even thermoplastic toilet seats.[455] We are literally surrounded by carbon.[456]

The best-known uses of petroleum are associated with transportation. Recent U.S. data show:

> "Of the approximately 7.21 billion barrels of total U.S. petroleum consumption in 2016, 47% was motor gasoline, 20% was distillate fuel (heating oil and diesel fuel), and 8% was jet fuel."

Science, chemistry, current lifestyles and human longevity based on crude oil will all need to be reinvented if we are to achieve a carbon-free society.[457]

Real-World Issues Will Delay Decarbonization

Outside of all the everyday, lifesaving products derived from crude oil, there are real-world factors that will hinder the attempt to transition away from carbon. In January-February 2019, world oil prices were weakened due to Chinese data that indicated a slowdown in the country's economy. In late January, China reported its 2018 GDP growth rate at 6.6 percent, "the weakest in nearly three decades."[458] As a likely result, the transition to carbon-free electric vehicles (EVs) will also be slowed as cheaper gas and oil incentivize global consumers to drive larger cars and SUVs. Cheap gas means more carbon-based vehicles. Additionally, more crude oil will be refined into petroleum and thus be spread globally through cheaper and more accessible consumer products.

Further complicating the transition is the expectation for the energy industry to increase its spending in the coming years. A large majority of top energy executives "found that respondents planned to either maintain or increase capital expenditure (CAPEX) in 2019."[459] Those respondents, according to the DNV GL (the company completing the industry wide survey), included 791 top energy professionals. DNV GL concluded in its report:

> "Despite greater oil price volatility in recent months (2018-2019), our research shows that the sector (oil, natural gas, crude oil, coal) appears confident in its ability to better cope with market instability and longer-term lower oil and gas prices."[460]

According to the DNV GL survey, firms are attempting to reduce their carbon footprint only because they are being told to do so, and "46 percent of respondents believed high oil prices could delay the industry's shift toward decarbonization" in order to make short-term profits from improved efficiencies and best practices.[461] In both cases, please note, whether oil prices are high or low, carbon still increases.

Pipelines are also being built to deliver oil and natural gas in unexpected places. A January 2019 statement from Cyprus, Greece, and Israel confirms their intention to construct the EastMed gas pipeline, explaining that it "comes from an emerging alliance between the three countries who must move forward cautiously in the face of neighboring States' opposition."[462]

If this pipeline is built in one of the most dangerous regions in the world, it would become one of the longest and deepest underwater gas pipelines anywhere, and one "that is expected to deliver approximately 10 billion cubic meters (BCM) of natural gas to the European Union (EU) through Greece and Italy."[463]

To counter Russian influence in the EU and to diversify its natural gas imports away from Vladimir Putin, the EU has fully supported this project. The EastMed project could fulfill approximately "10-15% of the EU's projected natural gas needs."[464] The United States has weighed in with its own support, "As it sees the growing trilateral alliance as a bulwark of democracy and stability in a largely authoritarian and war-torn region."[465]

What's striking about the amoral, brutish, "Hobbesian world" of geopolitics—one of self-interested, political survival—is that it trumps all well-intentioned environmental virtues, including the quest for a carbon-free society.[466] If countries can counter Putin's growing authoritarian power, and at the same time grow their own economies, they will likely choose economic advancement and geopolitical power over a carbon-free world.

As discussed in earlier chapters (*Introduction* and *How China and India View Energy*), the gasoline glut taking place worldwide has been ongoing since 2014, as a result of U.S. oil and natural gas flooding world markets. The decades-old oil and refined gasoline trade is rapidly being killed off and replaced with cheaper, abundant, scalable, reliable, and profitable U.S. oil.[467] This type of oil is considered "light oil," which yields plenty of gasoline to meet short-term, as well as future world demands with excess supply. Making the prospects for a carbon-free world even more remote is the fact that, since 2018, China has begun exporting more oil while adding to its refining capacity. President Xi Jingping of China is on record as seeking "energy security" for China and has directed state energy firms to rapidly increase E&P (exploration and production) of Chinese oil and natural gas.[468]

The difficulties of moving to a carbon-free society are sadly illustrated by another geopolitical situation. There has finally been some progress reported in the bitter civil war in South Sudan, a war involving the use of abducted child soldiers. But even this crippling problem hasn't stopped that country from seeing its oil output increase by 34 percent in 2018, bringing output up to 175,000 barrels per day (bpd).[469] The takeaway is inescapable and appalling: Not even one of the most horrific conditions known to mankind—the use of children as weapons of war—has stopped South Sudan from trying to join world energy markets.[470]

Moving to a carbon-free society means *the elimination of all fossil fuels*. Therefore, the use of natural gas that is explored and produced (E&P) and then refined into liquid natural gas (LNG) would also be eliminated. If that transpired, business interests and governments would stand to lose trillions of dollars. The use of LNG derivatives has exploded since 2017. Derivatives are defined in finance "As a contract that derives its value from the performance of an underlying entity… i.e., liquid natural gas."[471] By the end of 2018 derivative trade "Ballooned to 23 percent of total world LNG supply. Volumes are still a fraction of those for Brent crude, but the rising liquidity in trading is evidence that the market is maturing for fossil fuel derivatives."[472]

Industry experts now view the future as one of natural gas refined into LNG. This is causing "more money to be tied up in LNG futures than in coal." It is a good bet that if the goal of a carbon-free society means that global financial markets will lose money, that goal will take a back seat to LNG's future and the growing derivative market.[473]

It is also likely that China will actually decide if the world will ever attain a carbon-free or healthier environment. China is now funding global coal projects more than any other country. China insists it is cutting coal use. At the same time, however, President Xi is developing markets abroad to sell Chinese coal. China has financed roughly a quarter of all worldwide coal projects, with Bangladesh, Vietnam, South Africa, and Pakistan the main recipients of that Chinese largess.[474]

In order to assist in limiting global emissions, the World Bank, International Monetary Fund (IMF), the United Nations (UN), and multinational investment firms and banks tend to limit, or restrict coal-fired power-plant investments. Not surprisingly, Chinese state-owned enterprises and policy banks are now becoming the "lenders of last resort" for coal-fired power. This is detailed in a January 2019 report from the Institute for Energy Economics and Financial Analysis (IEEFA) titled, *China at a Crossroads: Continued Support for Coal Power Erodes China's Clean Energy Leadership*.[475]

Chinese financial institutions have pledged, committed, or offered funding of more than $35.9 billion for 102 gigawatts (GW) of "coal-fired power now being developed outside the country," the IEEFA report said.[476] Until China changes that policy, a carbon-free society will not become a reality,

Russia also poses impediments to achieving a carbon-free society. Russia, which did not sign the Paris Climate Agreement, has been China's largest oil supplier since 2016. More than 1.43 million bpd of Russian oil ended up in Chinese ports between 2016-2018; that figure rose to 19.7 percent in 2018, and is expected to grow higher.[477] Chinese and Russian energy companies and refineries do *not* follow the same strict environmental standards as the U.S., the EU, and large exporting nations like Norway.

Russia understands that it can't compete with U.S. oil and gas production coming from shale deposits in states like Texas South Dakota, and Pennsylvania. So, to strengthen its competitive position against the U.S., Russia has joined the organization known as OPEC +. (The Organization of Petroleum Exporting Countries founded in 1960 in Baghdad, and based in Vienna, has 14 member nations plus Russia, hence the name, OPEC +.) OPEC + will do everything it can to ensure that prices remain above $40 per barrel. Kirill Dmitriey, head of the state-backed Russian Direct Investment Fund, said at an early January

2019 World Economic Forum in Davos, Switzerland, "Oil prices $40 per barrel and lower, that is not healthy for the Russian economy."[478]

The Russians will not make the mistake of allowing excess oil supply to be dumped onto world energy markets as it was in 2014, causing prices to crash.[479] With oil prices being stable, the transition to a carbon-free society—i.e., moving away from fossil fuels—becomes even harder.

With U.S. oil and gas production booming from shale, deep-earth mineral deposits, the world's top energy producer, Saudi Arabia, decided to make heavy investments in U.S. natural gas production. Saudi Aramco, Saudi Arabia's state-run oil and gas company, is actively seeking to acquire natural gas in Texas, Pennsylvania, Oklahoma, Colorado, New Mexico, and Louisiana. The aim is to "become a global gas player," according to the company's CEO.[480] The Saudis and Russians are investing billions in such fossil fuel energy. Neither country is attempting the transition to a carbon-free, electricity-run world.

The *Introduction* to this book asserts that U.S. oil production could grow over 15 million bpd under current regulatory, technological, and drilling conditions. A snapshot map from the U.S. Energy Information Administration confirms our assertion, and shows another sizable reason that the requirements to switch over to a carbon-free society will be nearly impossible under the current economic environment.[481] U.S. drilling activity shows no signs of slowing unless President Trump is defeated by a Democratic who opposes E&P for fossil fuels on public and private land. The figure below shows where U.S. continental drilling for oil and natural gas is heaviest and gives the names of the deep-earth mineral formations.

Figure 9-2

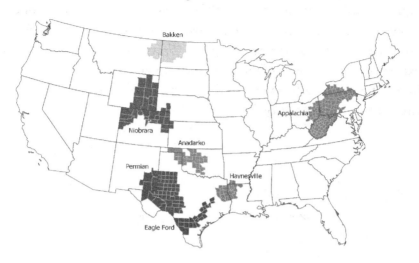

The only thing that could stop the U.S. shale oil and gas growth, and thus help the move toward a carbon-free society, will be Investors wanting better financial returns. This shift from production growth to shareholder returns is now a priority; "U.S. shale companies have badly trailed the S&P 500 for years."[482] Investors seeking rates of return in the double-digits could force shale drillers into bankruptcy and thus aid the move toward carbon-free companies and societies.

Astonishingly, it seems, a bunch of roughnecks stationed in the backward parts of the rural South has been able to upend foreign policy, national security, international geopolitics, U.S. domestic politics, and the entire worldwide environmental movement. <u>For the purposes of this chapter and section, this is the number-one factor holding back the requirements of transitioning to a carbon-free society</u>.

The EIA basically said as much in its *Annual Energy Outlook for 2019* (AEO) with projections out to 2050. The biggest takeaway is that the "U.S. will become a net energy exporter in the 2020s, due to surging natural gas and oil production."[483] A carbon-free reality takes another major blow when you realize that the U.S. hasn't been a net energy exporter since 1953. More key takeaways from the AEO are:

"The large increases in crude oil, natural gas and natural gas plant liquids (NGPL) production and NGPLs having the highest production growth while accounting for almost one-third of cumulative U.S. liquids productions during the projection period. The power sector experiences a notable shift in fuels used to generate electricity, driven in part by historically low natural gas prices and increased natural gas-fired electricity generation."[484]

Figure 9-3

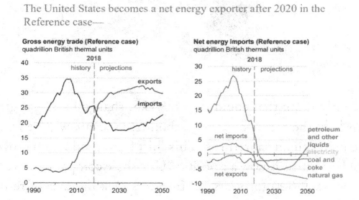

California is the exception in the U.S. since the state has increased crude oil imports from 5 percent in 1992 to 57 percent in 2018 to meet daily energy needs.[485] The AEO (on p.152) highlights the fact that the U.S. and other leading industrialized nations are not projecting a carbon-free future or society for decades to come. The statement reads:

> "Total industrial delivered energy consumption grows by 0.9% per year on average from 2018-2050. Energy consumption grows more slowly than economic growth because of increasing energy efficiency."[486]

That is fantastic news for the US, global energy growth and increased energy efficiency in the industrial sector, but it doesn't indicate that the basic requirements for a carbon-free society are being met.

It does mean that fossil fuel production companies have abundant reasons to ramp up growth to meet electrical consumption needs. In early 2019, the French multinational, fossil fuel E&P firm, Total SA (NYSE: TOT), asserted "that it would launch its largest exploration campaign in years in 2019."[487] On the heels of that announcement by Total SA, Exxon declared that it "gave the go-ahead to double the capacity of its Beaumont, TX refinery," and that "The expansion would launch the facility into the top spot as the country's (U.S.) largest refinery."[488]

An often-overlooked question in the transition to a carbon-free world is what to do with the tremendous amounts of oil and natural gas in the United States. Historically, undeveloped countries like South Sudan will not hesitate to take the billions, and possibly trillions of dollars of economic benefits from fossil fuel and renewable energy activity, over choosing a carbon-free world.

But <u>Shouldn't</u> We Move to a Carbon-Free World?

National Geographic magazine has a section on its website titled "A Blueprint for a Carbon-Free America." The portal leads to beautifully designed pages that completely dismiss fossil fuels and nuclear while touting renewables. Statistical breakdowns are given showing how solar (on and offshore), wind (on and offshore), hydroelectric power plants, and other forms of non-carbon energy resources can power our nation.

Click on a drop-down menu and select your state to view projections on how carbon-free renewables can meet your state's energy needs.[489] One problem the Blueprint never addresses is that components for solar panels, windmills, and the concrete to build hydroelectric dams that generate electricity all have their origins in crude oil. The co-author of this book, Ronald Stein (an engineer with 50 years of experience), explains how oil is needed for renewables to work:

> "All of the materials used by the 17 infrastructures that the American Society of Civil Engineers (ASCE)

will be reporting on in the upcoming 2019 Infrastructure Report Card for California, <u>inclusive of all the materials used in the wind, solar and electric vehicle industries, have their materials made from the chemicals and by-products manufactured from crude oil</u>."[490]

National Geographic does not explain how much carbon is added into the air when renewables need "over 1,000 times more space than fossil fuels."[491] Material and land issues for renewables will need addressing before the requirements for a carbon-free world can be met.

Leading up to the Paris Climate Agreement in May 2015, The World Bank released a book, *Decarbonizing Development – Three Steps to a Carbon Free Future*. This is their blueprint to achieve a carbon-free society and the requirements it says are necessary for this goal to be attained. Unfortunately, the authors never lay out an achievable blueprint for how to wean the world from fossil fuel, its products, and nuclear energy; nor do they seem to understand how electricity is generated, or how to work around the major obstacle posed by the dilute and intermittent nature of renewables.[492]

In fairness to the World Bank's book, it does lay out what it would take to achieve a carbon-free world by 2100:

> "It argues that the following 'action items' are needed: Act early with an eye on the end-goal; Go beyond prices with a policy package that triggers changes in investment patterns, technologies and behaviors; Mind the political economy and smooth the transition for those who stand to be most affected."[493]

The nuts and bolts of the book/report actually appear in a press release/article put out after publication. The World Bank believes zero-net-emissions can be achieved when coupled with:

> "A well-planned, robust, economic growth that emphasizes four areas. The work starts with a shift from relying on fossil fuels for electricity to using clean

energy that decarbonizes electricity. With increasing amounts of clean energy following, a massive shift to electrification can then increase access to clean energy and displace polluting fuels. Improving energy efficiency helps lower the demand. Keeping natural carbon sinks healthy through better forest and land management helps offset emissions by absorbing and storing carbon."

The press release is sprinkled with inspiring terms like "developing public transportation," "improving energy efficiency," and "reduced pollution." Let's start with the first item in that series, developing or increasing public transportation. Actually, a carbon-free society and public transportation have little to do with one another.

Let's look at the facts of public transportation in just the United States. Transportation expert Randal O'Toole summed up public transportation data from 2017-2018 and surmised:

> "Using statistics from the Federal Transit Administration, ridership declined in all of the nation's 38 largest urban areas. Two of the fastest growing urban areas – Austin lost 19.5 percent and Charlotte lost 15.4 percent of riders – US transit systems receive $50 billion a year in taxpayer subsidies. The data suggests the public prefers to get around in cars and SUVs."[494]

Public transportation and high-speed rail are the linchpins for the get-off-carbon movement.

The stubborn facts are that people simply do not want to leave the convenience and safety of their personal vehicles in the United States—and globally.[495] Further, if you do away with fossil fuels, and the 6,000 or so products that have their origins in crude oil, how do you replace all the jobs, taxes, and economic activity that oil, natural gas, coal, and renewables make possible?

Without crude oil, you cannot build solar panels, wind turbines, or the infrastructure needed for hydroelectric dams. We are veering into dangerous territory in believing the world will be carbon-free under current technological constraints.

Is Natural Gas the Answer?

For states going to 100% renewables for their electricity in order to achieve a low or carbon-free society, the theory is that natural gas for electric generation will be replaced mainly by solar and wind farms. California is leading the world in the attempt to make this vision a reality. California's challenge in generating clean energy and electricity is reflected in the graph below.

Figure 9-4

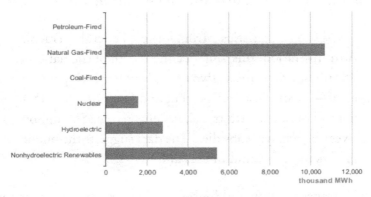

The obvious problem with this idealistic line of thinking is that nothing offers abundant, scalable, reliable, affordable, flexible, and job-creating energy like natural gas. If you adhere to the carbon-free societal goal and believe the requirements are within reach, this chapter has shown example after problematic example that must be dealt with before a world fully fueled by carbon-free energy and electricity can be achieved.

Natural gas, however, <u>could</u> lead to lower carbon output, as the United States has recently demonstrated. It became the only industrialized, mature economy (possessing one of the world's largest manufacturing sectors) to decrease its emissions enough to meet the Kyoto Protocol environmental goals. The U.S.-based conservative think tank, American Enterprise Institute (AEI), did analysis on the *2018 BP Statistical Review of Global Energy* and worked with University of Michigan economist Mark Perry and found:

> "The United States achieved the largest decline in carbon emissions in the world for the 9th time this century. AEI reported that in 2017, U.S. carbon emissions decreased by more than 42 million tons. Despite departing from the Paris Agreement, the U.S. significantly reduced its carbon footprint this year (2017). This remarkable success can be attributed to substituting natural gas for coal."[496]

This was achieved when the U.S. began to rely more on natural gas than on coal.[497] Natural gas <u>can</u> meet the requirements of moving toward a cleaner society. Natural gas for energy and electricity leads to cleaner air without lowering life expectancies, human progress, or job-growing economies.

Conclusion

The zeal to rid the world of carbon, if turned loose on our existing industries and modes of living could lead to environmental disasters equal to, or even surpassing, those they seek to prevent. Carbon is the most abundant element on the planet. Its elimination from human activity would require draconian, restrictive land-use policies, plus trillions in tax subsidies. It would also require us as a society to figure out just how we will be able to rely exclusively on renewables as a dependable energy and electrical source. The metropolises of Beijing,

New Delhi, Bangkok, New York, and Los Angeles, along with other major cities, don't have the infrastructure, electrical grids, or monies to pay for these carbon-free energy and electrical features. It is worth noting that Australia elected a new government in May 2019 based on the rejection of carbon-free electricity and the transitioning to renewables over fossil fuel.[498]

How do you make people change their commuting patterns and preference for global travel that have done more for globalization than free trade? The fact is, you don't. What you do instead is make maximum use of natural-gas power plants while researching carbon storage and effective methods to achieve clean coal technology and safer uses of nuclear energy. Then, respectfully, you ask the environmental movement to stop demonizing issues like melting glaciers as an imperative for going carbon-free without delay. Especially when the exactly opposite weather phenomenon is occurring in countries such as Greenland and Iceland.[499]

You advocate more sensible plans and do away with grandiose solutions. Simple policy goals can be achieved, such as better airline routes to smaller towns, cities, and tribal areas globally. You choose natural gas power plants over dirty Chinese, Indian, and Australian coal-fired power plants.

This chapter has attempted to highlight real-world scenarios when it comes to energy and electricity. Ratepayers, consumers, and job-creators all need to be driving the conversation of how to achieve a lower-carbon and, eventually, a carbon-free society without wrecking human advancement.

EVs highlight this dilemma. Private enterprise is more likely to build affordable electric vehicles "as opposed to firms receiving taxpayer-funded subsidies to build government-directed projects."[500] The often-overlooked truth about EVs is that they are decades away from being a carbon-free transportation option.

General Motors (GM) announced they are going "all electric, but it doesn't expect to make money off battery-powered cars until early next decade."[501] But, remember, GM is a publicly traded company with a fiduciary responsibility to its shareholders, and board members to turn a profit. How long will GM be able to lose money to gain "green-virtue-signaling-credibility" before some activist shareholder, hedge fund, or group of investors takes legal action against CEO Mary Barra for this decision?[502] Even Tesla remains unprofitable with its Model 3, a lower-priced "middle-of-the-road" EV.[503]

Until energy literacy is increased among consumers, the use of oil, natural gas, coal, and nuclear will continue to grow in the U.S., the EU, India, China, Australia, all of Asia, and Africa.[504] Currently, the only reasonable way to achieve a carbon-free or a low-carbon society is through wide-scale deployment of nuclear energy.[505] Natural gas will lower emissions while backing up renewables that are incapable of supplying constant, reliable energy. Please note, however, the natural gas-renewals combo still won't achieve zero-carbon energy or electricity.

The authors hope they have demonstrated that while achieving a carbon-free society and world is a laudable goal, it remains decades away. Meanwhile, there are better alternatives for achieving cleaner air, continued economic growth, and the ability for billions to acquire lifesaving energy and electricity.

Chapter Ten

Energy and National Security
By Ronald Stein

Summary

This chapter is dedicated to California, which has the world's fifth-largest economy. The Golden State is crusading to reach 100 percent intermittent electricity from renewables, but still needs nonelectric energy to support its essential infrastructures and commerce.

The United States is now a net exporter of crude oil (i.e., with crude oil exports exceeding imports), but the insurmountable problem of no current pipelines over the Sierra Nevada mountains results in California being an "energy island" with no easy access to the oversupply of U.S. crude oil east of the Sierra.

As a result, California is the only state importing most of its oil. California's reliance on foreign crude has grown to 57 percent and is increasing each year to fill the void of production losses in Alaska and California.

Energy and National Security

California is the only state in the union that currently imports most of its crude oil energy from foreign countries. In fact, since the state operates what is, in effect, the world's fifth-largest economy, its ever-increasing dependency on foreign countries for its crude oil requirements not only causes inflationary challenges for its citizens and businesses but has the potential to put our national security at risk.

While the state's crusade toward 100 percent renewables continues, the intermittent electricity resulting from all those wind and solar farms ("100 percent by 2045"[506]) has caused the state to increase its imports of crude oil to meet its insatiable energy demands. California could decrease its growing dependency on foreign crude oil simply by increasing in-state crude oil exploration, but environmentally correct state leadership refuses even to consider such a plan.

And California's energy problems don't stop there. Adding EV-charging requirements onto its grid while simultaneously removing from that grid continuously uninterruptible electricity generation by nuclear and natural gas, plus the expected difficulties of finding and procuring huge acreage for renewable solar and wind farms, may also factor in the unwitting formula for statewide economic disaster.

According to the Energy Information Institute (EIA), California currently imports about 29 percent of its electricity, two to three times as much as states like Virginia, Ohio, Maryland, and Tennessee.[507]

The two prime movers of transportation, the jet turbine and the diesel engine, provide the backbone of our national prosperity for both commerce and recreation. The demand for thousands of products refined from crude oil other than gasoline fuel—that is, the multitude of chemicals and by-products as well as aviation fuel, diesel fuel, and asphalt that both the military and all civilian infrastructures are dependent upon—directly support our current lifestyles. Modern high-energy societies enjoy a much higher standard of living than their historical predecessors, and these gains have naturally led to expectations of continued lifestyle improvements.[508]

California is an "energy island" inhabited by roughly 40 million citizens and situated between the Pacific Ocean and the Arizona/Nevada state lines, with no existing pipelines possible over the Sierra Nevada mountains. Daily energy use for California's 145 airports[509] (inclusive of 33 military, 10 majors, and more than 100 general aviation) is 13 million gallons of aviation fuels,[510] or one-fifth of the nation's jet fuel consumption. California's 35 million registered vehicles[511] are consuming 10 million gallons a day of diesel and 42 million gallons a day of gasoline for those 90 percent of state-registered vehicles that are not EV's.[512]

The basis for California becoming a national security risk is that in-state crude oil production and Alaskan oil imports are both in decline, and thus unable to help meet California's energy needs. The state's solution has been to increase crude oil imports from foreign countries from 5% in 1992 to a shocking 57% in 2018, at a cost of more than $60 million dollars a day—and increasing each year.[513]

To understand why California's choice not to increase in-state crude oil production may have national security repercussions, we need only look at the vast amount of in-state energy reserves in question. For starters, California has the largest shale reserves[514] and ocean crude oil reserves in the country in the Monterey Shale[515] and Pacific Ocean.[516] There are approximately two billion barrels offshore Santa Barbara that are discovered, estimated, and producible, but subject to state and federal moratoria on production. The larger reserves are within seven miles of the coast. This number is significant in that, with recently proven slant-drilling technology, formations within seven miles of shore are accessible mostly from land-based slant drilling with no offshore spill risk.[517]

It is estimated that oil seepage for a single six-mile stretch along the Santa Barbara coastline averages 10,000 gallons of oil each day (240 barrels). Every 12 months about 86,000 barrels of oil seep into the ocean—the equivalent of the quantity of oil spilled in the 1969 Santa Barbara oil spill. Every four years the volume of oil seepage equates to the 1989 Exxon Valdez spill. Since 1970, the quantity of oil that has seeped naturally into the Santa Barbara Channel equals approximately thirty-one "1969" oil spills.[518]

In 2017, California imported crude oil at an annual rate of more than 354 million barrels[519] from oil-rich foreign countries, which, at a price of $60 a barrel,[520] equates to Californians sending about $60 million a day to foreign nations. That's $21.2 billion a year—all to feed the progressive state's secret crude oil energy habit! In addition, those foreign countries have less stringent environmental regulations than California and transport their crude oil in air-polluting ships to California ports on a daily basis from Saudi Arabia, Ecuador, Colombia, Iraq, Kuwait, Brazil, and Mexico and elsewhere.

In a recent Rand research study on imported oil being a threat to U.S. national security,[521] the country would definitely benefit from policies that diminish the sensitivity of the world's fifth-largest economy (i.e., California) to an abrupt decline in the supply of foreign crude oil.

Figure 10-1

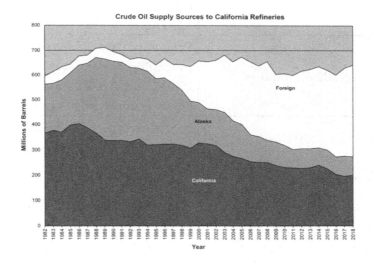

Figure 10-1
Observations of Illustration

Foreign crude oil imports	In 1992 California imported 5% from foreign sources but has been constantly increasing each year since. The state's reliance on foreign crude for its energy needs had grown to 57% in 2018 at a cost of $60 million a day and is increasing each year to fill production losses in AK and CA.
Alaska crude oil imports	Peak imports via ships from Alaska to California ports were in the late 1980s, but Alaska production has been declining every year since.
California in-state crude oil production	Ever since the mid-1980s, in-state crude oil production has been on a relatively constant decline.

The states' choice— to continue exporting $60 million of its dollars to oil-rich nations on a <u>daily</u> basis in order to obtain crude oil from foreign countries—may be exposing America to serious national security pressures. In addition, those foreign countries have less-stringent environmental regulations than California and transport their crude oil via air-polluting ships to California ports.

In another show of anti-oil advocacy, many California lawmakers threw their support behind AB 345. The bill, proposed during the 2019 California legislative session by Al Muratsuchi (D-Los Angeles), calls for a 2,500-foot setback between residences and any new oil industry operations. The effect would be to further reduce in-state oil production by more than half.

Although the bill did not pass the Legislature in 2019, it may make a rerun in 2020. "AB 345 would mandate a 2,500-foot health and safety buffer zone between new oil and gas wells and sensitive land uses, which include schools, day care centers, residential homes, and hospitals, thereby creating a safe distance between drilling operations and vulnerable populations in order to avoid serious public health and safety risks and impacts," Muratsuchi told The Real News Network (TRNN). "Oil and gas extraction produce air toxics, including volatile organic compounds like benzene and formaldehyde, fine and ultra-fine particulate matter, and hydrogen sulfide. Other risks include water contamination, toxic chemicals spills, and explosions."

AB 345 has the enthusiastic support of organizations ranging from 350 South Bay Los Angeles, California Environmental Justice Alliance, Californians Against Fracking, Consumer Watchdog, Greenpeace, Physicians for Social Responsibility, Center on Race, Poverty, & the Environment and Sunrise Movement Bay Area.

That large a reduction in production would result in an increase of the state's daily costs of importing oil from foreign countries from $60 million a day to an estimated $90 million a day, every dollar of that being "exported" to oil-rich foreign countries.

California is thus right in line with Putin's desire to encourage the "leaders" of the 184 ratifying countries of the Paris Accord to delay and eventually stop any further exploration of deep-earth minerals by diverting those countries' efforts toward intermittent renewables of wind and solar for electricity.

Russia's president is doing his best to stop fracking in the USA. He even provides funding to support anti-fracking movements, as documented by the 2018 report by the U.S. House of Representatives Committee on Science, Space, and Technology.[522]

California is the most populous state with the most robust economy in the U.S. Indeed, its economy is the fifth largest in the world. California has used its economic position to step up as a leader on climate change. Under the banner of reducing carbon emissions into the world's atmosphere, the state pioneered a system of subsidies for wind and solar that sparked a global boom in manufacturing those technologies. However, the unintended consequences of that environmental leadership may be increasing rather than decreasing emissions.[523]

Over the years the California Air Resources Board (CARB) and Air Quality Management District (AQMD) have both been viewed by the business community as being overbearing and business-unfriendly, especially since California is already the most environmentally regulated location on planet earth. As if to confirm its anti-business bias, the CARB, with the passage of Assembly Bill (AB) 617 (C. Garcia, 2017), has now established the Community Air Protection Program.

In the years ahead, CARB will be looking for recommendations to be taken under advisement to direct its "emissions" work from 10 communities throughout California. Local Steering Committees will be stocked with CARB's hand-picked community volunteers from local residents, businesses, and agencies. CARB's goal, no doubt, will be to find locals who are already in agreement with the radical environmentalist "BANANA" acronym ("Build-Absolutely-Nothing-Anywhere-Near-Anyone"). It seems predictable (though incomprehensible) that these local "advisory" groups will attempt to micromanage existing federal and state emissions standards and set even lower standards for their communities, standards that may not be in the best interests of the rest of the state's 40 million residents.

The unintended consequences of such actions by any of the Community Air Protection Program Local Steering Committees would necessitate CARB and the AQMD taking those recommendations under advisement and/or going through the legal and regulatory activities required to make changes to existing federal and state emission standards. Again, any such changes to existing emission standards would have financial impacts on all state residents.

Today, we are constantly being bombarded with reminders and progress reports about achieving California's plans to reduce greenhouse gas emissions 40 percent below 1990 levels by 2030 and to achieve an 80 percent reduction from 1990 levels by 2050.

California's flagship climate-change policy legislation, Assembly Bill 32, the Global Warming Initiative, was signed into law in 2006 when California was a minuscule contributor to the world's greenhouse gases (GHGs). Statistically, the world is generating annually about 46,000 million metric tons of GHGs while California has been generating about 429 million metric tons, which is less than one percent of the world's contributions.[524]

Now, more than a decade after the passage of AB 32, California remains the most environmentally regulated location in the world, yet still contributes a minuscule less-than-one percent[525] and has had little to no impact on the reduction of the other 99 percent of global GHG emissions.

Many in the Golden State are working hard on conservation and to produce hydrocarbon energy efficiently, reliably, and safely, and many others are working just as hard to develop alternative energy sources that will efficiently, reliably, and safely produce carbon-neutral energy. But despite those well-meaning efforts, the state's energy needs continue to grow in order to maintain a sustainable energy future for its growing economy as well as its people, vehicles, and businesses.

The latest data from the California Energy Commission (CEC) show California fuel consumption at its highest level in years.[526] As a likely result, continuation of the state's dependency on foreign countries for its energy needs seems to be in the state's short-term, if not long-term future, which may not be in the best interests of U.S. national security.

Most of California's 40 million citizens are probably unaware that their state is an "energy island," bordered by the Pacific Ocean on the west and the Sierra Nevada mountains on the east. The state's daily need to support its 145 airports[527] (inclusive of 33 military, 10 majors, and more than 100 general aviation) is 13 million gallons of aviation fuels. In addition, its 35 million registered vehicles[528] (of which 90 percent are <u>not</u> EVs) are consuming 10 million gallons a day of diesel and 42 million gallons a day of gasoline. All that expensive fuel comes at a heavy cost to consumers.

Since foreign refineries, and U.S. refineries outside California, all have less stringent environmental regulations than California, any aviation, diesel, or gasoline refined outside the state for in-state use (since so many of the state's refineries have closed) will lead to increased global emissions and excessive importing costs.

As a result of the state's overregulation's, its emissions crusade, the subsidizing funds required by low-power-density renewables, and the state's general high cost of living, California households are paying more than 40% more, and industrial users are paying more than 100% higher than the national average for electricity[529] (according to 2018 data from the U.S. Energy Information Administration[530]). Those costs are expected to increase significantly with the implementation of SB 100.

In addition, Californians continue to pay almost $1 per gallon more for fuel[531] than the rest of the country due to a) the state's sales tax per gallon, which is one of the highest in the country; b) refinery reformatting costs per gallon; c) cap-and-trade program compliance costs per gallon; d) low-carbon fuel standard program compliance costs per gallon; and e) renewable fuels standard program compliance costs per gallon.

More costs onto fuels are projected by 2030 from cap-and-trade and the low-carbon fuel standard[532] that may add another $1-to-$2 per gallon.

Continuation of that emissions crusade at the expense of the state's 40 million citizens, and continued funding for the high-speed train, will further fuel the growth of California's homeless and poverty populations (see below).

Despite higher energy bills, public opinion has remained supportive of the state's energy transition and its strategy to cut emissions. That support is apt to shift, however, once politicians resolve the debate about how their targets match reality. Either they will have to abandon the environmental goals and live with more pollution than they've promised, or they will have to force through painful and even more expensive measures to further limit emissions.

With energy and fuel costs among the nation's highest, California continues to suffer the highest percentage of people in poverty and homeless, a welfare crisis so acute that it shocks the world:

- California has the largest numbers of Unsheltered People Experiencing Homelessness per the 2018 data from the U.S. Department of Housing and Urban Development.[533]
- State-by-State Poverty rates, geographically adjusted, place California's highest in the nation at 23.8%.[534]

- California spends more than $100 billion toward welfare, which is more than the next two (New York and Texas) on the list combined, according to U.S. Census Bureau data.[535]

To minimize world GHG emissions and control costs of fuels on California's little energy island, the moral reasoning is to provide Californians with affordable and reliable energy and jobs by manufacturing those fuels in the most stringently environmental locations in the world, which means in-state, for use by one of the world's largest economies, which is also within the borders of California.

So, to meet the daily needs of the state's transportation requirements, more than 60 million gallons of aviation, diesel, and gasoline fuels are manufactured daily within California, as noted, the most environmentally regulated location on earth.

California's South Coast Air Quality Management District (SCAQMD) has proposed an option that would ban a critical refinery process technology at two Southern California refineries, a technology that is required for manufacturing cleaner-burning gasoline. These two refineries operate hydrofluoric acid (HF) alkylation units that use a modified form of HF (MHF), the latest advance in catalyst technology that enhances worker and community safety. Although the SCAQMD already approved this technology, the Agency is now considering banning use of MHF via Proposed Rule 1410 and is in process of developing a regulation to better mitigate the risk from—or possibly to phase out—the use of hydrofluoric acid at the two Southland refineries.

As a result of a June 2019 meeting, the SCAQMD voted not to ban the acid and work toward developing agreements with refineries in Torrance and Wilmington that would allow them to keep using the industry standard modified hydrofluoric acid but with enhanced safety measures. This subject may reach a conclusion in November 2019 when the SQAQMD Board is scheduled to vote on the resolution not to ban the acid.

The HF or MHF technology is currently in use at 50 U.S refineries (page 54 of the following link),[536] but banning that technology in

California, which, as explained, is an "energy island" to its almost 40 million citizens, would likely result in both major fuel producers being shut down, according to the California Energy Commission (CEC).

This would put the state at the mercy of fuels to be imported from foreign countries or other states (fuels produced with less environmental regulations) and would result in permanent spikes in fuel costs and higher GHG emissions[537] to the world.

In fact, with no pipelines feasible over the Sierras, the result of closing two California refineries would be higher costs to consumers and higher emissions to the world, in exchange for providing Californians with fuels imported from other countries or states with less stringent environmental regulations. And, not incidentally, there is inadequate storage infrastructure to manage imports at the level those refinery phase-outs would require.

The closing of even one of California's dozen in-state refineries (as part of the crusade to reduce emissions) will not only negatively impact the state's economy, but also our national security, for the following reasons (several of which have been mentioned earlier):

1. When AB32 was signed into law in 2006, California contributed 1 percent to the world's GHGs.
2. Today, more than a decade later, California still contributes less than 1 percent, but the result of that crusade is that residential users are paying more than 40 percent more for electricity than the rest of the country; industrial users are paying more than 100 percent for electricity[538] than the rest of the country; and drivers are paying almost an extra $1 more for fuel than the rest of the country.
3. The inflationary impact on the California economy of higher minimum wages may also be a contributing factor to the state's having the highest poverty and homeless populations in America.
4. To minimize world GHG emissions and control costs of fuels on California's little energy island, the moral reasoning is to provide Californians with affordable and reliable energy and

jobs by manufacturing those fuels in the most stringently environmental locations in the world, for one of the world's largest economies, which is within the borders of California.
5. But there is inadequate storage infrastructure at California's ports to manage importing finished refinery products at the level a phase-out of in-state refinery manufacturing would require.
6. EVs utilize the marketing term "clean and green" because these vehicles have no tailpipe. In reality, however, the EV "tailpipe" exists miles away at the power plants that generate the continuously uninterruptible power to charge the EV's batteries, and at the refineries that produce the chemicals to manufacture all the products needed to make the car.[539]

Despite state and private-electric vehicle incentives and charging-station infrastructure investments that have resulted in more than 50% of all EVs in the country being registered in California,[540] the U.S. Energy Information Administration data show fuel consumption in the state has increased steadily four years in a row with California fuel consumption currently at the highest level since 2009.[541]

Up and down the West Coast, California has 15 ports: Los Angeles, Long Beach, Oakland, Richmond, Port Hueneme, San Diego, Martinez, San Francisco, Benicia, Stockton, Crockett, Sacramento, Redwood City, Eureka, and Alameda.

California's imports and exports of goods[542] in July 2018 alone amounted to more than $36 billion in imported goods and $14 billion in exported goods. Again, that's for one month. Popular commodities passing through U.S. West Coast ports of entry include electronics, computers and computer equipment, automotive parts, plastics, industrial supplies and materials, fuel and oil, and clothing.

According to the U.S. Energy Information Administration (EIA), the United States is now the largest global crude oil producer,[543] surpassing Russia and Saudi Arabia. The American shale boom has important security implications as well, as America is now less dependent on crude oil from the turbulent Middle East. Except for California.

For California to access the oil shale boom from the rest of the country would require that oil to transit the Panama Canal to reach California ports. There are, of course, other options for transporting crude oil—by truck or rail—but these have been overwhelmingly ruled out by environmental activists.

The get-off-fossil-fuels leaders (*e.g.*, Al Gore, former California Governors Jerry Brown and Arnold Schwarzenegger, Tom Steyer, and current Governor Gavin Newsom) are crusading to pursue intermittent renewable electricity from wind and solar in order to "save the planet." Unfortunately, these visionaries seem oblivious to the fact that all of the industries that use fossil fuels to "make products and move things" (which support all the world economies) are increasing, not decreasing, their fossil fuel usage each year. The developed world has become accustomed to the lifestyles provided by all the myriad products that are based on fossil fuels.

The potential impact on the world's fifth-largest economy of an upset occurring to imported shipments of crude oil from foreign countries could be extremely detrimental to national security for the following reasons (some which have been touched on):

1. The California "energy island" is separated from the rest of the country by the Sierra Nevada mountains, giving the state "zero" access to the oversupply of American crude east of the Sierras. The U.S. now has the status of being a net exporter of oil—except for California.
2. In the event of a reduction in those foreign crude oil imports, the ability to manufacture the chemicals that make up the many crude-oil by-products will be impacted, adversely affecting the military, airlines, cruise ships, supertankers and container shipping, and trucking infrastructures.
3. With a shortage of the thousands of products from crude oil, California's ability to maintain its flow of more than $50 billion in imported and exported goods every month will also be impacted negatively.

4. With a shortage of the 13 million gallons a day of aviation fuels for California's 145 airports (inclusive of 33 military, 10 major, and more than 100 general aviation), aviation, transportation, and commerce will be impacted negatively.
5. California's ability to continue fueling cruise liners that use around 80,000 gallons of fuel per-day per-liner[544] will be impacted negatively.
6. Refusing to drill for oil in America's largest reserves, located in California, is an economic risk the California public has so far been willing to accept, but this may not be in the best interests of national security. In a state with the highest percentage of poverty and homelessness, the public may not be aware that California is sending more than $60 million each day to Saudi Arabia, Ecuador, Colombia, Iraq, Kuwait, Brazil, Mexico, and elsewhere for the crude oil energy the state requires.

California contributes less than 1% of the world's emissions.[545] Assembly Bill 32 (AB 32) mandates California reduce its greenhouse gas emissions 40% to 1990 levels by 2020. In September 2018, Senate Bill 100 (SB 100) was signed into law, mandating that California generate 100% clean energy by 2045,[546] which includes renewables, non-carbon emitting sources (hydro) and battery storage. "Clean electricity" from SB 100 is required to generate 100% clean energy by 2045, but electricity cannot replace the fuels needed for aviation, cruise liners, container shipping, and the transportation infrastructure that collectively moves $50 billion of imported and exported goods each month.

With California already having trillions of debt obligations,[547] the state's crusade to reach 100% clean energy by 2045[548] is contrary to the international forecast by the EIA for electrical generation by source, a majority of which is projected to be generated by nuclear, natural gas, and coal. Yet California continues to target 100% of its electricity to be generated from renewables in 2045, thus:
- There will be no electricity generated from nuclear in California in 2045
- No electricity generated from natural gas in California by 2045

To meet the goal of 100% clean energy by 2045,[549] growth in renewables will be required to replace the electricity generation by nuclear and natural gas,[550] as the Nuclear Power plant at Diablo Canyon will be closing in 2025.

Figure 10-2

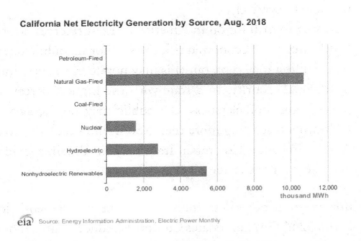

Figure 10-2
Observations of Illustration

Huge challenges are facing California to achieve 100% of its electricity being generated from renewables in 2045, thus:
The Diablo Canyon Nuclear will close in 2025, thus there will be no electricity generated from Nuclear in California after 2025.
Natural Gas provides more than 50% of the state's power, but the goal is for no electricity being generated from Natural Gas in California by 2045.

Developing nations need abundant, scalable, reliable, affordable, and flexible energy. The Green New Deal (GND) being proposed by New York Representative Alexandria Ocasio-Cortez (AOC) for intermittent renewable electricity is most likely unaffordable even for "rich" nations;

and even if it were affordable, it is a completely irresponsible plan to run every economic platform across the globe. Many of the world's inhabitants survive in deplorable economic and living conditions where the GND cannot work.

Infrastructure projects in the U.S. are not controlled by the federal government, or state governments, or local governments. They have fallen under the total control of powerful and popular organizations such as NIMBY, BANANA, SOBBY, NAMBI, and NIABY (see definitions below). Thus, the GND idea for a "super grid" to distribute intermittent electricity is a folly that has no chance of ever happening.

For those not familiar with the various acronyms for organizations that put up opposition to proposed developments in their local area and initiate a swarm of lawsuits to stop or indefinitely delay projects, here is a short list:

- NIMBY – "Not In My Back Yard"
- BANANA – "Build Absolutely Nothing Anywhere Near Anything"
- SOBBY – "Some Other Bugger's Back Yard"
- NAMBI – "Not Against My Business or Industry"
- NIABY – "Not In Anyone's Backyard"

The predictable onslaught of lawsuits from the above-listed powerful organizations presents significant infrastructure hurdles even for the most worthwhile projects, and insurmountable hurdles for bogus pork-barrel projects that rightfully deserve to be kept from progressing.

Further, any GND-type "super grid" will be unable to support the two prime movers that have done more for the cause of globalization than any other: the diesel engine and the jet turbine. Both get their fuels from oil. Without the transportation, there is no commerce.

Airlines are accommodating 4 billion passengers per year. There are more than 40,000 airports of which more than 1,200 are commercial airports. There are about 39,000 planes in the world, including all commercial and military planes. Airlines are consuming more than 225 million gallons of aviation fuels <u>per day</u> to move almost 10 million passengers and other things <u>per day</u>, and those figures are increasing every year.

Boeing, one of the world's largest aircraft manufacturers, says that 39,620 new planes will be needed over the next 20 years. This estimate puts the number of aircraft in the world at 63,220 by 2037. Passenger projections for 2036 are in excess of 7 billion.

More than 300 cruise liners are accommodating 25 million passengers per year. Fuel consumption is around 80,000 gallons of fuel per day, per liner. As a side note, billions of vehicle trips to and from airports, hotels, ports, and amusement parks are also increasing each year.

Electricity alone, especially intermittent electricity from renewables, has not, and will not, run the world's economies, as electricity by itself is unable to support the energy demands of the military, airlines, cruise ships, supertankers, container shipping, trucking infrastructures, and our space program. Again, without transportation, there is no commerce since globalized road and air travel dominate most people's lives.

The National Aeronautics and Space Administration (NASA) now pays Russia to Uber our astronauts and scientists to and from the International Space Station.

The intermittent electricity from wind, solar, or from batteries and storage units made from exotic materials like cobalt and lithium <u>cannot</u> supply the thousands of products from petroleum that are demanded by every transportation infrastructure and required for electricity generation, medications, cooling, heating, manufacturing, and agriculture. Indeed, virtually all the products that are the basis of everyone's standard of living in the developed world are made from petrochemicals. These incredible building blocks have not only made possible the movement of goods and people anywhere in the world but have led to reduced infant mortality and extended life spans.

Land requirements for wind and solar are huge compared to the land area needed for electricity from zero-emission nuclear. To generate the same electricity, wind needs almost 100 times the land area and solar requires 8 times the area of a nuclear plant. To make matters worse, renewable sites require wind and sun, uncontrollable commodities that are mostly unavailable in continuous and uninterrupted supply around the country.

In view of all the foregoing, the conclusion is unavoidable. A national "super grid" for supplying vast amounts of intermittent electricity, as proposed by Rep. Ocasio-Cortez's Green New Deal, is a socially and economically irresponsible idea.

According to International Energy outlook,[551] the strongest growth in electricity generation is projected to occur among the developing, non-OECD nations (those not among the 36 member states of the Organization for Economic Co-operation and Development). Increases in non-OECD electricity generation are projected to average 2.5%/year from 2012 to 2040, as rising living standards increase demand for home appliances and electronic devices, as well as for commercial services, including hospitals, schools, office buildings, and shopping malls.

Solar and wind represented a small portion of electricity generation in 2016.[552] Historically, wind and solar renewables have provided intermittent electricity coupled with storage systems in early stages of development, all of which makes renewables at this time incapable of powering the huge California economy on a continuously uninterruptible basis.[553] Energy consumption in the USA per the EIA:[554]

> The pattern of fuel use varies widely by sector. For example, petroleum provides about 92% of the energy used for transportation, but only 1% of the energy used to generate electricity.[555]

California's great weather, plus its overregulation's, the emissions crusade, and the subsidizing funds required by low-power-density renewables have all been contributory to the general high cost of living in the state. California household users are paying more than 50% more, and industrial users are paying more than 100% of the national average for their electricity[556] [557] according to 2018 data from the U.S. Energy Information Administration.[558] Those costs are expected to increase significantly with the implementation of SB 100 for the state to reach 100 percent reliance on renewable electricity from wind and solar and small hydroelectric plants by 2045.

Figure 10-3

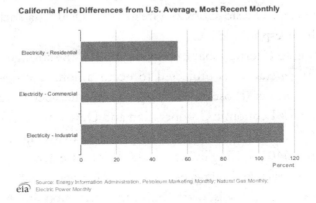

Figure 10-3
Observations of Illustration

California household users are paying <u>more</u> than 50% more than the national average for electricity.
California industrial users are paying <u>more</u> than 100% than the national average for electricity.

Figure 10-4

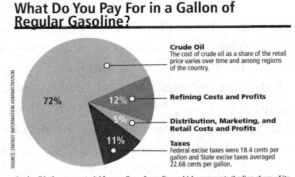

Californians continue to pay almost $1 more per gallon of fuel than the rest of the country due to a) taxes per gallon, which are some of the highest in the country; b) refinery reformatting costs per gallon; c) Senate Bill 32 cap-and-trade program compliance costs per gallon; d) Senate Bill 32 low-carbon fuel standard program compliance costs per gallon; and e) renewable fuels standard program compliance costs per gallon. With Californians paying an extra dollar for fuel, we should have the best transportation infrastructure in America. However, that dollar supports twenty-one California Climate Investment Programs administered through different California agencies.[559]

More costs onto fuels are projected by 2030 from cap-and-trade and the low-carbon fuel standard that may add another $1-to-$2 per gallon to fuel.[560]

Apparently, Disneyland daily admission prices and gasoline prices are both relatively inelastic products, meaning that changes in prices have little influence on demand.

It may sound shocking, but there are no economic reasons just to manufacture the chemicals and by-products from crude oil from which we derive thousands of products that are part of every transportation infrastructure, electricity generation, cooling, heating, manufacturing, agriculture, and that are used in everyone's daily lives.

The primary economic reasons that refineries even exist is to manufacture the aviation, diesel, and gasoline fuels for our nation's military and transportation industries; only incidental, though of surpassing importance to society, are the thousands of chemicals and by-products manufactured from crude oil.

As noted above, with the inflationary costs of regulations and subsidizing, Californians are paying more for electricity and fuels. This is no doubt part of the reason that the state has been experiencing a net exodus of citizens every year for decades, i.e., more leaving the state than moving into the state. Is California becoming a Land of NIMBY, i.e., a state for elites only, since no one else will be able to afford to live there except the homeless[561] and illegal immigrants?

The essential energy questions for the world's fifth-largest economy need to focus on finding a workable, sustainable balance across equally important concerns for the economy, everyone's shared sense of social equality, everyone's impact on the environment, and a truly sustainable energy future.

Many in California are working hard to produce hydrocarbon energy efficiently, reliably, and safely, and many others are working hard to develop alternative energy sources that will efficiently, reliably, and safely produce carbon neutral energy. Yet despite all those appreciable efforts, California's energy needs continue to grow along with its numbers of people, vehicles, and businesses.

Until electricity storage technology can support intermittent electricity from wind and solar, the state will continue to need redundant fossil fuel backups for those windless and cloudy days in order to provide continuously uninterruptible electricity to the economy.

As illustrated in previous chapters by the U.S. Energy Information Administration (EIA) in their Annual Energy Outlook, with projections of Energy Consumption by Sector to 2030,[562] and the EIA energy consumption projections to 2050 by fuel,[563] electricity alone, especially intermittent electricity from renewables, has not, and will not, run the fifth-largest economy in the world, or any other world economies. Electricity by itself is unable to support the energy demands of the military, airlines, cruise ships, supertankers, container shipping, and trucking infrastructures. Nor can intermittent electricity from wind and solar provide the thousands of products from petroleum that are essential to every transportation infrastructure, electricity generation, cooling, heating, manufacturing, agriculture, and from which we derive virtually every product used on our jobs and in our homes.

Chapter Eleven

The Weaponization of Energy
By Todd Royal

Summary

Russia knows that a major (and perhaps the principal) reason the Allies won World War II, and have led the world for over seventy years since the end of the war, is their greater access to oil, petroleum, natural gas, and coal than was available to the Axis Powers of Germany, Italy, and Japan. These were the vital energy sources the Allies needed for fueling their planes, tanks, ships, troop movements, and supply convoys.

China, Russia, Iran, and North Korea know that the desire for renewable electricity embodied in the Paris Accord cannot support 100 percent of the industries that use deep-earth minerals/fuels to "make thousands of products and move things" to support economies that are busily <u>increasing</u> their use of fossil fuels.

Energy has always been a main factor in human development, and that is especially true of today's complex international, political, and economic systems that have been in place since the end of WWII. Whoever controls energy, controls the world. Oil and natural gas are the weapons now being used—much as militaries have always been used—for both offensive and defensive purposes.

The Weaponization of Energy

The weaponization of energy has been defined as "the intersection between international security, politics, and energy." Today's system of energy, as defined by the United States, Russia, China, and Iran, takes cognizance of the fact "that every shift in global energy patterns has brought with it changes in international politics." Countries, companies, and individuals will "shape grand strategies" to meet their energy needs from reliable fossil-fuel sources, namely oil, natural gas, and coal.[564] The aggressive pursuit of fossil fuels in the last hundred years is one of the biggest issues facing our contemporary world, because modern economies run off energy and electricity and depend upon more than 6,000 products that come from crude oil.[565]

Fossil fuels, rather than renewables (solar and wind), are being used more and more as weapons in the arenas of foreign policy, natural security, and international relations. Whoever controls these fossil fuel resources will decide how economies grow and whether we live under democratic or authoritarian governments. Unfortunately, no one weaponizes its oil and natural gas resources in the systematic way Russia does; in Russia's case to politically influence the European Union (EU), Central Asia, and any country dependent on Russia for energy. Russia is one of the world's largest oil producers. Only in 2018 did the U.S. become a counterbalance to Russian production.[566] Since 2017:

> "The U.S. has increased its oil production by nearly 3 million barrels per day as the result of fewer regulations, more federal leasing, and the continuing brilliance of American frackers and horizontal drillers. It appears there is still far more oil beneath U.S. soil than has ever been taken out. The United States remains the largest producer of natural gas and second-greatest producer of coal." [567]

This caused the American economy to grow by 4.2% in the second quarter of 2018, 3.4% in the third quarter, and added a record amount of jobs at the end of December 2018.[568] U.S. Gross Domestic Product (GDP) is now $1.7 trillion larger than in January 2017, and the U.S. economy is $8 trillion times larger than the GDP of China, thanks in large part to the exploration and production (E&P) of oil, natural gas, and coal.[569] On the other hand, Russia, the Organization of the Petroleum Exporting Countries (OPEC), and China all use their energy resources not to improve the lives of their citizens, but as weapons to gain more land, resources, and control. Whose economy do you want growing, that of the U.S. or those of Russia, Iran and China?

Our new energy self-sufficiency means that the U.S. and the Western world are no longer bound to police and care for the Middle East *ad infinitum*. Before the U.S. hydraulic fracturing (fracking) revolution, Saudi sheiks, authoritarian monarchs, and Islamic terrorists could leverage Western governments and companies by using oil as a carrot and a stick, since the entire world was desperate for OPEC oil to fill up their gas tanks, power their economies, and heat and cool their homes. The days of a $4-$10 gallon of gas controlled by OPEC are thankfully over with the U.S. now flooding world markets with oil and natural gas.[570]

Energy as a Weapon in Vladimir Putin's Russia

Energy's sole mission is no longer about furthering human progress, not when Russia seeks to dominate places like war-torn Syria, Ukraine, most of Central Asia, and the entire EU. Russian efforts to control the supply of fossil fuels are intended to slow or stop the U.S. from increasing any type of crude oil or natural gas production. It follows, then, that the Russians are adamantly against U.S. fracking efforts and very supportive of efforts by any environmentalist group or wealthy individuals to slow or stop crude oil and natural gas E&P within U.S. and European borders. Former North Atlantic Treaty Organization (NATO) Secretary-General Anders Fogh Rasmussen, upon leaving NATO in 2014 when his tenure expired, told journalists that:

"Moscow was coordinating opposition to fracking in order to promote dependence on Russian oil and gas. As part of their sophisticated information and disinformation operations [they] engaged actively with so-called non-governmental organizations – environmental organizations working against shale gas – to maintain European dependence on imported Russian gas."[571]

There have been Kremlin-funded efforts specifically targeted to stop, curtail, or severely weaken U.S. fracking of crude oil and natural gas in states like Texas, North Dakota, Colorado, Oklahoma, Louisiana, and Pennsylvania.[572]

Figure 11-1

Russia uses its vast energy resources exactly the way the Soviet Union used its nuclear weapons in the Cold War to control nations and scare global citizens.[573] Russia now has the ability "to increasingly wield oil as a geopolitical tool, spreading its influence around the world and challenging the interests of the United States.[574] Geopolitics has been defined as "How a country's geography and location affect its foreign, economic (think energy) and military policy."[575] Vladimir Putin's Russia is challenging Western Democratic organizations like NATO and the EU by attacking them through their dependence on Russian oil and natural gas.[576]

The invasion and annexing of Crimea by Russia in 2014 brought the weaponizing of energy assets to the world's attention.[577] Russia wants to rule Crimea and Ukraine and is using natural gas energy assets as a focal point in the battle.[578] The Crimea is a peninsula on the southern coast of the Ukraine, surrounded by the Black Sea and the Sea of Azov. When the Soviet Union collapsed in 1991, the Autonomous Republic of Crimea was formed, with special international status accorded to Sevastopol, the largest city on the Peninsula. The 1997 Partition Treaty on the Status and Conditions of the Russian Black Sea Fleet allowed the Ukraine and Russian navies to be headquartered together in Sevastopol. Under the 2010 Kharkiv Pact, Ukraine extended Russia's lease of their part of the naval facilities <u>in exchange for discounted natural gas, but the pact was unilaterally terminated by Russia when it invaded and annexed the Crimea in 2014</u>.[579]

Ukraine declared martial law in late November 2018 over Russian aggression and Putin's apparent plans to bring Estonia, Latvia, Lithuania, and the Ukraine also into a "buffer zone of influence."[580] Other lesser-known former Soviet satellite countries now under Russian sway are the country of Georgia, the Republic of Abkhazia in northwestern Georgia, the Republic of South Ossetia in North Georgia, the Azov Sea in Eastern Europe (considered a northern extension of the Black Sea), and the Strait of Kerch that connects the Black Sea and the Sea of Azov while separating the Kerch Peninsula of Crimea in the west from the Taman Peninsula of Russia's Krasnodar Krai in the east.[581, 582] By gaining control of the Ukraine, Russia would be taking at least a sizable step toward reconstituting the "buffer zone" it had during the Cold War.

These former Soviet Union satellite states are all located near Russia or Central Asia. More to the point, these countries are all controlled by Russia's military and its supply of natural gas. Russian-controlled energy firms Gazprom and Rosneft will not allow deliveries of petroleum and natural gas to these countries if Putin doesn't like how they are behaving. Thus, once again, Russian energy assets are weaponized to control behavior. Gazprom is the more lethal company since it is majority-government-owned through the Russian Federal Agency for State Property Management.

In a less obvious sense, just as lethal to international security, human progress, and longevity are U.S. and Western environmental leaders and organizations championing the get-off-fossil-fuels platform. These vocal champions include former Vice President Al Gore, former California Governor's Jerry Brown and Arnold Schwarzenegger, and fossil fuel investor turned environmentalist Tom Steyer.[583, 584, 585] Each of these celebrity advocates for intermittent renewable electricity from wind and solar, by the way, has billions tied up in renewable investments.[586, 587, 588]

Al Gore and others of his apocalyptic persuasion have made more than a few environmental predictions that did not come true. As an example, Mr. Gore said on December 13, 2008, "the entire North 'polarized' cap will disappear in five years."[589] Obviously it hasn't. Groups like *Climate Policy Initiative* now want $5 trillion to combat climate change without saying how these monies would be used.[590] The Stanford University engineering department predicted that increased temperatures would lead to greater human conflict without offering any evidence.[591] The prediction website, FiveThirtyEight.com, reported in late 2018, "Human Behavior Might Be the Hardest Part of Climate Change to Predict."[592] Once again, zero evidence was offered to back up this prediction.

Vladimir Putin uses false environmental narratives to fund and do away with Western natural gas. Were he successful, of course, the world would have to rely more heavily on Russian oil and natural gas. It only took $200 billion for the Apollo space program to send a man to the moon, but trillions are being demanded to solve environmental issues without even the semblance of a working plan in place for how any of it is supposed to happen. Despite all the sweeping assertions by politicians and celebrities, there is still no "settled science" or "scientific consensus" as to whether climate change is caused by human activity.

The climate was significantly hotter hundreds of millions, and even thousands of years ago—by seventeen degrees—long before the Industrial Revolution or a planetary population in the billions. Dr. Walter E. Williams of George Mason University clarifies this vexing scientific conundrum:

> "Today CO2 concentrations worldwide average about 380 parts per million. This level of CO2 concentration is trivial compared with the concentrations during earlier geologic periods. For example, 460 million years ago, during the Ordovician Period, CO2 concentrations were 4,400 ppm, and temperatures then were about the same as they are today. With such high levels of CO2, at least according to the warmers, the Earth should have been boiling."[593]

Other periods of history, like the Paleocene-Eocene Thermal Maximum (PETM), were warmer than today, with average global temperatures as high as 73 F.[594]

For the get-off-fossil-fuels crowd, global warming and climate change are the vehicle of choice to gain control and money the same way Putin uses oil and natural gas to control the EU and countries that were once under the Soviet Union's communist system. Environmentalist Tom Steyer has made billions off building and investing in coal-fired power plants but has never completely divested himself of those holdings. Other leaders of the get-off-fossil-fuels movement became even more pro-renewable in 2016 when "Renewables received 94 times more in U.S. federal subsidies than nuclear and 46 times more than fossil fuels per unit of energy generated."[595]

Putin loves when Western billionaires help him disturb global peace and prosperity.[596] Putin weaponizes his energy resources and funds environmental movements, anti-fracking and anti-fossil fuel ventures, because he knows the world is increasing its usage of fossil fuels each year.[597] Increasingly popular renewables will also need Russian oil and natural gas because:

"Windmills require petroleum every single step of their life cycle. If they can't replicate themselves using wind turbine generated electricity, they are not sustainable."[598]

Here is an even more disturbing fact about wind power, one that also benefits Russian energy:

"Oil is used from start to finish – from mining to crushing ore and smelting it, to delivery to the fabrication plant to the supply chains for 8,000 parts in a wind turbine to the final delivery site."[599]

Putin knows also that renewables have many serious limitations yet to be overcome. By pushing renewables, he gains additional leverage from those governments that embrace renewables over fossil fuels to their detriment. Duplicitous energy behavior abounds, however. India signed the Paris Climate accords but is increasing fossil fuel use with its "1.3 billion customers, its oil imports increasing 5% a year and isn't expected to level off anytime soon."[600] Clearly, this isn't strictly a U.S. or EU spectacle; environmental trickery and folly are worldwide phenomena.

The world is now accustomed to prosperity that includes global infrastructures, industrialization, and military security based on fossil fuel.[601] Long before becoming a geopolitical expert, Vladimir Putin was a colonel in the KGB. His years of KGB service taught him that, in the last two centuries, both Napoleon and Hitler's armies invaded Russia. Using Russian oil and natural gas as a weapon, and buffer, against another attack has allowed Russia to "hook" Germany on Russian natural gas.[602] The entire EU now relies on two Russian energy giants—Gazprom and Rosneft—to control their supply of natural gas.[603]

The various Central Asian countries that regained their freedom after the collapse of the Soviet Union now also find themselves dependent on Russian oil and natural gas to power their emerging market economies.[604] Without this flow of energy from Russia, these countries and governments cannot survive.[605]

Turkey was once a reliable NATO ally, but, with the completion of the Gazprom-approved TurkStream natural gas pipeline in 2019, Turkey is under the thumb of Gazprom.[606] If further evidence of Russia's influence is needed, in 2018 Turkey defied NATO's objections to purchase Russia's lethal S-400 anti-missile weapon, a weapon "that poses a serious security risk if integrated into NATO hardware."[607] With the TurkStream pipeline and S-400 purchase, Turkey now has better relations with Russia and Iran than with the U.S., the EU, NATO, Israel and the Sunni-Muslim nations of Saudi Arabia, the United Arab Emirates, Bahrain and Egypt.[608]

This weaponized prosperity from fossil fuels can be used as well against free-market capitalism (as has been done in the Crimea, with devastating side effects such as increases in infant mortality and decreases to life spans).[609] Fossil-fueled progress has also allowed the movement of goods and people anywhere in the world via the diesel engine and jet turbine.[610] Putin uses all this to better influence the United Nations Security Council and European capitals that need Russian energy to power their comfortable lifestyles.

Putin is, in effect, playing energy chess while the rest of the world is playing energy checkers.[611] The unnerving part about Russian geopolitical savvy, and Western energy naivety, is that Moscow sees itself as having been in a state of war since 2005, with energy being its main funding component to subvert democracies, control nation-state economies, and hinder political institutions.

On January 18, 2005, Russian Defense Minister Sergei Ivanov told his country's Academy of Military Sciences, "There is a war against Russia under way, and it has been going on for quite a few years."[612] Minister Ivanov never defined who or what entity was at war against Russia, but it's not surprising that Putin and his Defense Minister hold these schizophrenic views.[613]

Using energy as a weapon allows Moscow to gain billions from oil and natural gas sales to Europe and Asia. These monies are then leveraged to gain land, naval bases, army outposts, and political influence in Syria, the EU, the Black Sea, Crimea, Southeast Asia, and, as we have seen, on the U.S. political process. Putin is able to conduct advanced cyber warfare activities, distribute dirty money to corrupt governments, and generally wreak global havoc. This has been called "Putinomics," and it also involves his paying off the elites in Russian society to keep his corrupt government in place.[614]

Western governments could slow Putin's reign of chaos by maintaining crippling sanctions on Putin's economic holdings and the elites in his government. A next step would be to leverage Western holdings of oil and natural gas against Moscow's efforts. It can't be stressed enough how energy sales through Russian companies Gazprom and Rosneft are used "<u>to subvert pro-Western regimes and gain a free hand for its polices of aggression throughout vast regions, like the entire European Union and Eastern Europe</u>."[615] An encouraging note, however, is that one staunch Russian ally, Belarus, is apparently tiring of Putin's geopolitical adventures using energy.[616]

From the Baltic States to Eastern Europe—including Poland and Black Sea-bordered countries—Moscow has used its energy weapons "to corrupt politicians, parties, institutions and buy up media."[617] Hungary and Bulgaria can't survive without Russian energy, and their pipelines are conduits for big Russian gas users farther west, namely Italy and Germany.

Countering this Russian energy weaponization has taken on greater focus in the Trump administration. The U.S. is drilling at an unprecedented rate for domestic shale oil and natural gas. Under Trump's America First energy plan (whether good or bad, depending on how you view him, as well as climate change, clean energy, and geopolitics in general), shale production in Texas, North Dakota, Oklahoma, and Louisiana are changing the world.[618]

Indeed, just Texas itself began "reshaping the world" in 2018 after becoming, in effect, the world's third-largest oil and natural gas producer.[619] Texas is a striking illustration of how U.S. shale E&P through fracking has become a national security weapon for the U.S.[620] U.S. Marines or NATO forces are no longer needed to invade countries if the U.S. can instead export oil and natural gas.

Here's how it works:

Prosperity, national security, and cleaner environments go hand-in-hand. The unintended consequences of other nations getting off fossil fuels (while Russia uses its energy like a nuclear arsenal) won't reduce emissions or ensure world peace, because additional coal, oil, and natural gas power plants are needed as backups for renewables.[621] Russia, China, Iran, and North Korea would all welcome the U.S. and other mature economies eliminating fossil fuels. None of those four countries or their leaders, however, has ever indicated any inclination to do without oil, petroleum, natural gas, coal, or nuclear energy.[622]

China Weaponizing Energy, Trade, and Politics

China, even more than Russia, wants to "remake the world order" that has been in place for over seventy years, particularly if it harms the U.S.[623] China has actually encouraged California (through its support of Tom Steyer) to block oil and natural gas drilling, resulting in thousands of businesses leaving the Golden State.[624] Outside of the U.S. and EU, no other country or continent considers doing away with fossil fuel exploration and production.[625] China, like Russia, does everything it can to strengthen and encourage the Western environmental movement in its misguided efforts to kill fossil fuels.[626] If they are successful in manipulating environmentalists to destroy oil, natural gas, coal, and nuclear, China and Russian will have virtually ended U.S. dominance in world affairs.

Abolishing fossil fuels would also do away with most medications; with fertilizers that feed the world; and all forms of transportation that require gasoline or electricity. Without access to crude oil byproducts, and thus access to reliable, scalable, affordable, and flexible energy, global death tolls will rise. What country could possibly wish to bring about a global catastrophe resulting in shortened life spans and dramatic decreases in living standards? China is the answer; indeed, China believes it stands to profit from such dire events.

Regardless of which rival powers are behind the curtain pulling all the energy strings, the West is definitely moving to eliminate fossil-fuel prosperity and hand the world over to Chinese authoritarians, a ruthless Russian dictator, and the Iranian Ayatollahs without ever understanding the concept of weaponization of energy.[627] China is definitely aligning itself with Iran in its efforts to make 2019 and beyond difficult for the Middle East. Despite heavy U.S. sanctions, Iran's economy from oil and natural gas is starting to improve, and its military-terrorist proxies, led by Hezbollah, Hamas, Yemen's Houthi tribes, the Muslim Brotherhood, and Shia paramilitary militias, are attacking the global economy daily.[628]

President Trump seems to understand, for better or worse, through a trade war with China, that only coercive action will change such behavior.[629] The U.S. is winning the trade war, and this can be used to stop China aligning with Russia and further weaponizing their energy and trade assets.[630] Energy will continue to define 21st century prosperity, economic growth and global peace.[631]

Trade between nations, as exemplified by Japan's December 2018 trade agreement with the U.S., means free trade is alive and well. But without stable, reliable, scalable, flexible, and affordable energy, this agreement won't reach its full potential.[632] Energy, and its weaponization, defines trade. Whoever controls fossil fuel energy resources in 2019 and beyond will control the world, as populations continue growing in Africa, India, and Southeast Asia. China wants that control to emanate from Beijing.

But American energy producers have been rewriting the global-energy playbook, along with standards of behavior. The U.S. is now exporting record amounts of oil and natural gas to China, India, and Kuwait. With the confidence of U.S. shale producers at an all-time high, they have forced oil prices lower, deflated OPEC's power and stripped the ability of OPEC + (Russia and Saudi Arabia leading this coalition) to outflank trade war tariffs against China.

U.S. shale oil is now being weaponized in much the same way OPEC used oil to punish U.S. President Richard Nixon for supporting Israel during the 1973 Yom Kippur War.[633] OPEC's oil embargo hurt a fragile U.S. economy then, but the organization of oil exporters no longer has the power to set world oil market prices and punish perceived enemies the way they did to Nixon in 1973.[634]

The U.S. now has power over China from unlimited amounts of oil and natural gas. The U.S.' power increased in 2018 by surpassing Russia and Saudi Arabia to become the world's biggest oil producer, with total crude output climbing to roughly 11.7 million barrels per day (mbp); additionally:

> "Oil production from seven major U.S. shale basins is by year end 2018 expected to surpass 8 million bpd for the time, the U.S. Energy Information Administration said."[635]

In five to ten years America will be energy independent (though some U.S. politicians have asserted that this is already the case). In fact, this will become the new norm if U.S. domestic politics don't strip the ability of shale-heavy states to keep breaking E&P records. If current U.S. production keeps pace in shale-rich states, the U.S. will top 15 mbp between 2020 and 2022. In December 2018 the EIA's *Short-Term Energy Outlook* announced, "The U.S to average 12.1 mb/d in 2019 up sharply from a 10.9 mb/d average in 2018."[636]

China and Russia will respond by <u>manipulating prices and supply to countries and political entities like the EU that are overly dependent on their natural gas and oil</u>.[637] From 2017 onward, China and Russia have been making corrupt energy deals in Venezuela, Syria, Saudi Arabia, Turkey, and Iranian oil field auctions.[638] China has even invested more than $4 billion in Kurdistan in Iraq oil fields in an effort to hurt the U.S., NATO, the EU, and any U.S. allies in Asia.[639]

Natural gas is the newest weaponized energy source upon which China is deeply dependent to fuel its economy. The U.S. is now on par with any Liquefied Natural Gas (LNG)-producing country and has been since "The first shipment of U.S. LNG from the lower 48 states left in February 2016 and now the U.S. exports LNG to Europe, Asia, Southeast Asia, South America and the Middle East."[640]

This effectively blocks China and Russia from becoming bosom buddies since China needs U.S. LNG. Russia sustains further damage to its energy prestige when close allies like Bulgaria, Romania, and Serbia (all of whom have been double-crossed by Russia over natural gas deliveries) also welcome heavy U.S. LNG exports that keep prices low during cold Eastern European and Central Asian winter months.[641]

The U.S. needs to ensure abundant supplies to Western and Eastern Europe and to encourage supplies from any country (think Turkey) that now aligns itself with China and Russia.[642] The small Mediterranean island nation of Cyprus is vulnerable to pressure from nearby Turkey (which administers the island's northern third), but they are blessed with hydrocarbons (oil, natural gas, rare minerals) that can be drilled for in their exclusive economic zone (EEZ).[643] This poses another counter to Russian energy giants Gazprom and Rosneft, which are selling billions in oil and natural gas to China."[644] By selling energy to "the Balkans, Eastern Europe, and Asia" that traditionally buy from Middle Eastern dictators and Russia, Washington is finding another way to block the geopolitical energy strategies of Beijing and Moscow.[645]

To further illustrate the benefits of energy's diplomatic power without starting a war, there is a long-running conflict along the shared border, or "Neutral Zone," between Saudi Arabia and Kuwait. The dispute is over which country gets "to restart idled oil fields in [the] disputed territory."[646] These oil fields have the capacity to produce upwards of 500,000 bpd but have been offline for years over political disagreements. The Trump administration used heavy-handed diplomatic measures on both countries to resolve their differences "with an eye on shrinking supply from Iran." That is the kind of geopolitical influence that energy offers without ever firing a shot.

Chinese and Asian LNG demand is "expected to quadruple by 2030."[647] The avenues for geopolitical influence and the de-weaponization of energy using LNG exports and new LNG terminals (like the Qatar-proposed Golden Pass in Texas to offset the Arctic LNG-2 terminal in Russia) confirm that fossil-fuel energy has never been more important.[648]

Energy historian Daniel Yergin's book, *The Prize,* gives one of the best socioeconomic historical accounts of how fossil fuels changed the world.[649] Mr. Yergin's follow up book, *The Quest: Energy, Security and the Remaking of the Modern World,* introduced the weaponizing of energy, oil, and hydrocarbons as a political concept informing every aspect of a nation's foreign and domestic policies.[650] In his second book Yergin clearly showed that the fight between great nation-states is over oil and natural gas <u>and not renewable energy</u>. This truth has become increasingly apparent when we look at China and Russia both weaponizing energy, and the U.S. using its newfound shale influence to influence and control world events.[651]

No great leader or nation cares about windmills, solar panels, hydroelectric, or biomass. They care about oil, natural gas and coal, the reliable fossil fuels that win wars and run nations.[652] This energy realism (over environmental idealism) allows China even more than Russia to attempt to displace the U.S. leadership and democracy that have been in place for over seven decades.[653] It is why Russia, with Chinese backing, has proposed more than 90 percent of new capital expenditure (CAPEX) "on planned and announced crude and natural gas projects in the Former Soviet Union (FSU) over the period 2018-2025."[654]

The U.S. Responds to China and Russia

China and Russia will continue weaponizing their oil, natural gas, coal, and nuclear energy resources. This realization caused the U.S. to release the 2018 U.S. National Defense Strategy (NDS) that "announced the return of great power competition."[655] The Cold War of energy is at the vanguard of this strategic shift.[656] The developing world is the next frontier for the energy wars and continued weaponization of hydrocarbons. The solutions offered by the NDS to the developing world in Africa, Southeast Asia, and India, which are also experiencing the fastest population increases, are "mass immigration and rapid transition to renewable clean energy," but <u>without offering fossil fuel</u>

energy the way China and Russia will to alleviate billions living under wretched conditions.[657]

The *World Bank Population Estimates and Projections* and the *BP Statistical Review of World Energy* revealed more than half of the world's 7.7 billion people—approximately, 4.2 billion—live in the Asia/Southeast Asia/Pacific region; this includes China, India, Pakistan, Bangladesh, and Indonesia.[658]

The world's population will grow by 25% between 2020-2050, but Africa should cause the most distress with more than 600 million people lacking electricity, power, or energy at this time.[659] Africa will increase from 2.2 billion people in 2020 to 2.5 billion by 2050; current 2018-2019 African population estimates are at 1.3 billion. In other words, Africa will add, "1.2 billion people to its population, whereas the rest of the world combined will add another 0.8 billion by 2050." China's first overseas military base is now located in the African nation-state of Djibouti.

Energy weaponization and access to reliable, scalable, affordable, and flexible energy are the leading issues, along with food and water security, that must be addressed moving forward by world leaders, policymakers, and non-government organizations (NGOs).

Over a hundred years ago, Prussian General Carl von Clausewitz stated, "War is the continuation of politics by other means."[660] It is certainly true that accelerated development of natural resources should protect the environment, but pretending that renewable energy can meet billions of African children's needs for education, clean water and shelter is not only foolish, but also morally wrong.

Even technologically-savvy Los Angeles is investing billions in fossil fuels.[661] California denies reality by claiming they will be using only clean, carbon-free energy for the fifth-largest economy in the world and now the most populous state in the U.S.[662] This type of overhyped and untruthful energy rhetoric only encourages China and Russia to weaponize energy at an ever faster pace. A continuation of these actions will result in millions of Africans, Asians, and Indians being denied the better-quality lives from the West that reliable energy could provide them; and forces them to turn instead to dictators in China, Russia, and Iran in order to meet their energy, electricity and economic needs.

Conclusion

Instead of letting people die, starve, or live unfulfilled lives due to zero access to energy resources, natural gas power plants should be installed rather than unstable, intermittent solar and wind farms that do nothing to alleviate crippling poverty or stop Russia, China, or Iran from aiding the developing world. Environmentalism, as practiced by Tom Steyer, Al Gore, Jerry Brown, and Arnold Schwarzenegger, will lead to future global conflicts in the same way that Neville Chamberlin's foreign policy gave the green light to Hitler's European expansionism. It should be clear by now that <u>environmental and social equity means nothing in the amoral world of geopolitics</u>.

Will the U.S. and its allies be accused of imperialism, sexism, racism, and the other-isms that pass as deep thought today if they flood world markets with additional fossil-fuel resources to counter Russian and Chinese energy aggression? Yes, of course, these accusations will be made. But the alternative is the weaponization of natural resources in Africa, India, China, *et al.*, to serve the malign purposes of presidents Putin of Russia and Xi of China.

Scarcity makes no sense when abundant global energy sources are available. What <u>does</u> make eminent sense is investing in fossil-fuel power plants for energy consumption in Africa and by billions of people elsewhere similarly in desperate need of energy; as well as stopping the "nihilism of mass immigration." These are moral and just causes that, if steadfastly pursued, can also put a stop to the rampant weaponization of energy.[663]

The current path of demonizing fossil fuel won't lift billions out of energy poverty, but it will serve to fortify Putin's resolve. Western media outlets that back the get-off-fossil-fuels crowd do not seem to understand those geopolitical realities. Building electrical lines powered by natural gas is a great pathway to successfully countering Putin and his authoritarian minions by promoting democratic capitalism, energy-sufficient nation-states, and continents with market economies, a pathway capable of leading billions out of despair.[664]

For the sake of peace and eliminating undue suffering in our time, let us hope and pray that this happens. If not, Putin and Xi will win—and nuclear war will loom as a real possibility.[665]

The weaponization of energy is a complex geopolitical issue with national security and foreign policy implications that affect literally every person on the planet. If the Ukraine, a NATO Membership Action Plan (MAP) applicant since 2008, can be bullied, annexed, and invaded without consequences from the West, then again Putin wins.[666] Looking at foreign policy decisions through the lens of energy can lead either to chaos or the deterring of determined enemies like Vladimir Putin. "Leading from behind" and the "resets" favored by the Obama administration won't help the Ukraine or other Russian border states under Putin's systematic assault.

Viewing energy through the prism of stopping authoritarians and moving international relations toward the U.S.-led order is the best hope for the world in this perilous century. It may also be our best hope for forestalling another global war.

Chapter Twelve

Climate Change
By Ronald Stein and Todd Royal

Summary

Neither humans nor fossil fuels were present during the five warming cycles that melted the icebergs of the five previous ice ages. Also, it should be noted, only 12 percent of the earth's surface is habitable by humans.

Humans have been monitoring temperatures since we've had meteorologists, which is about the last 150 years. On a 24-hour clock, those 150 years in which we've been monitoring temperatures (out of the 4.5 billion earth has been around) represent 0.00288^{th} of a second!

Today's CO2 concentrations worldwide average about 380 parts per million. Four hundred and sixty million years ago, CO2 concentrations were 4,400 ppm, and temperatures then were about the same as they are today.

Obviously, natural forces greater than humans and fossil fuels caused those five previous warming cycles, which prompts the question: How can humans' minuscule presence on earth possibly be the cause of the next warming cycle?

In answering that question, are we not drawn to the conclusion that the one constant on earth is that the climate is <u>always</u> changing?

Climate Change

We are being constantly bombarded with rhetoric to the effect that 97% of all scientists believe that mankind has played a role in changing the earth's climate. Yet common sense tells us that no large group of people on our planet could ever reach 97% agreement on anything, even the world being round!

Contrary to the oft-repeated 97% argument, the godfather of all letters objecting to the climate change alarmism, the Oregon Global Warming Petition Project[667] circulated by the Oregon Institute for Science and Medicine and signed by more than 31,000 American scientists (including more than 9,000 with doctorates), states:

> There is no convincing scientific evidence that human release of carbon dioxide, methane, or other greenhouse gases is causing or will, in the foreseeable future, cause catastrophic heating of the earth's atmosphere and disruption of the earth's climate. Moreover, there is substantial scientific evidence that increases in atmospheric carbon dioxide produce many beneficial effects upon the natural plant and animal environments of the earth.

The world's complex climate has been around for more than 4.5 billion years. During all those eons of its existence, the earth has gone into and out of at least five major ice ages, and five warming cycles that melted those icebergs, with only the sun and moon being around to witness these epochal changes. Noticeable by their absence, during the five warming cycles that melted the icebergs, were humans and fossil fuels.

Figure 12-1

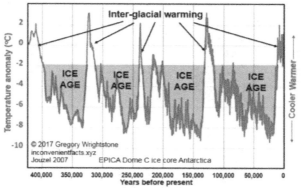

Figure 12-1
Observations of Illustration

Neither humans nor fossil fuels were present during the five warming cycles that melted the icebergs of the five previous ice ages.
In addition, only 12 percent of the earth's surface is habitable by humans.
Obviously, natural forces greater than humans and fossil fuels caused those five previous warming cycles, so can humans' minuscule presence on earth be the cause of the next warming cycle?
Can we avoid the conclusion that the one constant on earth is that the climate is <u>always</u> changing?

Figure 12-2

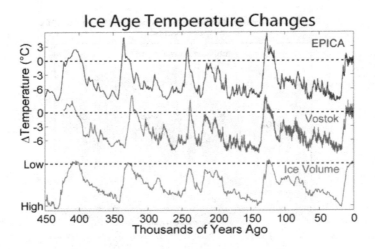

Figure 12-2
Observations of Illustration

There have been at least five major ice ages in the Earth's history (the Huronian, Cryogenian, Andean-Saharan, Karoo Ice Age, and the current Quaternary Ice Age).
What causes the Earth's climate to change? We think of the climate we enjoy today as "normal"; however, the planet's climates are always changing.
In times past, Britain was hot enough for hippos to live in Norfolk.
At other times, ice has covered the country for tens of thousands of years. Global climate change has usually occurred very slowly over thousands or millions of years.

We're also being bombarded with warnings that CO2 levels are higher than ever, but when we look at CO2 levels over the last 600 million years, we see some interesting data that totally contradict today's alarmist CO2 headlines.

Figure 12-3

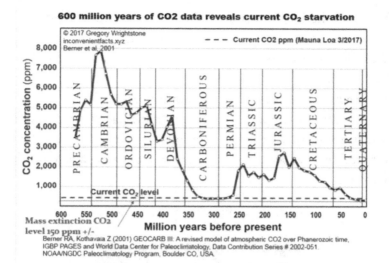

Figure 12-3
Observations of Illustration

Today's CO2 concentrations worldwide average about 380 parts per million.
Today's level of CO2 concentration is trivial compared with the concentrations during earlier geologic periods.
600 million years of CO2 data reveal current CO2 starvation vs. CO2 levels in the past.
460 million years ago, during the Ordovician Period, CO2 concentrations were 4,400 ppm, and temperatures then were about the same as they are today. With such high levels of CO2, the Earth should have been boiling.

Contrary to the non-stop mantra of the media and the so-called "experts" that today's CO2 concentrations are unprecedented, our current geologic period, the Quaternary, has seen the lowest average levels of carbon dioxide in the Earth's long history.

During each of the last four ice ages, CO2 concentration fell below 190 ppm. At the end of the last ice age, it fell to 182 ppm, thought to be the lowest in the Earth's history. Why is this alarming? Because below 150 ppm, most terrestrial plant life cannot exist.

CO2 levels were many multiples of 400 ppm during virtually all of Earth's history.

From a historical perspective, an atmospheric CO2 concentration of 400 ppm is almost scraping the bottom of the barrel. Over the Earth's history, atmospheric CO2 concentrations have ranged from 180 ppm to 7000 ppm. On that scale, today we are in fact barely above the Earth's record lows.

Figure 12-4

Worrying that 400 ppm is too high is like worrying about your fuel tank overflowing when it reaches the 1/8 mark during filling.[668] At 400 ppm CO2 levels are, in historical terms, actually dangerously low.

Our current geo period (Quaternary) has the lowest CO2 levels in all of Earth's history. The average CO2 level dating back to the Precambrian was 2,600 ppm. Our current level of ~406 ppm (January 2017) is tiny in comparison to Earth's historical levels. The real risk is CO2 starvation. (https://twitter.com/GillesnFio/status/1122384430054682625)

It should be obvious to impartial observers of the long-term data that, rather than experiencing excessively high levels of carbon dioxide, we are in fact in a period of CO2 starvation. While short historical periods are used to support apocalyptic visions of life in a world with slightly increased CO2, perspective is everything: the increase of approximately 120 ppm since the beginning of the Industrial Revolution is barely recognizable when viewed in the context of a longer section of Earth's CO2 history.

Over the billions of planetary years, ice ages have come and gone, and sea levels have risen and fallen. Temperatures have swung wildly going into and out of the ice age periods, with virtually no human presence nor fossil fuel energy usage over those billions of years. Fossilized sea animals are somewhat common to find in the "mountains" as a result of those weather swings over the billions of years.

The spread of humans[669] and their large and increasing population has had a profound impact on large areas of the environment and millions of native species worldwide. Advantages that explain this evolutionary success include a relatively larger brain, which enable high levels of abstract reasoning, language, problem-solving, sociality, and culture through social learning. Humans use tools to a much higher degree than any other animal, are the only extant species known to build fires and cook their food, and are the only extant species to clothe themselves and create and use numerous other technologies and arts.

Humans are uniquely adept at using systems of symbolic communication (such as language and art) for self-expression and the exchange of ideas, and for organizing themselves into purposeful groups. Curiosity and the human desire to understand and influence the environment and to explain and manipulate phenomena (or events) have provided the foundation for developing science, philosophy, mythology, religion, anthropology, and numerous other fields of knowledge.

Though most of human existence has been sustained by hunting and gathering in band societies, increasing numbers of human societies began to practice sedentary agriculture approximately 10,000 years ago, domesticating plants and animals, thus allowing for the growth of civilization. These human societies subsequently expanded in size, establishing various forms of government, religion, and culture around the world, unifying people within regions to form states and empires. With access to fossil fuels, the rapid advancement of scientific and medical understanding in the 19th and 20th centuries led to the development of fuel-driven technologies and infrastructures and increased life spans, causing the human population to rise exponentially.

If the Earth were 24 hours old,[670] how old would humankind be? Ever wondered what the beginning of existence would look like if it was tracked and measured on a 24-hour clock? What if we charted the history of earth on a clock? When and where did humankind come into existence during the creation of life?

Condensing all the information about the history of earth into a 24-hour time period, we find that Humans have existed only for 77 seconds!

Figure 12-5

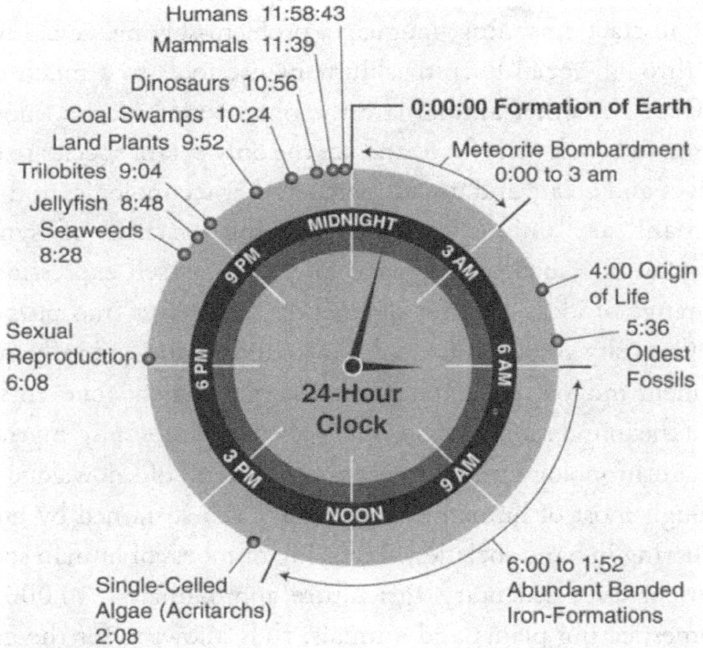
Humans 11:58:43
Mammals 11:39
Dinosaurs 10:56
Coal Swamps 10:24
Land Plants 9:52
Trilobites 9:04
Jellyfish 8:48
Seaweeds 8:28
0:00:00 Formation of Earth
Meteorite Bombardment 0:00 to 3 am
MIDNIGHT
3 AM
6 AM
9 AM
NOON
3 PM
6 PM
9 PM
24-Hour Clock
4:00 Origin of Life
5:36 Oldest Fossils
Sexual Reproduction 6:08
Single-Celled Algae (Acritarchs) 2:08
6:00 to 1:52 Abundant Banded Iron-Formations

Figure 12-5
Observations of Illustration

If midnight marks the formation of Earth on the clock, dinosaurs, mammals, and humans would be last in the line of creation. In fact, human history doesn't begin until 11:58:43 p.m.!
It's interesting to notice that even the simplest forms of life didn't exist until 4 a.m.
Dinosaurs lived and died in almost 30 minutes!
Doesn't it make one realize how truly vast the existence of earth is, and that humans are just a tiny part of it?
Looking back just a few short centuries, as humans began controlling their lifestyles from the horse-and-buggy days (before the discovery of oil and the invention in the early 1900s of the automobile and airplane), life expectancy was 40 to 50 years, infant mortality rates were high, and weather-related deaths were huge.
Humans have been monitoring temperatures for about the last 150 years, i.e., about how long we've had meteorologists. The warming we have had over the last 150 years is so small that if we didn't have meteorologists and climatologists to micromanage the data, we wouldn't have noticed it at all. <u>On a 24-hour clock, those 150 years that we've been monitoring temperatures (out of the 4.5 billion the earth has been around) represent 0.00288th of a second!</u>

Today, on the basis of this minuscule 150-year time-frame, we are micromanaging and forecasting earth's demise as caused by humans and fossil fuels, when the only things around during the first 4.5 billion years was the sun, which goes through 11-year cycles of massive sunspots and solar flares,[671] and the moon that is moving farther and farther from the earth every year.

When the quantity of CO_2 in the atmosphere increases, the temperature of the Earth also rises. This in turn would contribute to a warming of the oceans. Warm oceans are less able to absorb CO_2 than cold ones, so as the temperature rises, the oceans release more CO2 into the atmosphere, which in turn causes the temperature to rise again. This process is known as feedback.

Viewed from space, the majority of the Earth's surface is covered by oceans.[672] Oceans, in fact, make up 71 percent of the planet's surface, leaving the remaining 29 percent for land, and most of that 29 percent is uninhabitable!

Figure 12-6

Figure 12-6
Observations of Illustration

The total land mass of 29 percent comprises both uninhabitable deserts and mountains, and habitable areas:
The uninhabitable area is 17 percent of the earth's surface.
Deserts make up about 10 percent of the earth's surface.
Mountains make up another 7 percent of the surface.
The habitable surface area is only 12 percent.

> Discounting the uninhabitable surface area of deserts and mountains, the habitable land mass is about 12% of the earth's surface.

Today, only 12 percent of the earth's surface is land mass habitable by humans, animals, and vegetation. And it's up for discussion as to whether humans, animals, plants, fossil fuels, Mother Nature, or the sun's strength and sunspot activity, or the moon's changing distance from the earth, or any or all of the above factors have contributed to past and current climate changes, and how they may impact future changes in the climate.

Without the existence of human beings or fossil fuels to blame for the previous ice ages, and the warming cycles that melted the ice, we are left with a troublesome question. Namely, how can the presence of humans and fossil fuels, for "0.00288th of a second" on the "24-hour clock," on the 12 percent of the earth's surface that is habitable land mass, have any influence as compared to all the natural forces that have caused the five previous warming cycles and climate changes over the last 4.5 billion years?

Figure 12-7

![Figure 12-7: Heat capacity of air: 1005 J/kg/K. Heat capacity of ocean water: 3993 J/kg/K. Global Calculation of all air and ocean mass Energy content in Joules/Degree Kelvin. Air: 5×10^{21}. Ocean: 5.6×10^{24}. Source: http://noconsensus.wordpress.com/2011/04/05/234-5/]

Figure 12-7
Observations of Illustration

Liquid water is far denser than air.
Dense liquid water in the oceans is a huge reservoir of stored energy.
The oceans contain greater than 1,000 times more energy than the atmosphere; this means that earth's atmosphere as a whole—regardless of which gases make up the atmosphere—cannot warm the oceans in any significant amount.
And this means the oceans are warming the atmosphere.
The oceans are controlling the weather and climate on earth, not the atmosphere.
Direct and indirect solar radiation, as well as volcanic, and tectonic forces resulting from gravity, warm the oceans.

Two prominent organizations have come up with the answer, the National Oceanic and Atmospheric Administration (NOAA) and the United States National Climatic Data Center (NCDC). According to both:

1. The <u>primary</u> force is the <u>sun</u> that heats the earth's oceans and land;
2. Then, secondarily, the earth's oceans and land heat the atmosphere. The atmosphere is <u>not</u> heating the earth, it's the sun.
3. Finally, then, and only after the above two factors have had their primary and secondary effects, increasing air temperature does increase sea surface temperature.

With the facts thus laid before us, we are forced to the conclusion that the one constant on earth is that the climate is <u>always</u> changing.[673]

Returning to the matter of greenhouse gases, the sequence, again, is that the sun heats the earth, and then the earth heats the atmosphere. The atmosphere is not heating the earth. According to the laws of thermodynamics, energy only flows from higher-energy earth to the lower-energy atmosphere. Earth (oceans and land) heats the air, not the reverse. Where can we measure this effect in the natural world? After detrending (i.e., removing seasonal variations) the sea-surface temperatures versus air temperatures, we see in the illustration above (Figure 12-7) that increasing air temperature <u>always follows</u> increasing sea surface temperature.

In the second part of this chapter my co-author, Todd Royal, will describe how politics and emotion have overtaken rationality when it comes to the global warming/climate change debate.

The Global Warming and Climate Debate Has Been Politicized

Dr. Frank Luntz, the Republican political pundit and pollster, realized that the public and elected officials did not understand the concept of "global warming." Therefore, in a brilliant political move, he came up with the phrase "climate change."[674] This helped sell the theory of man-made global warming. The problem with politicizing the weather in this way is that no one has ever accurately predicted the weather.

Computer models are only digital predictions, yet increasingly they are being pressed into service as pawns in local, county, state, federal and even presidential elections. These easily manipulated predictions are now being used to justify increased government budgets, governmental control over energy, and, if extreme climate-change advocates have their way, to shut down more and more aspects of our lives and choices as consumers. Here, indeed, is a "manufactured crisis," to use a current phrase, a crisis the public is being told that it should pay, and pay heavily, to "fix." Meanwhile, Al Gore and an extremely vocal faction of wealthy California environmentalists (Arnold Schwarzenegger and Tom Steyer prominent among them) are peddling doomsday fears about global warming and climate change that have no basis in our planetary history or applicable science.

Consider, for instance, that in January 2012, 16 eminent scientists published an article in the *Wall Street Journal* titled, "No Need to Panic About Global Warming." The authors included the president of the World Federation of Scientists, a Princeton University professor of physics, a Hebrew University professor of astrophysics, and Professor Mojib Latif, a climate expert at the Leibniz Institute at Kiel University in Germany and member of the U.N. Intergovernmental Panel on Climate Change (IPCC), the world's most significant organization arguing for man-made global warming.[675] There is absolutely no basis for dismissing the closely reasoned arguments of these individuals and the thousands of others who are skeptical of the modern "gospel" of man-made, anthropogenic global warming and climate change. For further proof, readers are invited to read and research the more than 9,000 scientists who have signed the *Oregon Petition*.

Readers are also recommended to check endnote 8 (at the end of this chapter) for a list of rational and reputable books that question "the science is settled claim" and the ongoing purge of "deniers" while trying to soberly understand the issue of anthropogenic global warming and climate change.[676] There *is* another side to this vital debate, because the claims about global warming and climate change need to be vetted and debated, so it can be determined whether man is, or is not, the cause of current warming and cooling trends.

For instance, the claim is made again and again that man is the cause of high $CO2$ levels that started with the Industrial Revolution and continue today. There are several problems with that argument, however, as summarized below:

> "Today's $CO2$ concentrations worldwide average about 380 parts per million. This level of $CO2$ concentration is trivial compared with the concentrations during earlier geologic periods. For example, 460 million years ago, during the Period, $CO2$ concentrations were 4,400 ppm, and temperatures then were about the same as they are today. With such high levels of $CO2$, the Earth should have been boiling."[677]

Anyone sincerely interested in finding the truth about global warming and climate change should adopt at least an agnostic or "realist" position in regard to its causes based solely on the following facts:

> "According to the Climate.gov website, the current global average temperature is roughly 'shy' of 60 degrees Fahrenheit. About 55 million years ago – just after the age of the Dinosaurs – the era known as the Paleocene-Eocene Thermal Maximum (PETM) saw average global temps as high as 73-degree Fahrenheit. As humans only showed up about 100,000 years ago, Ron and I can both say, 'PETM WAS NOT OUR FAULT.'"[678]

Nearly ten years ago, a popular technology website catalogued "700 papers supporting climate realism."[679] Another review of scientific literature at that time found "over 450 peer-reviewed papers challenging man-made global warming."[680] Again, the *Oregon Petition* provides over 9,000 qualified challenges to the notion of man-made global warming and/or climate change. The following paragraphs provide a brief survey of current research contributing to the collapsing narrative of man-made global warming and climate change.

As mentioned, we are incessantly told that 97 percent of all scientists agree that man is causing irreversible global warming and climate change. That statistical statement is false.[681] Here is the truth of the matter:

> "A recent study reported in the peer-reviewed *Organization Studies* found that just 36 percent of earth scientists and engineers believe that humans are creating a climate change crisis. A majority of the 1,077 respondents in the survey believe that nature is the primary cause of recent global warming and climate change."[682]

Contrary to the 97% rhetoric, the godfather of all letters objecting to the climate change alarmism, the Oregon Global Warming Petition Project (the *Oregon Petition*), circulated by the Oregon Institute for Science and Medicine and signed by more than 31,000 American scientists (and including more than 9,000 with doctorates), states unequivocally:[683]

> There is no convincing scientific evidence that human release of carbon dioxide, methane, or other greenhouse gases is causing or will, in the foreseeable future, cause catastrophic heating of the earth's atmosphere and disruption of the earth's climate. Moreover, there is substantial scientific evidence that increases in atmospheric carbon dioxide produce many beneficial effects upon the natural plant and animal environments of the earth.

Man as the prime cause of global warming and climate change took another hit when a March 2019 NASA study found the famous Jakobshavn glacier in Greenland (an ice mass that in 2012 was found to be "retreating about 1.8 miles and thinning nearly 130 feet annually) was starting to grow again at about the same rate in the past two years (2016-2018)."[684] The NASA study was published in late March 2019 in *Nature Geoscience*.[685] Past natural variability seems to be the explanation for the unexpected results, which point to a likely failure to thoroughly vet the supposed scientific consensus that "demands to prove that rising CO2 is causing an effect like melting Greenland ice."[686]

What about the role of the sun in determining and causing the Earth's climate to change or warm? According to Professor A. Balasubramanian from the Centre for Advanced Studies in Earth Sciences, University of Mysore:

> "The climate of a region (or whole earth) is determined by radiation energy of the sun, and its distribution and temporal fluctuations. The long-term

state of the atmosphere is a function of variety of interacting elements. They are: Solar radiation, Air masses, Pressure systems (cyclone belts), Ocean Currents, Topography."[687]

CO2 is one of many factors that influence regional and global temperatures. There are serious questions about the role CO2 has played during warming trends in the 20th and thus far in the 21st century. Climate scientist Vijay Jayaraj cites these weather facts to make the case that the earth is actually in danger of global cooling:

> "There is poor correlation between CO2 emissions and global temperature. Between 2000 and 2018, global temperature showed no significant increase despite a steep increase in carbon dioxide emissions from anthropogenic sources. The same was the case between the years 1940 and 1970. When carbon dioxide concentration increases at a constant and steady rate and temperature doesn't follow the pattern, we can be certain that carbon dioxide is not the primary driver of global temperature."[688]

MIT atmospheric physicist Richard Lindzen, one of the world's leading climatologists, believes CO2 is not the main factor in global warming and climate change. He questions whether the earth is warming, cooling or somewhere in between. Dr. Lindzen is considered by some a "climate-science denier" and skeptic simply because he questions whether CO2 is the main driver of weather![689]

Climate scientists acknowledge that life on earth happens through the Earth's positioning in the solar system relative to the sun, and that "the sun is the biggest influencer and driver of global temperature."[690] NASA's original home page on its website acknowledged "the sun's impact on our climate system."[691] But NASA took that statement down over political pressure to say man and CO2 emissions are killing the planet.

Freedom of speech and scientific debate have been, and continue to be, squelched in regard to this crucial issue. CO2 has been officially designated as prime mover in the global warming and climate change debate. This short-circuits the asking of any questions about how the sun affects weather and global temperature. This is a huge mistake for many reasons, including the ignoring of relevant scientific data:

> "[In] Central Europe, for example, temperature changes since 1990 coincided more with the changes in solar activity than with atmospheric CO2 concentration. The same has been true globally, and across centuries. The Maunder Minimum (1645-1715) and Dalton Minimum (1790-1830) – periods of low solar activity – were responsible for the coldest periods of the Little Ice Age. Likewise, increased solar activity in the Roman Warm Period (~250 B.C. to A.D. 400) and Medieval Warm Period (~A.D. 950-1250) brought warmer temperatures on Earth. Hundreds of peer-reviewed scientific papers affirm the overwhelming impact of solar activity on Earth's temperature."[692]

Should we be seriously contemplating global cooling? A number of climate scientists believe "another major cooling" is likely to happen in this century.[693] However, does that prove correlation? No, it doesn't. But "observations of sunspot activity" at the Space Weather Prediction Center of the National Oceanic and Atmospheric Administration (NOAA) do "indicate that there has been a lull in solar activity during the past 18 years."[694]

During this same 18-year period there "has been no significant warming which can prove and show direct correlation between solar activity and global average temperature."[695] NASA has admitted a cooling trend based on the "evidence for the lull in solar activity."[696]

Recent scientific studies confirm "the next solar cycles (25 and 26) could be similar to the Maunder and Dalton Minima that plunged much of the world into disastrous cold."[697] The peer-reviewed scientific journal, *Astrophysics and Space Science,* in February 2019 suggested the dire possibility of the solar minimum having already begun.[698] That indicates the strong probability that a Little Ice Age could be under way. But contradictions are inherent when it comes to predicting weather. No one understands the cycles of weather, much less if man can cause or affect it, one way or the other.

The Damage From Environmental Politics

The leaders of today's environmental movement—Al Gore and Tom Steyer come to mind—cannot refrain from making apocalyptic predictions. Fortunately for the rest of us (and even for them), these false prophets of doom have so far compiled a 100 percent record of inaccuracy (except, of course, for dire events safely predicted to happen decades in the future). But, unfortunately, their wildly inaccurate predictions actually do wreak havoc. As a prime example, Al Gore's anti-global-warming jihad, by relentlessly promoting ill-conceived environmental policy, has had devastating effects on local areas and entire nations.

Seasonal flooding has reached near-catastrophic levels in the U.S. due to the "green insanity" inflicted in the Missouri River Basin, Nebraska, Iowa, and South Dakota. This began when "Congress in 2004 under pressure from environmental organizations approved a revision to the Master Water Control Manual (MWCM)."[699]

This allowed the U.S. Corps of Engineers—with authority from the U.S. Congress—to flood eight states in accordance with new environmental revisions to the MWCM. Flood control was no longer a priority; instead the politicized green movement, thanks to its own rising tide of membership, media visibility and strength, was able to make "wild rivers" the fashionable new priority.

The MWCM's original mandate was flood control, but suddenly they had the Corps of Engineers "utilizing dams in a way for which they were never designed – to attempt to mimic the natural cycles of the river through the season." In consequence, environmental emotion prevailing over reason has inflicted billions in flood damage, destroying farms, homes, and roads, all in the cause of "wild rivers" being returned to their natural habitat.

California suffered some of the worst wildfires in its history in mid-2018. Pacific Gas & Electric is now in bankruptcy over the damages from entire towns burning to the ground because of faulty electrical infrastructure, high winds, and environmental regulations that prevented excess brush and dead trees from being cleared throughout cities, towns, forests, and wilderness areas.[700] Yet, rather than reassess these ill-advised policies, top state policymakers and political leaders have instead blamed:

> "Climate change as an excuse for California's recent wildfires and even criticized those addressing California's poor forest management and community development policies as being a huge contributor to these wildfires."[701]

In a clear rebuke of state officials, however, a February 22, 2019, California Department of Forest and Fire Protection (Cal Fire) report pointedly did <u>not</u> include climate change as a leading cause for the devastating wildfires. Instead the report specifically noted:

> "An epidemic of dead and dying trees, and the proliferation of new homes in the wildland urban interface (WUI) magnify the threat and place substantially more people and property at risk than in preceding decades."[702]

Forest-management practice and action plans within specific at-risk communities need to be implemented. Blaming climate change is a false canard that excuses the incompetence of elected officials, along with environmental regulations and organizations that stand to profit from the global warming and climate change narrative.

The Cal Fire report clearly laid out priorities, which include:

"Suspending onerous regulatory requirements to use prescribed fires to thin out dense brush areas, set specific priorities for removal of dead trees, excessive forest undergrowth to reduce fuel (fire) and restore forest health. 35 specific high-priority fuel reduction areas in state that cover more than 90,000 acres of forest land need immediate action."[703]

The report identified 25 million acres of California wild lands at <u>very high or extreme fire heat risk</u>—over half the state—and additional estimations in the report put 15 million acres of California forest in some need of restoration.[704]

To implement Cal Fire's recommendations will require cooperation from the California governor, Legislature, and dozens of state agencies and regulatory entities at both state and federal level. Likely, none of these recommendations will be implemented, even on a limited basis. California is a one-party state (Democratic), and its 2020 presidential candidate, Senator Kamala Harris, Governor Gavin Newsome and former Governor Jerry Brown all believe in, and receive (or have received) significant political support from, the global warming and climate-change movement.[705]

Misguided legislators who mistakenly enable destructive floods and forest fires would seem to be the most extreme example of environmentalism run amok. But think again. What about letting children make environmental policy and wreck entire industries in the process? Yet that is exactly what happened—and is still happening. A 9-year old Vermont boy, using made-up statistics, launched the ban-plastic-straws movement to the detriment of jobs and technological progress in the plastics sector.[706]

We are repeatedly told that the U.S. is causing a plastic tsunami of straws littering our oceans, rivers, and drinkable waterways. This is false. The World Economic Forum did an analysis on the issue and found:

> <u>"That more than 8 million tons of plastic end up in the ocean every year. Most of the plastic washed into the oceans, 90% of it come from just 10 rivers in Asia."</u>[707]

Ten river systems from Asia carry 90 percent of all global plastic waste that floats into oceans. Letting a 9-year-old be taken seriously and using his theory to begin destroying the plastics industry by mandating that businesses, governments, and entire continents ban plastic straws is both laughable and seriously dangerous.

Yet the ban-plastics-straws crusade is the essence of today's global and U.S.-based environmental movement. Facts take a back seat to feel-good sentiment so long as it pushes the global warming and climate change story forward. No one counts the cost to taxpayers or the incremental curtailment of human progress.

There seems to be an unending supply of people, organizations, officials, and government leaders who, in the name of saving our planet, keep recycling the same global-warming and climate-change scares to gain more money and political power. Yet none of their predictions come true, and the idea of translating scientific facts into sound environmental policy is rarely, if ever taken into consideration.[708]

Claiming that the U.S., Europe, or other modern countries are environmental hellholes as a way of smearing capitalism so that radical environmentalists like Al Gore, Tom Steyer, Bill McKibben, and Naomi Klein can earn billions off renewable energy is the worst form of environmental hypocrisy. These people halt "mining, logging, fossil fuels extraction and condemn communities to poverty."[709]

When continents, countries, states, regions, cities, towns, and villages are free to use their natural resources, the result is invariably an increase in human thriving, productivity, and even longevity, along with a corresponding decrease in human suffering. Unfortunately, the focus of today's radical green movement is on naming and shaming the next environmental evildoer rather than on coming up with real-world solutions. For these green-eyed visionaries, sadly, "it's not really about pollution or reducing CO_2 emissions or solving the energy needs of the neediest and making the world cleaner and healthier."[710]

America and American companies or other modern countries or multinational firms often provide the only means for developing countries to gain access to better lives or the resources to clean up their environments. Environmentalists should be praising America for this technological outreach; and if anyone really wants to demonize, they should start with India and China for the damage both countries are doing to global health. America and its environmental allies are, by any scientific measure, part of the "pollution solution":

> "Since 2005, U.S. carbon dioxide emissions have fallen by 758 million metric tons. It's the largest decline of any country in the world, <u>while China's and India's CO_2 emissions mushroomed by 3 billion and 1 billion metric tons respectively</u>."[711]

If the U.S., the EU, NATO, U.S. allies in Asia, Fortune 500 countries, and sovereign nation funds under the collective Western security umbrella don't stop this fixation on global-warming and climate-change being the crux of every policymaking decision, then China, Russia, Iran, and North Korea may eventually destroy the whole post-WWII, liberal, U.S.-led order.

Global warming and climate change may indeed pose the greatest national security threat now facing the world. Not because of all the implausible doomsday scenarios, but because environmental policy that considers only global warming and climate change has taken center stage all itself, while relegating important issues of national security, foreign policy, and basic economics into the background. If man is overly warming the earth, the question should be asked: How do we reverse course without ruining countries and continents? Environmentalists seem completely unaware that radical solutions (like the "Green New Deal") would open up the entire world to violence, pestilence, famine, destruction, and even eventual slavery under some form of communism or socialism.

For some reason, leading environmental organizations, such as the Rockefeller Fund and Sierra Club, always overlook human progress when touting their global warming and climate change credentials. Even worse in their collaboration with the undoing of Western technological progress are the Europeans. Their continuing embrace of the Paris Climate Agreement, global warming, and climate change comes without any specific policy answers on how to combat either phenomenon if it is actually proved to be man's fault. Environmentalism trumping common sense will only embolden the Chinese, Russians, Iranians, and North Koreans to further menace the West's freedom and liberal way of life.

The EU, led by Germany, is killing NATO over global warming and climate change.[712] Germany continues orienting its entire country toward renewable energy, which has been proven not to work, while refusing to meet its security obligations under NATO treaties.

Germany offers an additional example of how environmental thinking can actually subvert security issues. Germany plans on buying its natural gas from the Russian Nord Stream 2 pipeline. At the same time the Germans are setting up their entire national security apparatus for possible cyber-attack and Chinese control by allowing Huawei Technology, a Chinese multinational telecommunication equipment and consumer electronics manufacturer, to build in Germany their next generation 5G mobile networks. Ren Zhengfei, a former engineer from the Chinese military, founded Huawei in 1987.

Global Warming and Climate Change: Total Political War?

Those who dare question global warming and climate orthodoxy, or even the scarcity-of-resources argument, are labeled as "climate deniers." The result of such intellectual intolerance is that a full and fair vetting of global warming and climate change claims is never allowed to proceed. The goal obviously is not factual accuracy leading to carefully reasoned conclusions. The goal, political rather than scientific, is simply to win at all costs. What will such "winning" look like? Here is another doomsday prediction, one we pray does <u>not</u> come to pass. Ultimate victory for the radical environmentalists could result in shutting down all human progress and constraining, even crippling, human ingenuity. And that kind of total political war could ignite actual wars that could spreading across the globe.[713]

The authors of this book consider themselves climate agnostics searching for the truth, and then logically opting, at some reasonable point, for the most workable answers and prescriptions moving forward. By 2020 the "Asian Century" will begin, and with the environmental destruction coming from Asia's rivers along with their use of coal, nuclear, and natural gas, we in the West need to ponder this basic question: What do we care about more? Dismantling all our hard-won technological advantages in hopes of eradicating global warming and climate change? Or bringing billions of people in Asia, India, and Africa out of crippling poverty and environmental annihilation?[714]

*

Here's a final suggestion as a postscript: Why not arrange a debate between Al Gore or Tom Steyer on one side, say, and Bud Bromley[715] or Dr. Judith Curry[716] on the other? The latter two are prepared to explain and fully support all the reasons why global warming and climate change are not man's fault. Unlike Gore and Steyer, moreover, neither stands to lose trillions of taxpayer dollars and political prestige should they be proved wrong.

Ronald Stein
Founder and Ambassador for Energy & Infrastructure
PTS Advance

As founder of PTS Advance (Principal Technical Services – 1995), Ronald Stein has developed one of the most successful and innovative family owned professional services firms in California. Known as the leader in delivering staffing solutions to the 12 major oil refineries in the state, the business has since transformed to support a range of staffing, consulting, project services and business process outsourcing solutions to the wider Energy & Infrastructure and Life Sciences industries.

Over the last decade, Ron has become the private business spokesperson for the energy and infrastructure industries through his more than 100 published Op Ed articles that provide an education for the citizens as to what and why the energy infrastructures are the primary infrastructures that truly drives our economy.

At the 2018 Western State Petroleum Association (WSPA) Annual Conference, Ron was awarded the "President's Award for his Tireless Efforts Protecting and Promoting a Vibrant Oil and Gas Industry in the West". The November 2018 Press release that appeared on Yahoo Finance: **"Recognizing Greatness in the Oil and Gas Industry"** was shared with 17 million viewers. https://finance.yahoo.com/news/recognizing-greatness-oil-gas-industry-134100910.html

Ronald Stein, P.E.
Founder and Ambassador for Energy & Infrastructure

Ronald.Stein@PTSadvance.com
Twitter: @PTSFounder

Todd Royal

Independent public policy consultant in Los Angeles focusing on the geopolitical implications of energy

Todd Royal is an internationally published columnist and author with a growing consulting practice based in Los Angeles, California. His publication that is in the U.S. Library of Congress titled: "Hydraulic Fracturing and the Revitalization of the American Economy," helped launch his writing and consulting career. Todd took his time from working at Duke University on value chain analysis and using SWOT (strengths, weaknesses, opportunities, and threats) economic research into the $445 billion dollar global furniture industry, and current African aid programs administered by U.S. AID to complete groundbreaking research on how energy and economic recovery are intertwined.

After graduating from Pepperdine University's School of Public Policy with his Master's in Public Policy (M.P.P.) with highest honors in International Relations and State and Local Government, Todd began writing for OilPrice.com, The National Interest, Asia Times, USA Today, Yahoo Finance, Business Insiders, ModernDiplomacy.com,

SeekingAlpha.com, EurasiaReview.com, and the American Society of Civil Engineers on energy, foreign policy, national security, and California politics.

But Todd's focus began shifting heavily towards energy and how energy is used as a weapon by Russia, China and Iran every bit as much as their nuclear arsenals. His work on energy, foreign policy and national security has gotten the attention from industry leaders, energy organizations and State and Federal officials.

Todd Royal

Independent public policy consultant in Los Angeles focusing on the geopolitical implications of energy

ToddRoyal@yahoo.com

Twitter: @TCR_Consulting

Endnotes

Chapter Notes:
(Due to the dynamic nature of the Internet, the location of some of the more than 700 items cited in this work—and accessed at the time of writing—may change as menus, homepages, and files are reorganized.)

INTRODUCTION *Helping Citizens Become Energy-Literate*

1. CSU Bakersfield, Department of Geological Sciences, "What's Made from Crude Oil (a partial list of common products), 2018. Document can be downloaded if you type into Google: What do we make from oil?
2. U.S. Energy Information Administration, Independent Statistics & Analysis, "In 2018, the United States consumed more energy than ever before," www.EIA.gov, April 16, 2019. https://www.eia.gov/todayinenergy/detail.php?id=39092&src=email
3. The Engineering News Record reports that the International Energy Agency: Nuclear Power Will Be Needed to Meet Climate Goals https://www.enr.com/external_headlines/story?region=enr&story_id=bI65yJYEqabBfQ_3HmJ3xFRAv9A1mRPChM uuAgF4kadaDxlbiNv9jMwsNWsNwMuPUIkyYtZkulJdZN_ GPoQUvxIcV 37D 3hfK 72BFbIaRJ 0IsMVE 7NbM 2KqUnpFLSJGYu6RiLdDYQVup_UbO0UVSjzJIPOmkX

235

FcnUnAP3-SY6URE*&images_premium=1&define_caption=1&oly_enc_id=8565F2119945D0S

4. U.S. Energy Information Administration, Independent Statistics & Analysis, *International Energy Outlook 2018*, July 14, 2018. Next release date July 2019. https://www.eia.gov/outlooks/ieo/

5. Carlyle, Ryan, "Where can I find a comprehensive list of the 6,000 products made from petroleum? www.Quora.com, April 21, 2014. https://www.quora.com/Where-can-I-find-a-comprehensive-list-of-the-6-000-products-made-from-petroleum

6. U.S. Energy Information Administration, Independent Statistics & Analysis, "Oil: Crude and Petroleum Products *Explained*," www.EIA.gov, May 2018. https://www.eia.gov/energyexplained/index.php?page=oil_home

7. Global Data, *Power Transmission and Distribution Conductors, Update 2018 – Global Market Size, Competitive Landscape and Key Country Analysis to 2022*, www.GlobalData.com, December 2018. https://www.globaldata.com/store/report/gdpe1048emr--power-transmission-and-distribution-conductors-update-2018-global-market-size-competitive-landscape-and-key-country-analysis-to-2022/

8. van Beurden, Ben, Chief Executive Officer, Shell Oil, "Two billion people do not have access to reliable energy and electricity: this must change," www.linkedin.com, October 18, 2018. https://www.linkedin.com/pulse/two-billion-people-do-have-access-reliable-must-ben-van-beurden/

9. Parke, Phoebe, "Why are 600 Million Africans still without Power?" www.CNN.com, April 1, 2016. https://www.linkedin.com/pulse/two-billion-people-do-have-access-reliable-must-ben-van-beurden/

10. Gold, Russell, *The Boom: How Fracking Ignited the American Energy Revolution and Changed the World*," (Simon & Schuster, New York, NY), Page 265, April 21, 2015. https://www.amazon.com/Boom-Fracking-Ignited-American-Revolution/dp/1451692293/ref=sr_1_2?s=books&ie=UTF8&qid=1544497960&sr=1-2&keywords=the+boom

11 Daalder, Ivo H., Destler, I.M., "The Foreign Policy Genius of George H.W. Bush: How He Changed the Policy Process Forever," www.ForeignAffairs.com, December 4, 2018. https://www.foreignaffairs.com/articles/2018-12-04/foreign-policy-genius-george-h-w-bush?cid=nlc-fa_fatoday-20181204

12 Epstein, Alex, *The Moral Case for Fossil Fuels*, (Portfolio – Penguin Books, New York, NY), Entire book for the source. November 13, 2014. https://www.amazon.com/Moral-Case-Fossil-Fuels/dp/1591847443/ref=sr_1_1?ie=UTF8&qid=1544553425&sr=8-1&keywords=alex+epstein

13 Dr. Lehr, Jay, Harris, Tom, "Fear Over a Rising Sea is a Ruse," www.citizensjournal.us, December 2, 2018. http://citizensjournal.us/119523-2/

14 Emerson Smith, Joshua, "Climate contrarian uncovers scientific error, upends major ocean warming study," www.SanDiegoUnionTribune.com, November 13, 2018. https://www.sandiegouniontribune.com/news/environment/sd-me-climate-study-error-20181113-story.html

15 Editorials, *Investors Business Daily*, "Don't Tell Anyone But We Just Had Two Years of Record Breaking Cooling," www.Investors.com, May 16, 2018.

16 Editorials, *Investors Business Daily*. Ibid. 2018

17 Brown, Aaron, "Did You Know the Greatest Two Year Cooling Event Just Took Place?" www.RealClearMarkets.com, April 24, 2018. https://www.realclearmarkets.com/articles/2018/04/24/did_you_know_the_greatest_two-year_global_cooling_event_just_took_place_103243.html

18 Foster, Peter, "Peter Foster: Another report reluctantly admits that 'green' energy is a disastrous flop," www.Business.FinancialPost.com, November 22, 2018. https://business.financialpost.com/opinion/peter-foster-another-report-reluctantly-admits-that-green-energy-is-a-disastrous-flop

19 BP Statistical Review of World Energy, 2019, 68th Edition, Coal, Energy | Economics, www.BP.com, June 2019 release. https://

www.bp.com/en/global/corporate/energy-economics/statistical-review-of-world-energy/coal.html#coal-consumption
20. BP Statistical Review of World Energy, 2019, 68th Edition. Ibid. June 2019.
21. Global Warming Petition Project, Page accessed July 12, 2019. www.PetitionProject.org, http://www.petitionproject.org/index.php
22. Also see *The Polar Bear Catastrophe That Never Happened* by Canadian zoologist Susan Crockford (The Global Warming Policy Foundation, March, 2019)
23. Wettengel, Julian, "Climate goal failure warrants high Energiewende priority – gov advisors," www.CleanEnergyWire.org, July 28, 2018. https://www.cleanenergywire.org/news/climate-goal-failure-warrants-high-energiewende-priority-gov-advisors
24. News, Deutsche Welle (DW), "Germany awarded 'shameful' negative climate prize at COP 24," www.dw.com, December 7, 2018. https://www.dw.com/en/germany-awarded-shameful-negative-climate-prize-at-cop24/a-46642240
25. ESI Africa Edition 5, "Low emission tech can save coal's dominance," www.Esi-Africa.com, December 4, 2018. https://www.esi-africa.com/low-emission-tech-can-save-coals-dominance/
26. U.S. Energy Information Administration, Independent Statistics & Analysis, *International Energy Outlook 2018* (focusing on China, India and Africa), July 24, 2018. Next release date September 2019. https://www.eia.gov/outlooks/ieo/
27. Kotkin, Joel, "The first shots in the climate wars," www.OCRegister.com, December 9, 2018. https://www.ocregister.com/2018/12/09/the-first-shots-in-the-climate-wars/
28. Carrington, Daminan, "Tackle climate or face financial crash, say world's biggest investors: UN summit urged to end all coal burning and introduce substantial taxes on emissions," www.TheGuardian.com, December 9, 2018. https://www.theguardian.com/environment/2018/dec/10/tackle-climate-or-face-financial-crash-say-worlds-biggest-investors

Chapter One: Energy Density

29   Annual Energy Outlook 2018, February 6, 2018, U.S Energy Information Administration, Energy Information Administration (EIA) https://www.eia.gov/outlooks/aeo/

30   Foster, Peter, "Peter Foster: Another report reluctantly admits that 'green' energy is a disastrous flop," www.Business.FinancialPost.com, November 22, 2018. https://business.financialpost.com/opinion/peter-foster-another-report-reluctantly-admits-that-green-energy-is-a-disastrous-flop

31   2018, U.S. Energy Information Administration https://www.eia.gov/outlooks/aeo/pdf/AEO2018.pdf page 13

32   Energy Skeptic, Peak Energy & Resources, Climate Change, and the Preservation of Knowledge, "41 Reasons why wind power cannot replace fossil fuels," www.EnergySkeptic.com, December 14, 2018. http://energyskeptic.com/2018/wind/

33   Jeannine Anderson, January 10, 2017, www.publicpower.org coal, oil, natural gas and nuclear can satisfy the Four Imperatives: power density, energy density, cost and scale https://www.publicpower.org/periodical/article/eia-projects-flat-consumption-changing-fuel-mix-between-now-and-2050

34   Robert Bryce, May 11, 2010, Forbes.com primary energy came from oil, natural gas, and coal https://www.forbes.com/2010/05/11/renewables-energy-oil-economy-opinions-contributors-robert-bryce.html#732d46901403

35   Anjar Priandoyo, September 2, 2015, priandoyo.wordpress.com world's energy consumption forecasted out to 2030 https://priandoyo.wordpress.com/2015/09/02/summary-energy/

36   Goreham, Steve, "100 percent renewable energy-Poor policy for electricity ratepayers," www.cfact.org, October 18, 2018. http://www.cfact.org/2018/10/30/100-percent-renewable-energy-poor-policy-for-electricity-ratepayers/

37   Ranken Energy Corporation, "Products made from petroleum: With over 6000 products and counting, petroleum continues to be a crucial requirement for all consumers," www.Ranken-Energy.

com, 2017. Entire paragraph (except for Paleolithic Era quote) with a partial list of the 6,000 products and the graph is from this exhaustive source. https://www.ranken-energy.com/index.php/products-made-from-petroleum/

38 Dudley, Bob, Dale, Spencer, *BP (British Petroleum) Energy Outlook – 2018 Edition*, www.BP.com, February 20, 2018. https://www.bp.com/en/global/corporate/energy-economics/energy-outlook.html

39 Paul Rogers and Katy Murphy, September 10, 2018, Mercury News 100% clean energy by 2045 https://www.mercurynews.com/2018/09/10/california-mandates-100-percent-clean-energy-by-2045/

40 August 2018, U.S. Energy Information Administration electricity generation by Nuclear and Natural Gas https://www.eia.gov/state/?sid=CA#tabs-4

41 The San Bernardino County Board of Supervisors slammed the brakes on big solar projects https://www.latimes.com/business/la-fi-san-bernardino-solar-renewable-energy-20190228-story.html?fbclid=IwAR2qHGq3bahHme6SFErLsnyFi9UPIfBHIhvnOh3dU3OM7kUTMcEqYfN3pQA

42 Lomberg, Bjorn, Director of the Copenhagen Consensus Center, "Are Electric Cars Really Green," via PragerU for YouTube.com, www.prageru.com & www.youtube.com, August 13, 2017. https://www.youtube.com/watch?v=OrmVk5OA2QE

43 Anjar Priandoyo, September 2, 2015, priandoyo.wordpress.com world's energy consumption forecasted out to 2030 https://priandoyo.wordpress.com/2015/09/02/summary-energy/

44 Annual Energy Outlook 2018, February 6, 2018, U.S Energy Information Administration, Energy Information Administration (EIA) https://www.eia.gov/outlooks/aeo/

Chapter Two: Prosperous Societies and Energy

45 Moore, Tom, "You Will Never Guess What Kind of Weather is the The Deadliest?" www.Weather.com, (The Weather Channel),

	June 11, 2016. https://weather.com/science/weather-explainers/news/weather-event-fatalities-heat
46	The Telegraph August 2017 https://www.telegraph.co.uk/travel/travel-truths/how-many-planes-are-there-in-the-world/
47	Quora.com https://www.quora.com/How-many-airports-are-there-in-the-world-1
48	Airports Council International, April 9, 2018 https://aci.aero/news/2018/04/09/aci-world-releases-preliminary-2017-world-airport-traffic-rankings-passenger-traffic-indian-and-chinese-airports-major-contributors-to-growth-air-cargo-volumes-surge-at-major-hubs-as-trade-wars-thre/
49	Travel Week February 17, 2017 http://www.travelweek.ca/news/exactly-many-planes-world-today/
50	Index Mundi https://www.indexmundi.com/energy/?product=jet-fuel and https://www.statista.com/statistics/655057/fuel-consumption-of-airlines-worldwide/
51	Travel Week February 17, 2017 http://www.travelweek.ca/news/exactly-many-planes-world-today/
52	Flightradar24 https://www.quora.com/How-many-airplanes-are-in-flight-on-average-at-any-given-time-worldwide
53	The Telegraph August 2017 https://www.telegraph.co.uk/travel/travel-truths/how-many-planes-are-there-in-the-world/
54	Cruise Market Watch https://cruisemarketwatch.com/capacity/
55	Cruiseslovetoknow.com https://cruises.lovetoknow.com/wiki/How_Much_Fuel_Does_a_Cruise_Ship_Use
56	OilPrice.com, September 2018 https://oilprice.com/Energy/Energy-General/Diesel-Demand-Is-Set-To-Soar.html
57	The Geography of Transport Systems https://transportgeography.org/?page_id=5955
58	US Special Delivery, February 2017 https://www.usspecial.com/how-many-trucking-companies-in-the-usa/
59	Trucks.com, October 2016 https://www.trucks.com/2016/10/17/truckers-fuel-efficiency-alternative-fuels/

60 Green Car Reports, July 2014 https://www.greencarreports.com/news/1093560_1-2-billion-vehicles-on-worlds-roads-now-2-billion-by-2035-report

61 Ranken Energy Corporation, "Products made from petroleum: With over 6000 products and counting, petroleum continues to be a crucial requirement for all consumers," www.Ranken-Energy.com, 2017. Entire paragraph (except for Paleolithic Era quote) with a partial list of the 6,000 products and the graph is from this exhaustive source. https://www.ranken-energy.com/index.php/products-made-from-petroleum/

62 Poverty Facts and Stats http://www.globalissues.org/article/26/poverty-facts-and-stats

63 Goal: Reduce child mortality https://www.unicef.org/mdg/childmortality.html

64 Cancer Statistics 2018 https://www.cancer.gov/about-cancer/understanding/statistics

65 Deaths from Nuclear Energy Compared with Other Causes, February 2013, https://www.energycentral.com/c/ec/deaths-nuclear-energy-compared-other-causes

66 World Health Organization, https://www.who.int/airpollution/en/

67 World Health Organization, https://www.who.int/gho/phe/indoor_air_pollution/burden/en/

68 International Labour Organization, https://www.ilo.org/moscow/areas-of-work/occupational-safety-and-health/WCMS_249278/lang--en/index.htm

69 Road Safety Fact, https://www.asirt.org/safe-travel/road-safety-facts/

70 World Health Organization, https://www.who.int/mediacentre/news/notes/2013/make_walking_safe_20130502/en/

71 International Overdose Awareness Day, https://www.overdoseday.com/facts-stats/

72 UNODC, http://www.unodc.org/wdr2017/field/Booklet_1_EXSUM.pdf

73 Safety of Nuclear Power Reactors May 2018 http://www.world-nuclear.org/information-library/safety-and-security/safety-of-plants/safety-of-nuclear-power-reactors.aspx

74 List of nuclear and radiation accidents by death toll, http://www.unodc.org/wdr2017/field/Booklet_1_EXSUM.pdf

75 Plans For New Reactors Worldwide, April 2019, http://www.world-nuclear.org/information-library/current-and-future-generation/plans-for-new-reactors-worldwide.aspx

76 Nuclear-Powered Ships, May 2019, http://www.world-nuclear.org/information-library/non-power-nuclear-applications/transport/nuclear-powered-ships.aspx

77 Products from petroleum https://www.quora.com/Where-can-I-find-a-comprehensive-list-of-the-6-000-products-made-from-petroleum

78 Ranken Energy Corporation, "Products made from petroleum: With over 6000 products and counting, petroleum continues to be a crucial requirement for all consumers," www.Ranken-Energy.com, 2017. Entire paragraph (except for Paleolithic Era quote) with a partial list of the 6,000 products and the graph is from this exhaustive source. https://www.ranken-energy.com/index.php/products-made-from-petroleum/

79 December 22, 2018, Wikipedia https://en.wikipedia.org/wiki/Developing_country

80 Edward Ring, December 16, 2018, https://amgreatness.com/2018/12/16/how-globalism-is-the-real-authoritarianism/

81 November 15, 2017 https://www.amnesty.org/en/latest/news/2017/11/industry-giants-fail-to-tackle-child-labour-allegations-in-cobalt-battery-supply-chains/

82 The California Transparency in Supply Chains Act SB 657 https://oag.ca.gov/SB657

83 H.R.4842 - Business Supply Chain Transparency on Trafficking and Slavery Act of 2014 https://www.congress.gov/bill/113th-congress/house-bill/4842

84 Land use for electricity generation https://www.strata.org/pdf/2017/footprints-full.pdf

85 Nationwide killing of up to 4,200 bald eagles annuallyhttps://www.instituteforenergyresearch.org/renewable/wind/obama-allows-wind-turbines-legally-kill-eagles/

86 Wind turbines can trigger epileptic fits and seizureshttp://www.windaction.org/posts/14753-in-a-spin-professor-claims-wind-farms-can-cause-seizures#.XKOcEVVKiUl

87 EIA Energy International Outlookhttps://images.search.yahoo.com/yhs/search;_ylt=AwrUixMErZtcGh8At1IPxQt.;_ylu=X3oDMTByNWU4cGh1BGNvbG8DZ3ExBHBvcwMxBHZ0aWQDBHNlYwNzYw--?p=eia+energy+usage+chart&fr=yhs-pty-pty_packages&hspart=pty&hsimp=yhs-pty_packages#id=30&iurl=https%3A%2F%2Fupload.wikimedia.org%2Fwikipedia%2Fcommons%2Ff%2Ff5%2FWorld_energy_consumption%252C_1990-2040%252C_EIA_Energy_Outlook_2013.png&action=click

88 2017, Lawrence Livermore National Laboratory https://flowcharts.llnl.gov/content/assets/images/energy/us/Energy_US_2017.png

89 Kevin Chika Urama and Ernest Nti Acheampong, 2013, Stanford SoCal Innovation Review https://ssir.org/articles/entry/social_innovation_creates_prosperous_societies

90 Indur M. Goklany, 2011. Reson Foundation https://reason.org/wp-content/uploads/files/deaths_from_extreme_weather_1900_2010.pdf page6

91 Media Research Center (MRC), "Media Disguise Liberal Billionaire Tom Steyer as 'Climate Change Crusader,'" www.mrc.org, Page accessed December 7, 2018. https://www.mrc.org/articles/media-disguise-liberal-billionaire-steyer-'climate-change-crusader'

92 Dudley, Bob, Dale, Spencer, *BP (British Petroleum) Energy Outlook – 2018 Edition*, www.BP.com, February 20, 2018. https://www.bp.com/en/global/corporate/energy-economics/energy-outlook.html

93 Epstein, Alex, *The Moral Case for Fossil Fuels*, (Portfolio – Penguin Books, New York, NY), Entire book for the source. November 13, 2014. https://www.amazon.

	com/Moral-Case-Fossil-Fuels/dp/1591847443/ref=sr_1_1?ie=UTF8&qid=1544553425&sr=8-1&keywords=alex+epstein
94	December 14, 2018, Wikipedia refining processes https://en.wikipedia.org/wiki/Oil_refinery
95	2012, American Fuel and Petroleum Manufacturers The Bureau of Labor Statistics charts show that the petroleum-refining sector of health and safety is one of the safest industries to work in https://www.afpm.org/refinery_safety_at_a_glance/
96	September 14, 2017, U.S. Energy Information Administration https://www.eia.gov/todayinenergy/detail.php?id=32912
97	2017, Lawrence Livermore National Laboratory https://flowcharts.llnl.gov/content/assets/images/energy/us/Energy_US_2017.png

Chapter Three: World Wars I and II Were Both Won With Energy

98	World War I Map https://wiki--travel.com/detail/world-war-1-world-map-9.html
99	World War II Map https://www.mapsofworld.com/world-maps/world-war-ii-map.html
100	History in Images, Pictures of War, History, WW2, Original Source of Rare WW2 Images, "Hitler's Quest For Oil: Caucasus During WW2," www.HistoryImages.Blogpost.com, Site accessed June 26, 2019 for sourcing. https://historyimages.blogspot.com/2012/03/hitlers-drive-to-caucasus.html
101	Hanson, Victor Davis, *The Second World Wars: How The First Global Conflict Was Fought and Won*, (Basic Books, New York, NY), First Edition, October 2017. https://www.amazon.com/Second-World-Wars-Global-Conflict/dp/0465066984/ref=sr_1_1?crid=QJNUILOBNB8C&keywords=victor+davis+hanson+the+second+world+wars&qid=1551928702&s=gateway&sprefix=victor+davis+hanson%2Caps%2C443&sr=8-1

102 Bridges, Linda, "Tolkien, Lewis, and the Great War," www.NationalReview.com, September 3, 2015. https://www.nationalreview.com/2015/09/tolkien-lewis-and-great-war/

103 Miller, Keith, "How Important Was Oil in World War II?" Columbian College of Arts & Sciences, The George Washington University, History News Network, www.HistoryNewsNetwork.org, Site accessed June 26, 2019. https://historynewsnetwork.org/article/339

104 Hanson, *op. cit.*, Page 451. 2017.

105 World War I type-of-energy shown by the EIA https://www.eia.gov/todayinenergy/detail.php?id=11951#

106 Winegard, Timothy, C. for MilitaryHistoryNow.com, "Of Blood and Oil – How the Fight for Petroleum in WWI Changed Warfare Forever," www.MilitaryHistoryNow.com, November 9, 2016. https://militaryhistorynow.com/2016/11/09/of-blood-and-oil-how-the-fight-for-petroleum-in-ww1-changed-warfare-forever/

107 Poster depicting need to conserve energy in World War II https://www.gilderlehrman.org/sites/default/files/content-images/09520.web_.png

108 Economy, Elizabeth C., "The Problem With Xi's China Model," www.ForeignAffairs.com, March 6, 2019. https://www.foreignaffairs.com/articles/china/2019-03-06/problem-xis-china-model?utm_medium=newsletters&utm_source=fatoday&utm_content=20190306&utm_campaign=FA%20Today%20030619%20The%20Problem%20With%20Xi's%20China%20Model&utm_term=FA%20Today%20-%20112017

109 Map of China's recent incursions into the South China Sea http://www.southchinasea.org/files/2013/01/Disputed-claims-in-the-south-china-sea-Agence-France-Presse.jpg

110 Hanson, Victor Davis By Hillsdale College, "Victor Davis Hanson on China," www.Blog.Hillsdale.edu, June 7, 2019. http://blog.hillsdale.edu/online-courses/victor-davis-hanson-china

111 Decker, Phillip, "Russia Has Weaponized Energy," www.USNews.com, (US News & World Report), August 10, 2017. https://

www.usnews.com/opinion/world-report/articles/2017-08-10/how-the-us-can-fight-russias-weaponizing-energy

112 Map of former Soviet Union https://ribttes.com/wp-content/uploads/2014/11/Union-of-Soviet-Socialist-Republics.gif

113 Map of Soviet Union after it was broken up https://www.worldatlas.com/articles/what-countries-made-up-the-former-soviet-union-ussr.html

114 Royal, Todd, "The Geopolitical Implications of Renewable Energy," www.USAToday.com via Oilprice.com, November 8, 2017. https://www.usatoday.com/story/money/energy/2017/11/08/geopolitical-implications-renewable-energy/838203001/

115 Freedman, Russell, *The War To End All Wars: World War I*, (Clarion Books, Boston, MA), entire book, 1st edition, August 2, 2010. https://www.amazon.com/War-End-All-Wars-World/dp/0547026862/ref=asc_df_0547026862/?tag=hyprod-20&linkCode=df0&hvadid=266164555337&hvpos=1o1&hvnetw=g&hvrand=10286224376986937 18&hvpone=&hvptwo=&hvqmt=&hvdev=c&hvdvcmdl=&hvlocint=&hvlocphy=9031120&hvtargid=pla-762034650672&psc=1

116 Weinberg, Gerhard L., *A World at Arms: A Global History of World War II*, (Cambridge University Press, Cambridge, England), Pages 76-78, March 28, 2005. https://www.amazon.com/World-Arms-Global-History-War/dp/0521618266/ref=sr_1_1?keywords=weinberg+world+at+arms&qid=1552333644&s=books&sr=1-1-catcorr

117 Map of German U-Boat campaign in the Atlantic http://mapsontheweb.zoom-maps.com/image/103201314364

118 Map of JAPANESE GREATER EAST ASIA Co-PROSPERITY SPHERE http://worldwar2headquarters.com/HTML/Pearl Harbor/co-prosperity.html

119 Hanson. Ibid. Page 452. 2017.

120 Becker, Peter V., Dr., "The Role of Synthetic Fuel in World War II Germany," www.AirUniversity.AF.edu, July-August 1981. http://

www.airpower.maxwell.af.mil/airchronicles/aureview/1981/jul-aug/becker.htm

121 Hanson. *Ibid. 2017.*

122 O'Brien, Phillips Payson, *How the War Was Won: Air-Sea Power and Allied Victory in World War II (Cambridge Military Histories*, (Cambridge University Press, Cambridge, England), Pages 72-74, June 26, 2000. https://www.amazon.com/How-War-was-Won-Cambridge-ebook/dp/B00VAOVM2A/ref=sr_1_fkmrnull_1?keywords=O%27Brien+how+the+war+was+won&qid=1552345261&s=books&sr=1-1-fkmrnull

123 Murray, Williamson, Millett, Allan R., *A War To Be Won: Fighting The Second World War*, (Belknap Press, An Imprint of Harvard University Press, 3rd Printing Edition, Boston, MA), Page 52, November 22, 2001. https://www.amazon.com/War-Be-Won-Fighting-Second/dp/0674006801/ref=sr_1_1?keywords=murray+and+millett+a+war+to+be+won&qid=1552345936&s=books&sr=1-1-catcorr

124 MAP OF NORTH AFRICA CAMPAIGN FIGHTING https://tldesigner.net/world-war-2-in-europe-and-north-africa-map/world-war-2-in-europe-and-north-africa-map-roundtripticket-me-for-timeline-ii-1943-new-throughout-0/

125 MAP OF MIDDLE EAST OIL SUPPLIES https://www.geoexpro.com/articles/2014/02/how-much-oil-in-the-middle-east

126 Oil in decisive battles in World War II in or near Soviet Union http://www.visions.az/en/news/580/588903a7/

127 Vespa, Matt, "No Savior: New Study Torches Ocasio-Cortez's Global Warming Narrative for Green New Deal," www.Townhall.com, April 29, 2019. https://townhall.com/tipsheet/mattvespa/2019/04/29/facepalm-ocasiocortezs-green-new-deal-would-have-zero-impact-on-socalled-global-warming-n2545416

128 Winegarden, Wayne, "Green New Deal would cause a New Great Depression," www.OCRegister.com, March 12, 2019. https://www.ocregister.com/2019/03/12/green-new-deal-would-case-a-new-depression/

129 Egan, Matt, "America is set to surpass Saudi Arabia in a 'remarkable' oil milestone," www.CNN.com, March 8, 2019. https://www.cnn.com/2019/03/08/business/us-oil-exports-saudi-arabia/index.html
130 Egan, Matt, "America is set to surpass Saudi Arabia in a 'remarkable' oil milestone," www.CNN.com, March 8, 2019. https://www.cnn.com/2019/03/08/business/us-oil-exports-saudi-arabia/index.html

Chapter Four: Paris Accord Plans to Reduce Greenhouse Gases Miss the Mark

131 January 18, 2019 https://en.wikipedia.org/wiki/Paris_Agreement
132 December 7, 2018, https://www.climatechangenews.com/2018/07/12/countries-yet-ratify-paris-agreement/
133 United States House of Representatives Committee on Science, Space, and Technology report on Russian Attempts to Influence U.S. Domestic Energy Markets by Exploiting Social Media: 2018 report by the U.S. House of Representatives Committee on Science, Space, and Technology https://www.heartland.org/template-assets/documents/publications/House%20Science%20Committe%20Russian%20Attempts%20to%20Influence%20U.S.%20Domestic%20Energy%20Markets.pdf
134 December 9, 2012, Ralph Vartabedian, Los Angeles Times, http://notrickszone.com/2018/04/30/new-papers-intermittent-wind-power-preserves-increases-need-for-fossil-fuel-energy-generation/#sthash.k1KCoIHC.dpbs
135 July 24, 2018, U.S. Energy Information Administration https://www.eia.gov/outlooks/ieo/
136 Dr. Sarma Pisupati, Professor, Department of Energy and Mineral Engineering, College of Earth and Mineral Sciences International Energy outlook https://www.e-education.psu.edu/egee102/node/1929

137   The Cybersecurity and Infrastructure Security Agency (CISA) discusses 16 Sectors https://www.dhs.gov/cisa/critical-infrastructure-sectors#wcm-survey-target-id
138   Moore, Stephen, "'Who's the cleanest of them all?'" www.WashingtonTimes.com, August 19, 2018. https://www.washingtontimes.com/news/2018/aug/19/the-united-states-didnt-sign-the-paris-climate-acc/
139   Moore. Ibid. 2018.
140   Moore. Ibid. 2017

Chapter 5: How China and India View Energy

141   Population of the World, Population of China (2018), www.LivePopulation.com, Page accessed December 27, 2018. https://www.livepopulation.com/country/china.html
142   Population of the World, Population of India (2018), www.LivePopulation.com, Page accessed December 27, 2018. https://www.livepopulation.com/country/india.html
143   Armitage, Simon, *Sir Gawain and the Green Knight*, (Faber & Faber, London, England), www.Faber.co.uk, May 3, 2009. https://www.faber.co.uk/9780571223282-sir-gawain-and-the-green-knight.html
144   Rapier, Robert, "The U.S. Accounted For 98% Of Global Oil Production Growth In 2018," www.Forbes.com, June 23, 2019. https://www.forbes.com/sites/rrapier/2019/06/23/the-u-s-accounted-for-98-of-global-oil-production-growth-in-2018/#264056bb5125
145   Crooks, Ed, "The year in energy," www.FT.com, December 23, 2018. https://www.ft.com/content/2b420a2a-06c2-11e9-9fe8-acdb36967cfc
146   On The Issues, Every Political Leader on Every Issue, "George W. Bush on Energy & Oil," www.OntheIssues.org, September 12, 2018. http://www.ontheissues.org/Celeb/George_W_Bush_Energy_+_Oil.htm

147 Roberts, David, "The Green New Deal, explained," www.Vox.com, January 7, 2019. https://www.vox.com/energy-and-environment/2018/12/21/18144138/green-new-deal-alexandria-ocasio-cortez

148 Chiu, Dominic, "The East Is Green: China's Global Leadership in Renewable Energy," www.CSIS.org, (Center For Strategic & International Studies), Issue 13, Summer 2017, https://www.csis.org/east-green-chinas-global-leadership-renewable-energy

149 Crooks. Ibid. 2018.

150 Lelyveld, Michael, "China's Coal Use Climbs Despite Pollution Plans," www.RFA.org, (Radio Free Asia), July 7, 2018. https://www.rfa.org/english/commentaries/energy_watch/chinas-coal-use-climbs-despite-pollution-plans-07162018102732.html

151 Kool, Tom, "Why Have Oil Markets Turned So Bullish," www.OilPrice.com, January 8, 2019. https://oilprice.com/Energy/Energy-General/Oil-Rallies-On-Trade-Optimism.html

152 Installed Power Generation Capacity in China in the New Policies Scenario https://www.iea.org/weo/china/

153 Ye, Qi, Lu, Jiaqi, "China's coal consumption has peaked," www.Brookings.edu, January 22, 2018. https://www.brookings.edu/2018/01/22/chinas-coal-consumption-has-peaked/

154 Shearer, Christine, Yu, Aiqun, Nace, Ted, "Tsunami Warning: Can China's Central Authorities Stop a Massive Surge in New Coal Plants Caused by Provincial Overpermitting?" www.CoalSwarm.com, September 2018. http://coalswarm.org/trackers/a-shrinking-coal-plant-pipeline-mide-2016-results-from-the-global-coal-plant-tracker/

155 International Energy Agency (IEA), Market Report Series: Coal 2018 Analysis and Forecasts to 2023, www.IEA.org, December 18, 2018. https://www.iea.org/coal2018/

156 IEA. *Coal Report 2018*. Ibid. 2018.

157 U.S. Library of Congress, Global Legal Monitor, "China: 2020 Air Pollution Plan Released," www.LOC.gov, August 16, 2018. http://www.loc.gov/law/foreign-news/article/china-2020-air-pollution-action-plan-released/

158 Crooks. Ibid. 2018.

159 Stanway, David, Campbell, Joseph, "INSIGHT-Smog war casualty: China coal city bears brunt of pollution crackdown," www.Af.Reuters.com, (Reuters AFRICATECH section), November 26, 2018. https://af.reuters.com/article/commoditiesNews/idAFL4N1XV2BJ

160 Wright, Tom, Hope, Bradley, WSJ Investigation: China Offered to Bail Out Troubled Malaysian Fund in Return for Deals," www.WSJ.com, January 7, 2019. https://www.wsj.com/articles/how-china-flexes-its-political-muscle-to-expand-power-overseas-11546890449

161 Wright, Hope. Ibid. 2019.

162 Chan, Michelle, "How can China and California tout clean energy but still dirty their hands with fossil fuels?" www.SCMP.com, (South China Morning Post), September 7, 2018. https://www.scmp.com/comment/insight-opinion/united-states/article/2163160/how-can-china-and-california-tout-clean-energy

163 Niiler, Eric, "China Is Both The Best And Worst Hope For Clean Energy," www.Wired.com, December 4, 2018. https://www.wired.com/story/china-is-best-worst-hope-at-cop24-climate-summit/

164 CPEC China Pakistan Economic Corridor, CPEC-Energy Priority Projects, www.CPEC.gov.pk, Page accessed on January 8, 2019. http://cpec.gov.pk/energy

165 Ebrahim, Zoleen T., "Government unhappy, but Pakistan to stay with coal," www.Eco-Business.com, August 28, 2018. https://www.eco-business.com/news/government-unhappy-but-pakistan-to-stay-with-coal/

166 Grossman, David, "How Does Clean Coal Work?" www.PopularMechanics.com, August 23, 2017. https://www.popularmechanics.com/technology/infrastructure/news/a27886/how-does-clean-coal-work/

167 ESI Africa | Africa's Power Journal, "Low emission tech can save coal's dominance," ESI Africa Edition 5, www.ESI-Africa.com, December 4, 2018. https://www.esi-africa.com/low-emission-tech-can-save-coals-dominance/

168 ESI Africa. Ibid. 2018.

169 Hockenos, Paul, "Germany Is a Coal-Burning, Gas-Guzzling Climate Change Hypocrite," www.ForeignPolicy.com, November 13, 2017. https://foreignpolicy.com/2017/11/13/germany-is-a-coal-burning-gas-guzzling-climate-change-hypocrite/

170 AirClim, Air Pollution & Climate Secretariat, *Acid News*, No. 2, June 2018, www.AirClim.org, http://airclim.org/acidnews/germany-still-constructing-new-coal-power-stations

171 International Energy Agency, Data & Publications, *WEO-2017 Special Report: Energy Access Outlook*, www.webstore.IEA.org, October 17, 2017. https://webstore.iea.org/weo-2017-special-report-energy-access-outlook

172 Kitfield, James, "The US & China A Colder Peace or Thucydides' Trap?" www.BreakingDefense.com, December 12, 2018. https://breakingdefense.com/2018/12/the-us-china-a-colder-peace-or-thucydides-trap/

173 Egozi, Arie, "Israelis to US: Take On China Around Djibouti," www.BreakingDefense.com, November 28, 2018. https://breakingdefense.com/2018/11/israelis-to-us-take-on-china-around-djibouti/

174 Stratfor Worldview Assessments, "Why Banks in Morocco Are Spreading the Wealth Around Africa," www.Worldview.Stratfor.com, January 11, 2019. https://worldview.stratfor.com/article/why-banks-morocco-are-spreading-wealth-around-africa?utm_campaign=B2C%20%7C%20Newsletter%20%7C%20060818&utm_source=hs_email&utm_medium=email&utm_content=68947686&_hsenc=p2ANqtz-93NR06twYt0yb_v_1A8g5FX-5CsVnM1y01G9NjCi6DJMEwnaqkG43DmfKle1cSHCR6greQEoQC7IQL5w5cXTDo4tXu6w&_hsmi=68951496#/entry/jsconnect?client_id=633726972&target=%2Fdiscussion%2Fembed%3Fc%3D1547482458272%26vanilla_category_id%3D1%26vanilla_identifier%3D293586%26vanilla_url%3Dhttps%253A%252F%252Fworldview.stratfor.com%252Farticle%252Fwhy-banks-morocco-are-

spreading-wealth-around-africa%253Futm_campaign%253DB2C%252520%25257C%252520Newsletter%252520%25257C%252520060818%2526utm_source%253Dhs_email%2526utm_medium%253Demail%2526utm_content%253D68947686%2526_hsenc%253Dp2ANqtz-93NR06twYt0yb_v_1A8g5FX-5CsVnM1y01G9NjCi6DJMEwnaqkG43DmfKle1cSHCR6greQEoQC7IQL5w5cXTDo4tXu6w%2526_hsmi%253D68951496

175 International Energy Agency, Data & Publications, *The Future of Cooling: Opportunities for energy efficient air conditioning*, www.webstore.IEA.org, May 18, 2018. https://webstore.iea.org/the-future-of-cooling

176 Birol, Fatih, International Energy Agency, Data & Publications, *The Future of Cooling: Opportunities for energy efficient air conditioning*, Press release titled, "Air conditioning use emerges as one of the key drivers of global electricity-demand growth," www.IEA.org, May 18, 2018. https://www.iea.org/newsroom/news/2018/may/air-conditioning-use-emerges-as-one-of-the-key-drivers-of-global-electricity-dema.html

177 Fuxian, Yi, "Worse than Japan: how China's looming demographic crisis will doom its economic dream," www.SCMP.com, January 4, 2019. https://www.scmp.com/comment/insight-opinion/asia/article/2180421/worse-japan-how-chinas-looming-demographic-crisis-will

178 Wolf, Martin, "The future might not belong to China," www.FT.com, January 1, 2019. https://www.ft.com/content/ae94de0e-0c1a-11e9-a3aa-118c761d2745

179 Intergovernmental Panel on Climate Change (IPCC), *Global Warming of 1.5 Celsius*, (United Nations (UN), New York, NY), www.IPCC.ch, October 8, 2018. https://www.ipcc.ch/sr15/

180 U.S. Environmental Protection Agency (EPA), "Overview of Greenhouse Gases," www.EPA.gov, October 31, 2018. https://www.epa.gov/ghgemissions/overview-greenhouse-gases

Special note: also look at the definition of greenhouse gases at Wikipedia.com.

181 Burnett, H. Sterling, "Fossil Fuels Have, and Should Continue to Benefit Humanity," www.Townhall.com, January 9, 2019. https://townhall.com/columnists/hsterlingburnett/2019/01/09/fossil-fuels-have-and-should-continue-to-benefit-humanity-n2538701

182 Nongovernmental International Panel on Climate Change (NIPCC), About the NIPCC section, www.ClimateChangeReconsidered.org, Page accessed on January 14, 2019. NIPCC is part of The Heartland Institute.

183 Burnett. Ibid. 2019.

184 Nongovernmental International Panel on Climate Change (NIPCC), *Climate Change Reconsidered II: Fossil Fuels*, (The Heartland Institute, Arlington Heights, IL.), www.ClimateChangeReconsidered.org, December 4, 2018 release date. http://climatechangereconsidered.org/wp-content/uploads/2018/12/Summary-for-Policymakers-Final.pdf

185 Ritchie, Hannah, Roser, Max, Our World in Data, "Fossil Fuel," www.OurWorldinData.org, 2018. https://ourworldindata.org/fossil-fuels

186 Burnett. Ibid. 2019.

187 Fuxian, Yu, "Worse than Japan: how China's looming demographic crisis will doom its economic dream," www.SCMP.com (South China Morning Post), January 4, 2019. https://www.scmp.com/comment/insight-opinion/asia/article/2180421/worse-japan-how-chinas-looming-demographic-crisis-will

188 Royal, Todd, "The Unintended Geopolitical Consequences of Abortion," www.CaPoliticalReview.com, January 5, 2017. http://www.capoliticalreview.com/top-stories/the-unintended-geopolitical-consequences-of-abortion/

189 Clarke (Ret.), Sheriff David, "Abortion: The Black Community's Holocaust," www.Townhall.com, May 20, 2019. https://townhall.com/columnists/sheriffdavidclarke(ret)/2019/05/20/abortion-the-black-communitys-holocaust-n2546584

190 Edited by Bron Taylor, *Encyclopedia of Religion and Nature*, (Continuum International Publishing Group, New York, NY) Page 1211, August 10, 2008. https://www.amazon.com/Encyclopedia-Religion-Nature-Vol-Taylor/dp/1847062733/ref=sr_1_1?ie=UTF8&qid=1547519878&sr=8-1&keywords=encyclopedia+of+religion+and+nature

191 He, Wan, Goodkind, Daniel, Kowal, Paul, *An Aging World: 2015*, (United States Census Bureau Publication, Washington D.C.), www.Census.gov, March 28, 2016. https://www.census.gov/library/publications/2016/demo/P95-16-1.html

192 United Nations Educations, Scientific and Cultural Organization (UNESCO), Learning to Live Together section, section titled: "Poverty," www.UNESCO.org, 2017. http://www.unesco.org/new/en/social-and-human-sciences/themes/international-migration/glossary/poverty/

193 Nongovernmental International Panel on Climate Change (NIPCC), *Climate Change Reconsidered II: Fossil Fuels*. Ibid. 2018.

194 Burnett. Ibid. 2019.

195 Kotkin, Joel, "The first shots in the climate wars," www.OCRegister.com, December 9, 2018. https://www.ocregister.com/2018/12/09/the-first-shots-in-the-climate-wars/

196 Xuetong, Yan, "The Age of Uneasy Peace: Chinese Power in a Divided World," www.ForeignAffairs.com, January/February 2019 Issue. https://www.foreignaffairs.com/articles/china/2018-12-11/age-uneasy-peace?cid=nlc-fa_fatoday-20190118&utm_medium=newsletters&utm_source=fatoday&utm_content=20190119&utm_campaign=FA%20Today/Weekend%20011919%20How%20China%20Wants%20to%20Reshape%20the%20World%20Order&utm_term=FA%20Today%20-%20112017

197 Russell Mead, Walter, "Mike Pence Announces Cold War II: The administration is orchestrating a far-reaching campaign against China," www.WSJ.com, October 8, 2018. https://www.wsj.com/articles/mike-pence-announces-cold-war-ii-1539039480

198 Karlin, Mara, Coffman Wittes, Tamara, "America's Middle East Purgatory," www.ForeignAffairs.com, January/February 2019 Issue. https://www.foreignaffairs.com/articles/middle-east/2018-12-11/americas-middle-east-purgatory?cid=nlc-fa_fatoday-20190111&utm_medium=newsletters&utm_source=fatoday&utm_content=20190111&utm_campaign=FA%20Today%200111%20Deepfakes%20and%20the%20New%20Disinformation%20War&utm_term=FA%20Today%20-%20112017

199 Karlin, Wittes Tamara. Ibid. 2019.

200 Rothkopf, David, "Obama's 'Don't Do Stupid Shit' Foreign Policy," www.ForeignAffairs.com, June 4, 2014. https://foreignpolicy.com/2014/06/04/obamas-dont-do-stupid-shit-foreign-policy/

201 Mead, Walter Russell, "How American Fracking Changes the World," www.WSJ.com, November 26, 2018. https://www.wsj.com/articles/how-american-fracking-changes-the-world-1543276935

202 Larter, B., David, "Rebuilding 7th Fleet: The Navy's most scrutinized sailors correct course," www.NavyTimes.com, April 12, 2018. https://www.navytimes.com/news/your-navy/2018/04/12/rebuilding-7th-fleet-the-navys-most-scrutinized-sailors-correct-course/

203 Fuxian. Ibid. 2019.

204 Capital Economics, India Economics, India Economics Update, "Trade deficit to narrow further," www.CapitalEconomics.com, December 17, 2018. https://www.capitaleconomics.com/publications/india-economics/india-economics-update/trade-deficit-to-narrow-further-2/

205 Wolf, Martin, "Modi's India is on course to top China for growth," www.FT.com, (Financial Times), February 6, 2018. https://www.ft.com/content/e4998ab2-0a73-11e8-839d-41ca06376bf2

206 Wolf. Ibid. 2019.

207 Energypedia.com "India Energy Situation," Introduction, www.Energypedia.com, July 10, 2018. https://energypedia.info/wiki/India_Energy_Situation#Key_Problems_of_the_Energy_Sector

208 Energypedia.com. Ibid. 2018.

209 Government of India, Ministry of Power, "Power Sector at a Glance ALL INDIA," www.PowerMin.Nic.In, Last updated on December 11, 2018. https://powermin.nic.in/en/content/power-sector-glance-all-india

210 Office of the Registrar General & Census Commissioner, India, Ministry of Home Affairs, Government of India, *2011 Census Data*, www.CensusIndia.gov.in, 2011. http://censusindia.gov.in/2011-Common/CensusData2011.html

211 Energypedia.com, India Energy Situation, "Electrical Situation," Section, www.Energypedia.com, July 10, 2018. https://energypedia.info/wiki/India_Energy_Situation#Electricity_Situation

212 Stratfor | Worldview | Assessments, "Preparing for a Rematch at the Top of the World," www.Worldview.Stratfor.com, January 25, 2018. https://worldview.stratfor.com/article/preparing-rematch-top-world

213 Stratfor | Worldview | On Geopolitics, "India Struggles With Its Strategy for Becoming a Great Power," www.Worldview.Stratfor.com, March 23, 2018. https://worldview.stratfor.com/article/india-struggles-its-strategy-becoming-great-power

214 Conca, James, "U.S. CO2 Emissions Rise As Nuclear Power Plants Close," www.Forbes.com, January 16, 2019. https://www.forbes.com/sites/jamesconca/2019/01/16/u-s-co2-emissions-rise-as-nuclear-power-plants-close/?utm_source=FACEBOOK&utm_medium=social&utm_term=Valerie%2F&fbclid=IwAR3fv4n3fDm5jaOubqTMVY_rsGMSghwCYNFrRNX24pUew4YbpdENKotOzc#4c551bd77034

215 International Energy Agency (IEA), Nuclear Power, "Net growth in world's nuclear generation 2016-2040. www.IEA.org, 2019. https://www.iea.org/topics/nuclear/

216 Goh, Melissa, "China and India will lead the world's nuclear growth, experts say," www.CNBC.com, November 7, 2018. https://www.cnbc.com/2018/11/08/china-india-will-lead-global-nuclear-power-production-growth-experts.html

217 Goh. Ibid. 2018.
218 Shellenberger, Michael, "If Progressive Democrats Care So Much About The Climate, Why Are They Trying To Kill Nuclear Power?" www.Forbes.com, January 17, 2019. https://www.forbes.com/sites/michaelshellenberger/2019/01/17/if-progressive-democrats-care-so-much-about-the-climate-why-are-they-trying-to-kill-nuclear-power/#aff5b6588d5f
219 World Nuclear Association, "Nuclear Power in China," www.World-Nuclear.org, Updated January 2019. http://www.world-nuclear.org/information-library/country-profiles/countries-a-f/china-nuclear-power.aspx
220 Central Committee of the Communist Party of China, Beijing, China, *The 13th Five-Year Plan For Economic And Social Development Of The People's Republic Of China*, www.en.ndrc.gov.cn, 2006-2020. http://en.ndrc.gov.cn/newsrelease/201612/P020161207645765233498.pdf
221 International Atomic Energy Agency (IAEA), Power Reactor Information System, "Operational & Long-Term Shutdown Reactors," www. Pris.IAEA.org, Last updated January 18, 2019. Website is updated daily or weekly at the latest. Page written on date of update for research clarification. https://pris.iaea.org/PRIS/WorldStatistics/OperationalReactorsByCountry.aspx
222 Union of Concerned Scientists, Energy, "How is Electricity Measured?" Understanding watts, megawatts, kilowatt-hours, and more, www.UCUSA.org, Page accessed January 22, 2019. https://www.ucsusa.org/clean_energy/our-energy-choices/how-is-electricity-measured.html#.XEdV2y2ZOgw
223 International Energy Agency (IEA). Ibid. World Energy Outlook 2017.
224 Crooks, Ed, "The week in energy: A look ahead to 2019," www.FT.com, (Financial Times), January 5, 2019. Footnote is for the entire paragraph. https://www.ft.com/content/75c258ec-1087-11e9-a3aa-118c761d2745

225 Coal Plants by Country https://docs.google.com/spreadsheets/d/1I8GeKEfxPpwkQ_t0GQZx1GQm6MASclEtEtrQX3Y1nNc/edit#gid=0

226 Malm, Sara, "New Delhi is swamped in deadly smog as India's air quality nears 'severe level' category – and is blamed for 25% drop in tourists," www.DailyMail.co.uk, January 18, 2019. https://www.dailymail.co.uk/news/article-6606653/Delhis-dangerous-smog-sparked-tourist-industry-crisis.html

227 Gross, Neil, PhD, "Is Environmentalism Just for Rich People?" www.NYTimes.com, December 14, 2018. https://www.nytimes.com/2018/12/14/opinion/sunday/yellow-vest-protests-climate.html

228 Edited by Nikunja K Sundaray, Shri, Khardwaj, Shruti, Rai, Dr., with the Ministry of Environment, Forest & Climate Change: Bhawan, Paryavaran, Indira, Road, Bagh, Jor, *National Clean Air Programme* (NCAP), Ministry of Environment, Forest & Climate Change, Government of India, www. Moef.gov.in, 2019. http://www.moef.gov.in/sites/default/files/press-releases/NCAP%20Report%20Full.pdf

229 Morgan, Gwyn, "Gwyn Morgan: It's hard to be optimistic about 2019," www.TimesColonist.com, January 20, 2019. https://www.timescolonist.com/opinion/columnists/gwyn-morgan-it-s-hard-to-be-optimistic-about-2019-1.23605594

230 Thompson, Helen, "Broken Europe: Why the EU Is Stuck in Perpetual Crisis," www.ForeignAffairs.com, December 10, 2018. https://www.foreignaffairs.com/articles/europe/2018-12-10/broken-europe?cid=nlc-fa_fatoday-20190118&utm_medium=newsletters&utm_source=fatoday&utm_content=20190118&utm_campaign=FA%20Today%20011819%20Trump's%20Foreign%20Policy%20Is%20No%20Longer%20Unpredictable&utm_term=FA%20Today%20-%20112017

231 Ezrati, Milton, "The "Green New Deal" Is a Fiscal Fantasy," www.City-Journal.org, January 14, 2019. https://www.city-journal.org/green-new-deal-ocasio-cortez-krugman

232 Kaufman, Robert G., "Urging More from Our NATO Allies," Strategika, Issue 56, Hoover Institution, Stanford University, www.Hoover.org, January 17, 2019. https://www.hoover.org/research/urging-more-our-nato-allies#disqus_thread

233 World Coal Association, "Where is coal found?" www.WorldCoal.org, 2019. https://www.worldcoal.org

234 World Coal Association. Ibid. 2019.

235 Stratfor | Worldview | On Geopolitics, "Baleful and Benign: The Backyards of Great Powers," www.Worldview.Stratfor.com, August 22, 2017. https://worldview.stratfor.com/article/baleful-and-benign-backyards-great-powers#/discussions

236 Asia up to the North Pole and Russia https://geology.com/world/russia-satellite-image.shtml

237 Rogan, Tom, "Our most important alliance in 2019 will be with India. But two other foreign policy opportunities await," www.WashingtonExaminer.com, January 1, 2019. https://www.washingtonexaminer.com/opinion/our-most-important-alliance-in-2019-will-be-with-india-but-two-other-big-foreign-policy-opportunities-await

238 Stratfor | Worldview | On Geopolitics. India struggle with China, Ibid. 2018. Entire paragraph based upon this source.

239 Pearce, Elliot, "China and India: The Emerging Power Struggle of the 21st Century," www.BPR.Berkely.edu, (Berkeley Political Review), August 13, 2018. https://bpr.berkeley.edu/2018/08/13/china-and-india-the-emerging-power-struggle-of-the-21st-century/

Chapter 6: Renewable Electricity

240 Evans, Michael, "Renewable Energy," www.EarthTimes.org, April 30, 2011. http://www.earthtimes.org/encyclopaedia/environmental-issues/renewable-energy/

241 Crosby, Greg, "Down with big oil," www.TolucanTimes.info, March 22, 2012. http://tolucantimes.info/inside-this-issue/down-with-big-oil/

242 Shellenberger, Michael, "Had They Bet On Nuclear, Not Renewables, Germany & California Would Already Have 100% Clean Power," www.Forbes.com, September 11, 2018. https://www.forbes.com/sites/michaelshellenberger/2018/09/11/had-they-bet-on-nuclear-not-renewables-germany-california-would-already-have-100-clean-power/#4866c538e0d4

243 United Nations Development Programme (UNDP), "Goal 7: Affordable and clean energy," Sustainable Development Goals section. www.UNDP.org, 2019. http://www.undp.org/content/undp/en/home/sustainable-development-goals/goal-7-affordable-and-clean-energy.html

244 Ireland, Ed, "Renewable energy depends on fossil fuels," www.bseec.org, (Barnett Shale Energy Education Council), September 20, 2016. http://www.bseec.org/renewable_energy_depends_on_fossil_fuels

245 Aizhu, Chen, Meng, Meng, "Drill, China, drill: State majors step on the gas after Xi calls for energy security," www.Reuters.com, January 31, 2019. https://www.reuters.com/article/us-china-oil-exploration-analysis/drill-china-drill-state-majors-step-on-the-gas-after-xi-calls-for-energy-security-idUSKCN1PQ3PO

246 Economy, Elizabeth, C., "China's New Revolution: The Reign of Xi Jingping," www.ForeignAffairs.com, Essay May/June 2018 Issue. https://www.foreignaffairs.com/articles/china/2018-04-17/chinas-new-revolution?utm_medium=newsletters&utm_source=fatoday&utm_content=20190204&utm_campaign=FA%20Today%20020419%20Europe%20Tests%20the%20Boundaries%20on%20Iran&utm_term=FA%20Today%20-%20112017

247 Shellenberger, Michael, "The Reason Renewables Can't Power Modern Civilization Is Because They Were Never Meant To," www.Forbes.com, May 6, 2019. https://www.forbes.com/sites/michaelshellenberger/2019/05/06/the-reason-renewables-cant-power-modern-civilization-is-because-they-were-never-meant-to/#107098d9ea2b

248 Ireland. Ibid. 2016.

249 U.S. Energy Information Administration (EIA), Independent Statistics & Analysis, "Renewable Energy Explained," www.EIA.gov, Last updated July 13, 2018. https://www.eia.gov/energyexplained/?page=renewable_home

250 EIA. RE Explained. Ibid. 2018.

251 EIA. RE Explained. Ibid. 2018.

252 EIA. RE Explained. Ibid. 2018.

253 U.S. Energy Information Administration (EIA), Independent Statistics & Analysis, *International Energy Outlook 2017*, Table: World consumption of hydroelectric and other renewable energy by region. www.EIA.gov, 2017. https://www.eia.gov/outlooks/aeo/data/browser/#/?id=9-IEO2017

254 U.S. Energy Information Administration (EIA), Independent Statistics & Analysis, *International Energy Outlook 2018*, EIA test cases for high energy use and high-economic growth cases using Africa, China and India, and adding this data to the *International Energy Outlook 2017* projections. www.EIA.gov, July 24, 2018. https://www.eia.gov/outlooks/ieo/

255 Total Energy: Production: Crude Oil and Lease Condensate: https://www.eia.gov/outlooks/aeo/data/browser/#/?id=9-IEO2017

256 Desjardins, Jeff, Visual Capitalist, "All of these things can be made with one barrel of oil," www.BusinessInsider.com, September 28, 2016. https://www.businessinsider.com/things-that-can-be-made-with-one-barrel-of-oil-2016-9

257 Conoco Phillips Alaska, "What is Oil Used for?" www.Alaska.ConocoPhillips.com, 2019. http://alaska.conocophillips.com/what-we-do/oil-production/what-is-oil-used-for/

258 What Can You Make from one barrel of oil https://www.visualcapitalist.com/can-made-one-barrel-oil/

259 Scheld, Brian, "Permian Basin output to drive record-setting oil output for decades: US EIA," www.SPGlobal.com (S&P Global Platts), January 24, 2019. https://www.spglobal.com/platts/en/market-insights/latest-news/oil/012419-permian-basin-output-to-drive-record-setting-oil-output-for-decades-us-eia

260 Sheppard, David, "US becomes UK's top oil supplier for first time since Suez," www.FT.com, (Financial Times), February 5, 2019. https://www.ft.com/content/8be711e0-2931-11e9-a5ab-ff8ef2b976c7

261 Bellman, Eric, "Sri Lanka, Deep in Debt, Turns Increasingly to China for Loans," www.WSJ.com (U.S. Edition), January 29, 2019. https://www.wsj.com/articles/sri-lanka-deep-in-debt-turns-increasingly-to-china-for-loans-11548774001

262 Wright, Tom, Hope, Bradley, "WSJ Investigation: China Offered to Bail Out Troubled Malaysian Fund in Return for Deals," www.WSJ.com, January 7, 2019. https://www.wsj.com/articles/how-china-flexes-its-political-muscle-to-expand-power-overseas-11546890449?mod=article_inline

263 Shellenberger, Michael, "If Solar And Wind Are So Cheap, Why Are They Making Electricity So Expensive?" www.Forbes.com, April 23, 2018. https://www.forbes.com/sites/michaelshellenberger/2018/04/23/if-solar-and-wind-are-so-cheap-why-are-they-making-electricity-more-expensive/#203252c71dc6

264 Davidson, F. Todd, Tuttle, Dave, Rhodes Joshua D., Nagasawa, Kazunori, "Is America's Power Grid Ready for Electric Cars?" www.CityLab.com, December 7, 2018. https://www.citylab.com/transportation/2018/12/americas-power-grid-isnt-ready-electric-cars/577507/

265 Hurlbut, David, Zhou, Ella, Bird, Lori, Wang, Qin, *Transmission Challenges and Best Practices for Cost-Effective Renewable Energy Delivery across State and Provincial Boundaries*. (National Renewable Energy Laboratory, U.S. Department of Energy, Washington, D.C.), March 2017. Entire report for use as a source. https://www.nrel.gov/docs/fy17osti/67462.pdf

266 PJM Regional Power Transmission, United States. www.PJM.com, Page accessed February 6, 2019. https://www.pjm.com

267 PJM.com provided open-sourced information to show these wind and solar usage numbers. Charts and source were used by www.BurnMoreCoal.com, in article titled, "In bitter cold, wind falls to less than 1% of the Mid-Atlantic grid,"

January 31, 2019. https://burnmorecoal.com/2019/01/31/in-bitter-cold-wind-falls-to-less-than-1-of-the-mid-atlantic-grid/

268 Puko, Timothy, "From Beer to Casinos, Businesses Turn to Solar, Wind Power," www.WSJ.com, January 30, 2019. https://www.wsj.com/articles/climate-change-pushes-companies-to-buy-renewables-11548849602?mod=djem_EnergyJournal

269 Gilblom, Kelly, Wethe, David, "Baker Hughes Ponders 'Ecosystems' in Windmills, Solar Panels," www.Bloomberg.com, January 30, 2019. https://www.bloomberg.com/news/articles/2019-01-30/baker-hughes-ponders-windmills-solar-panels-for-oil-s-twilight

270 Bright Source Limitless, "Ivanpah: Solar Electric Generating System (ISEGS) in California's Mojave Desert," www.BrightSourceEnergy.com," Page accessed February 7, 2019 for information and source. http://www.brightsourceenergy.com/ivanpah-solar-project#.XFx_aS2ZN0I

271 Shellenberger, Michael, "Yes, Solar And Wind Really Do Increase Electricity Prices – And For Inherently Physical Reasons," www.Forbes.com, April 25, 2018. https://www.forbes.com/sites/michaelshellenberger/2018/04/25/yes-solar-and-wind-really-do-increase-electricity-prices-and-for-inherently-physical-reasons/#374a213017e8

272 Shellenberger. Ibid. 2018. https://www.forbes.com/sites/michaelshellenberger/2018/04/25/yes-solar-and-wind-really-do-increase-electricity-prices-and-for-inherently-physical-reasons/#374a213017e8

273 Environmental Progress, "Health and Safety," www.EnvironmentalProgress.org, Page accessed February 7, 2019. http://environmentalprogress.org/health-and-safety/#waste

274 Materials throughput by type of energy https://www.forbes.com/sites/michaelshellenberger/2018/04/25/yes-solar-and-wind-really-do-increase-electricity-prices-and-for-inherently-physical-reasons/#73bf3a7317e8

275 Bach, Natasha, "California Becomes 1st State to Require Solar Panels on New Homes. Here's How It Will Reduce Utility

Costs," www.Fortune.com, December 6, 2018. http://fortune.com/2018/12/06/california-solar-panels-new-homes/

276 A study for First Solar by The Brattle Group, *Comparative Generation Costs of Utility-Scale and Residential-Scale PV in Xcel Energy Colorado's Service Area*, www.Brattle.com, July 15, 2015. To delve further into Colorado's RE boondoggle involving Xcel Energy, please Google Xcel Energy Colorado renewable energy costs overruns, Cfact.org for verification. http://files.brattle.com/system/publications/pdfs/000/005/188/original/comparative_generation_costs_of_utility-scale_and_residential-scale_pv_in_xcel_energy_colorado's_service_area.pdf?1436797265

277 Entergy, "Backgrounder – A Comparison: Land Use by Energy Source – Nuclear, Wind and Solar," www.Entergy-Arkansas.com, Page accessed February 18, 2019. http://www.entergy-arkansas.com/content/news/docs/AR_Nuclear_One_Land_Use.pdf

278 Bryce, Robert, "All-renewable energy in California? Sorry, land-use calculation say it's not going to happen," www.LATimes.com, August 21, 2018. https://www.latimes.com/opinion/op-ed/la-oe-bryce-renewables-california-20180821-story.html

279 Jacobson, Mark Z., and 27 other authors, *Elsevier*, a Stanford Energy Department publication, www.web.Stanford.edu, July 22, 2014. http://web.stanford.edu/group/efmh/jacobson/Articles/I/CaliforniaWWS.pdf

280 Jacobson, Mark Z., "100% Wind, Water and Solar (WWS) All-Sector Energy Roadmaps for Countries, States, Cities, and Towns: Roadmaps to convert 139 countries of the world to 100% Wind, Water, and Sunlight (WWS) for all purposes," www.web.Stanford.edu, Page accessed February 7, 2019. Professor Jacobson research includes 2015-2019 for details of WWS conversion. http://web.stanford.edu/group/efmh/jacobson/Articles/I/WWS-50-USState-plans.html

281 Bryce. Ibid. 2018.

282 Wilburn, David R., *Wind Energy in the United States and Materials Required for the Land-Based Wind Turbine Industry From 2010-2030*. (U.S. Department of the Interior, Washington D.C.,

U.S. Geological Survey, Restin, VA.), 2011. Study completed under Democratic President Barack H. Obama's administration. Noted since is administration was heavy into global warming, climate change, RE and facts therefore don't have a conservative, Republican bent or bias towards fossil fuels instead of RE. https://pubs.usgs.gov/sir/2011/5036/sir2011-5036.pdf

283 Bryce. Ibid. 2018.

284 Nikolewski, Rob, "Wind energy in California: The good news and bad news," www.SanDiegoUnionTribune.com, August 28, 2017. https://www.sandiegouniontribune.com/business/sd-fi-california-wind-20170825-story.html

285 Power Technology, San Onofre Nuclear Generating Station (SONGS) California, Home page for informational purposes. Page accessed on February 7, 2019. https://www.power-technology.com/projects/san-onofre-nuclear-generating-california/

286 Kotkin, Joel, "California takes the prize for environmental virtue signaling – but not much else," www.OCRegister.com, August 18, 2018. https://www.ocregister.com/2018/08/18/california-takes-the-prize-for-green-virtue-signaling/

287 Dr. Lehr, Jay, Harris, Tom, "How Al Gore built the global warming fraud," www.Cfact.org, October 20, 2018. http://www.cfact.org/2018/10/20/how-al-gore-built-the-global-warming-fraud/

288 Fracking photos https://www.ipaa.org/fracking

289 Shellenberger. Ibid. 2018. https://www.forbes.com/sites/michaelshellenberger/2018/04/25/yes-solar-and-wind-really-do-increase-electricity-prices-and-for-inherently-physical-reasons/#374a213017e8

290 van Beurden, Ben, Chief Executive Officer, Shell Oil, "Two billion people do not have access to reliable electricity: this must change," www.Linkedin.com, October 18, 2018. https://www.linkedin.com/pulse/two-billion-people-do-have-access-reliable-must-ben-van-beurden/

291 Goldberg, Jonah, "Green New Deal Backers Embrace Their Fantasies," www.Townhall.com, February 8, 2019. https://townhall.com/columnists/jonahgoldberg/2019/02/08/

green-new-deal-backers-embrace-their-fantasies-n2541028?utm_source=thdaily&utm_medium=email&utm_campaign=nl&newsletterad=02/08/2019&bcid=f474ff7f07777dc0fd4d372af0dcd99b&recip=24783318

292 Goldberg. Ibid. 2019.

293 Althoff, David Jr., Altenburg, Robert, *Pennsylvania's Solar Future Plan: Strategies to increase electricity generation from in-state solar energy.* (State of Pennsylvania, Department of Environmental Protection and PennFuture Energy Center, Harrisburg, PA.) November 2018. https://www.dep.pa.gov/PASolarFuture/plan

294 U.S Energy Information Administration (EIA), Independent Statistics & Analysis, Electricity Data, ELECTRICITY DATA BROWSER, Average retail price of electricity, annual, www.EIA.gov, 2009-2017. https://www.eia.gov/electricity/data/browser/#/topic/7?agg=0,1&geo=g00000g&endsec=vg&freq=A&start=2009&end=2017&chartindexed=1&ctype=linechart&ltype=pin&rtype=s&maptype=0&rse=0&pin=

295 U.S. Energy Information Administration (EIA), Independent Statistics & Analysis, Electricity Data, ELECTRICITY DATA BROWSER, Average retail price of electricity (cents per kilowatthour), South Dakota. www.EIA.gov, 2009-2017. https://www.eia.gov/electricity/data/browser/#/topic/7?agg=0,1&geo=0000008&endsec=vg&linechart=ELEC.PRICE.SD-ALL.A-ELEC.PRICE.SD-RES.A-ELEC.PRICE.SD-COM.A-ELEC.PRICE.SD-IND.A-ELEC.PRICE.SD-TRA.A-ELEC.PRICE.SD-OTH.A&columnchart=ELEC.PRICE.SD-ALL.A&map=ELEC.PRICE.SD-ALL.A&freq=A&start=2009&end=2017&chartindexed=1&ctype=linechart&ltype=pin&rtype=s&maptype=0&rse=0&pin=

296 U.S. Energy Information Administration (EIA), Independent Statistics & Analysis, Electricity Data, ELECTRICITY DATA BROWSER, Average retail price of electricity (cents per kilowatthour), North Dakota. www.EIA.gov, 2009-2017. https://www.eia.gov/electricity/data/browser/#/topic/7?agg=0,1&geo=000000g&endsec=vg&linechart=ELEC.

PRICE.ND-ALL.A~&columnchart=ELEC.PRICE.ND-ALL.A&map=ELEC.PRICE.ND-ALL.A&freq=A&start=2009&end=2017&chartindexed=1&ctype=linechart&ltype=pin&rtype=s&pin=&rse=0&maptype=0

297 Nermec, Richard, "Bakken Production Records Continue, But Slowdown Predicted," NGI's Shale Daily, www.NaturalGasIntel.com, (NGI), December 17, 2018. https://www.naturalgasintel.com/articles/116819-bakken-production-records-continue-but-slowdown-predicted

298 U.S. Energy Information Administration (EIA), Independent Statistics & Analysis, Electricity Data, ELECTRICITY DATA BROWSER, Average retail price of electricity (cents per kilowatthour), Oklahoma. www.EIA.gov, 2009-2017.

299 U.S. Energy Information Administration (EIA), Independent Statistics & Analysis, Electricity Data, ELECTRICITY DATA BROWSER, Average retail price of electricity (cents per kilowatthour), Kansas. www.EIA.gov, 2009-2017. https://www.eia.gov/electricity/data/browser/#/topic/7?agg=0,1&geo=000008&endsec=vg&linechart=ELEC.PRICE.KS-ALL.A~~&columnchart=ELEC.PRICE.KS-ALL.A&map=ELEC.PRICE.KS-ALL.A&freq=A&start=2009&end=2017&chartindexed=1&ctype=linechart&ltype=pin&rtype=s&maptype=0&rse=0&pin=

300 U.S. Energy Information Administration (EIA), Independent Statistics & Analysis, Electricity Data, ELECTRICITY DATA BROWSER, Average retail price of electricity (cents per kilowatthour), Iowa. www.EIA.gov, 2009-2017. https://www.eia.gov/electricity/data/browser/#/topic/7?agg=0,1&geo=00000g&endsec=vg&linechart=ELEC.PRICE.IA-ALL.A~~~&columnchart=ELEC.PRICE.IA-ALL.A&map=ELEC.PRICE.IA-ALL.A&freq=A&start=2009&end=2017&chartindexed=1&ctype=linechart&ltype=pin&rtype=s&pin=&rse=0&maptype=0

301 Egan, Matt, "Texas to pass Iraq and Iran as world's No. 3 oil powerhouse," www.money.CNN.com, July 17, 2018. https://

money.cnn.com/2018/07/17/investing/texas-oil-iran-iraq-permian-basin/index.html

302 U.S. Energy Information Administration (EIA), Independent Statistics & Analysis, Electricity Data, ELECTRICITY DATA BROWSER, Average retail price of electricity (cents per kilowatthour), Texas. www.EIA.gov, 2009-2017. https://www.eia.gov/electricity/data/browser/#/topic/7?agg=0,1&geo=0000000002&endsec=vg&linechart=ELEC.PRICE.TX-ALL.A&columnchart=ELEC.PRICE.TX-ALL.A&map=ELEC.PRICE.TX-ALL.A&freq=A&start=2009&end=2016&chartindexed=1&ctype=linechart&ltype=pin&rtype=s&pin=&rse=0&maptype=0

303 U.S. Energy Information Administration (EIA), Independent Statistics & Analysis, Electricity Data, ELECTRICITY DATA BROWSER, Average retail price of electricity (cents per kilowatthour), Nevada. www.EIA.gov, 2009-2017. https://www.eia.gov/electricity/data/browser/#/topic/7?agg=0,1&geo=00000000002&endsec=vg&freq=A&start=2009&end=2017&chartindexed=1&ctype=linechart&ltype=pin&rtype=s&maptype=0&rse=0&pin=

304 U.S. Energy Information Administration (EIA), Independent Statistics & Analysis, Natural Gas, "Texas Natural Gas Prices Sold to Electric Power Consumers," www.IEA.gov, January 31, 2019. https://www.eia.gov/dnav/ng/hist/n3045tx3a.htm

305 Denning, Liam, "Texas Power: No Country for Old Thinking," www.Bloomberg.com, April 21, 2017. https://www.bloomberg.com/gadfly/articles/2017-04-21/griddy-launch-panda-thermal-bankruptcy-the-state-of-texas-power

306 Walton, Robert, "Exelon's Texas merchant subsidiary files for bankruptcy," www.UtilityDive.com, November 7, 2017. https://www.utilitydive.com/news/exelons-texas-merchant-subsidiary-files-for-bankruptcy/510253/

307 Martin, Chris, "Think Power's Expensive in Texas This Year? Just Wait Until 2019," www.Bloomberg.com, February 26,

308 NV Energy, *NV (Nevada) Energy Power Supply Assets*. Report for Governor of Nevada. 2018. http://energy.nv.gov/uploadedFiles/energynvgov/content/Programs/TaskForces/2017/NVE%20Supply%20Assets%20Data%20Request%20From%20GCEC%20TWG%20Consumer%20Investor%20Impacts.pdf

309 Shellenberger. Ibid. 2018. https://www.forbes.com/sites/michaelshellenberger/2018/04/25/yes-solar-and-wind-really-do-increase-electricity-prices-and-for-inherently-physical-reasons/#5126c617e84b

310 Hirth, Lion (2013): "The Market Value of Variable Renewables," *Energy Policy* 38, 218-236. doi:10.1016/j.eneco.2013.02.004. SPECIAL NOTE: Mr. Hirth asked his work be cited this way.

311 Shellenberger. Ibid. 2018.

312 Stein, Ronald, "Do Californians Support the State Being a National Security Risk on Imported Oil? www.FoxandHoundsDaily.com, February 11, 2019. http://www.foxandhoundsdaily.com/2019/02/do-californians-support-the-state-being-a-national-security-risk-on-imported-oil/

313 U.S. Energy Information Administration (EIA), Independent Statistics & Analysis, Electricity Data, ELECTRICITY DATA BROWSER, Average retail price of electricity (cents per kilowatthour), Hawaii. www.EIA.gov, 2009-2017. https://www.eia.gov/electricity/data/browser/#/topic/7?agg=0,1&geo=0000000000008&endsec=vg&freq=A&start=2009&end=2017&chartindexed=1&ctype=linechart&ltype=pin&rtype=s&pin=&rse=0&maptype=0

314 Nelson, Peter, Hayward, Steven F., *Energy Policy in Minnesota: The High Cost of Failure*, Center of the American Experiment, Minnesota's Think Tank. www.AmericanExperiment.org, October 10, 2017. https://www.americanexperiment.org/reports-books/energy-policy-minnesota-high-cost-failure/

[Note: Entry at top of page continues from previous page] 2019. https://www.bloomberg.com/news/articles/2018-02-26/think-power-s-expensive-in-texas-this-year-just-wait-until-2019

315 Hayward, Steven F., "The high cost of our failing wind policies," www.StarTribune.com, December 13, 2017. http://www.startribune.com/the-high-cost-of-our-failing-wind-policies/464005143/

316 Hayward. Ibid. 2017.

317 Lehr, Jay, Harris, Tom, "How Al Gore Built The Global Warming Fraud," www.Heartland.org (Heartland Institute), October 19, 2018. https://www.heartland.org/news-opinion/news/how-al-gore-built-the-global-warming-fraud

318 Osborn, Claire, "Georgetown renegotiating solar, wind power contracts," www.Statesman.com, December 16, 2018. https://www.statesman.com/news/20181216/georgetown-renegotiating-solar-wind-power-contracts

319 Shellenberger, Michael, Werbach, Adam, "It's the oil economy, stupid," www.SFGate.com, March 10, 2003.

320 Jenkins, Jesse, Muro, Mark, Nordhaus, Ted, Shellenberger, Michael, Tawney, Letha, Trembath, Alex, *Beyond Boom and Bust: Putting Clean Tech On a Path To Subsidy Independence*, www.Brookings.edu, April 18, 2012. https://www.brookings.edu/research/beyond-boom-and-bust-putting-clean-tech-on-a-path-to-subsidy-independence/

321 Rosenthal, Elisabeth, "2 studies conclude that biofuels are not so green after all," www.NYTimes.com, (New York Times), February 7, 2008. https://www.nytimes.com/2008/02/07/health/07iht-biofuel.5.9849073.html

322 Lustgarten, Abraham, FEATURE: "Palm Oil Was Supposed to Help Save the Planet. Instead It Unleashed Catastrophe: A decade ago (under the Obama administration), the U.S. mandated the use of vegetable oil in biofuels, leading to industrial-scale deforestation – and a huge spike in carbon emissions," www.NYTimes.com, November 20, 2018. https://www.nytimes.com/2018/11/20/magazine/palm-oil-borneo-climate-catastrophe.html

323 Shellenberger, Michael, "How Not to Deal With Climate Change," www.NYTimes.com, June 30, 2016. https://www.nytimes.

com/2016/06/30/opinion/how-not-to-deal-with-climate-change.html

324 Wilkes, William, Warren, Hayley, Parkin, Brian, "Germany's Failed Climate Goals A Wake-Up Call for Governments Everywhere," www.Bloomberg.com, August 15, 2018. https://www.bloomberg.com/graphics/2018-germany-emissions/

325 Wetzel, Daniel, "GERMANY RISKS TOTAL PERMANENT LOSS OF CONTROL OF ENERGIEWENDE, FEDERAL AUDIT OFFICE WARNS: Germany's Federal Audit Office has accused the government of a catastrophic mismanagement of the green energy transition (Energiewende). The wastage of resources is "unprecedented." www.TheGWPF.org, (The Global Warming Policy Forum), September 29, 2018. http://www.thegwpf.com/germany-risks-complete-loss-of-control-of-energiewende-federal-audit-office-warns/

326 STROM-REPORT BLOG, "ELECTRICITY PRICES IN EUROPE – WHO PAYS THE MOST," www.1-stromvergleich.com, 2019. https://1-stromvergleich.com/electricity-prices-europe/

327 Baynes, Chris, "Germany produces enough renewable energy in six months to power country's households for an entire year," www.Independent.co.uk, July 2, 2018. https://www.independent.co.uk/environment/renewable-energy-germany-six-months-year-solar-power-wind-farms-a8427356.html

328 Wettengel, Julian, "Climate goal failure warrants high Energiewende priority – gov advisors," www.CleanEnergyWire.org, June 27, 2018. https://www.cleanenergywire.org/news/climate-goal-failure-warrants-high-energiewende-priority-gov-advisors

329 Royal, Todd, "Can the EU Shake Its Russian Energy Habit?" www.GeopoliticalMonitor.com, January 4, 2018. https://www.geopoliticalmonitor.com/can-the-eu-shake-its-russian-energy-habit/

330 STROM-REPORT BLOG, "ELECTRICITY PRICES IN EUROPE – WHO PAYS THE MOST." IBID. 2019.

331 Bastasch, Michael, Energy Editor, "SPAIN ENDS SUBSIDIES TO NEARLY 40 PERCENT OF ITS WIND ENERGY CAPACITY," www.DailyCaller.com, February 7, 2014. https://dailycaller.com/2014/02/07/spain-ends-subsidies-to-nearly-40-percent-of-its-wind-energy-capacity/

332 StopTheseThings.com, "Ticket to Oblivion: Australia's $60bn Wind & Solar Subsidy Gravy Train Rolls Until 2031," www.StopTheseThings.com, April 16, 2018. https://stopthesethings.com/2018/04/16/ticket-to-oblivion-australias-60bn-wind-solar-subsidy-gravy-train-rolls-until-2031/

333 The Conversation, "FactCheck Q&A: are South Australia's high electricity prices 'the consequence' of renewable energy policy," www.TheConversation.com, March 25, 2018. https://theconversation.com/factcheck-qanda-are-south-australias-high-electricity-prices-the-consequence-of-renewable-energy-policy-93594

334 Fung, Brian, "Tesla's enormous battery in Australia, just weeks old, is already responding to outages in 'record' time," www.WashingtonPost.com, December 26, 2017. https://www.washingtonpost.com/news/the-switch/wp/2017/12/26/teslas-enormous-battery-in-australia-just-weeks-old-is-already-responidding-to-outages-in-record-time/?noredirect=on&utm_term=.02370cb97464

335 Fung. Ibid. 2017.

336 The FT View Australian Politics, "Energy is at the Roots of Australia's Political Crisis," www.FT.com, August 23, 2018. https://www.ft.com/content/2ad3c68c-a6cd-11e8-926a-7342fe5e173f

337 de Sisternes, Fernando J., Jesse D. Jenkins, and Audun Botterud, "The value of energy storage in decarbonizing the electricity sector," *Applied Energy* (in press, 2016). Authors requested source be cited this way unlike other sources throughout the chapter and book. http://web.mit.edu/ferds/www/Value_of_energy_storage_May_1_2016_pre-publication.pdf

338 Obama, Barack, President of the United States, U.S. Department of Energy, *Quadrennial Energy Review Part 1*, *Energy Transmission*,

Storage, and Distribution Infrastructure. (Office of the Executive, President of the United States, U.S. Department of Energy, Washington, D.C.). www.Energy.gov, April 2015. https://www.energy.gov/sites/prod/files/2015/07/f24/QER%20Full%20Report_TS%26D%20April%202015_0.pdf

339 Obama, Barack, President of the United States, U.S. Department of Energy, *Quadrennial Energy Review (QER) Part 2, Transforming The Nation's Electricity System: The Second Installment of the QER.* (Office of the Executive, President of the United States, U.S. Department of Energy, Washington, D.C.). www.Energy.gov, January 2017. https://www.energy.gov/sites/prod/files/2017/02/f34/Quadrennial%20Energy%20Review--Second%20Installment%20%28Full%20Report%29.pdf

340 Goreham, Steve, "100 percent renewable energy – Poor policy for electricity ratepayers," www.cfact.org, October 30, 2018. http://www.cfact.org/2018/10/30/100-percent-renewable-energy-poor-policy-for-electricity-ratepayers/

341 Shellenberger. Ibid. 2018. https://www.forbes.com/sites/michaelshellenberger/2018/04/25/yes-solar-and-wind-really-do-increase-electricity-prices-and-for-inherently-physical-reasons/#6d659aa17e84

342 Footnote in German, German Electricity Prices and Subsidies for "renewable energy feed-in tariffs," www.netztransparenz.de, 2017. https://www.netztransparenz.de/portals/1/Aktuelle_Daten_zu_den_Einnahmen-_und_Ausgabenpositionen_nach_AusglMechV_Dez_2017.pdf

343 Moore, Stephen, "Green is the New Red," www.Townhall.com, February 12, 2019. https://townhall.com/columnists/stephenmoore/2019/02/12/green-is-the-new-red-n2541187?utm_source=thdaily&utm_medium=email&utm_campaign=nl&newsletterad=02/12/2019&bcid=f474ff7f07777dc0fd4d372af0dcd99b&recip=24783318

344 Smil, Vaclav, "To Get Wind Power You Need Oil," www.Spectrum.IEEE.org, February 29, 2016. https://spectrum.ieee.org/energy/renewables/to-get-wind-power-you-need-oil SPECIAL

NOTE: Though the article focuses on wind the same processes he speaks of can be extracted for solar panels and Mr. Smil is the leading expert in the world on all forms of energy. See Mr. Smil's *Energy and Civilization* where he speaks about solar panels for verification.

345 Bailey, Ronald, "Power U.S. Using 100 Percent Renewable Energy is a Total Fantasy: New Research debunks a study claiming there's a low-cost way to power America using wind, solar and hydropower," www.Reason.com, June 21, 2017. https://reason.com/blog/2017/06/21/powering-us-using-100-percent-renewable

346 Bailey, Ronald, "How Much Will the Green New Deal Cost? Climate change is the excuse; radically remaking the American economy is the aim," www.Reason.com, February 7, 2019. https://reason.com/blog/2019/02/07/green-new-deal-democratic-socialism-by-o

347 Kruta, Virginia, Associate Editor, "'I WAS LAUGHING SO HARD I NEARLY CRIED': WSJ'S KIMBERLEY STRASSEL CAN'T GET OVER GREEN NEW DEAL," www.DailyCaller.com, February 7, 2019. https://dailycaller.com/2019/02/07/wsj-kimberley-strassel-green-new-deal/

348 Wind Action, "Facts, analysis, exposure to industrial wind energy's real impacts," www.WindAction.org, Page accessed February 14, 2019. http://www.windaction.org

349 Irfan, Umair, "Climate Scientists Debate Best Path Forward for Clean Energy," www.ScientificAmerican.com, June 1, 2016. https://www.scientificamerican.com/article/climate-scientists-debate-best-path-forward-for-clean-energy/

350 Christopher T.M. Clack, Staffan A. Qvist, Jay Apt, Morgan Bazillian, Adam R. Brandt, Ken Caldeira, Steven J. Davis, Victor Diakov, Mark A. Handschy, Paul D. H. Hines, Paulina Jaramillo, Daniel M. Kammen, Jane C.S. Long, M. Granger Morgan, Adam Reed, Varun Sivaram, James Sweeney, George R. Tynan, David G. Victor, John P. Weyant, Jay F. Whtacre, *Evaluation of a proposal for reliable low-cost grid power with 100% wind, water, and solar*, (Proceedings of the National Academy of Sciences of the United

States of America (PNAS), Washington, D.C.), www.PNAS.org, June 19, 2017. https://www.pnas.org/content/114/26/6722.full

351 Mooney, Chris, "A bitter scientific debate just erupted over the future of America's power grid," www.WashingtonPost.com, June 10, 2017. https://www.washingtonpost.com/news/energy-environment/wp/2017/06/19/a-bitter-scientific-debate-just-erupted-over-the-future-of-the-u-s-electric-grid/?utm_term=.f40ba7325b0d

352 Shellenberger, Michael, "Green New Deal Excludes Nuclear And Would Thus Increase Emissions – Just Like It Did In Vermont," www.Forbes.com, February 7, 2019. https://www.forbes.com/sites/michaelshellenberger/2019/02/07/green-new-deal-excludes-nuclear-and-would-thus-increase-emissions-just-like-it-did-in-vermont/#389b36b69afd

353 California Center for Jobs & the Economy, *A Closer Look At California's Cobalt Economy*, (California Business Roundtable, Sacramento, CA), www.CenterforJobs.org, January 2019. https://centerforjobs.org/wp-content/uploads/A-Closer-Look-At-Californias-Cobalt-Economy-2.pdf

354 Environmental Progress, *The Complete Case for Nuclear*, (Environmental Progress Publishing and Studies, Berkeley, CA), 2018. http://environmentalprogress.org/the-complete-case-for-nuclear/

355 Land Use by Electricity Source in Acres/MW Produced https://www.strata.org/pdf/2017/footprints-full.pdf

356 Where would you rather live? https://wattsupwiththat.com/2015/07/08/wednesday-wit-cartoon-by-josh

357 Solar Farm size photo : https://www.thisismoney.co.uk/money/investing/article-3078529/Are-giant-solar-farms-income-opportunity-ve-looking-for.html

358 Hydraulic fracturing photo http://www.hydrogenfuelnews.com/company-operating-uk-fracking-site-wants-to-increase-tremor-threshold/8536483/

359 Chen, Stephen, "China's ageing solar panels are going to be a big environmental problem," www.SCMP.com (South China

Morning Post), July 30, 2017. https://www.scmp.com/news/china/society/article/2104162/chinas-ageing-solar-panels-are-going-be-big-environmental-problem

360 Conca, James, "How Deadly Is Your Kilowatt? We Rank The Killer Energy Sources," www.Forbes.com, June 10, 2012. https://www.forbes.com/sites/jamesconca/2012/06/10/energys-deathprint-a-price-always-paid/#6c8fc46c709b

361 U.S Energy Information Administration, Independent Statistics & Analysis, FREQUENTLY ASKED QUESTIONS, "What is U.S. electricity generation by energy source?" www.EIA.gov, Last updated October 29, 2018. https://www.eia.gov/tools/faqs/faq.php?id=427&t=3

362 Krupp, Fred, Keohane, Nathaniel, Pooley, Eric, "Less Than Zero: Can Carbon-Removal Technologies Curb Climate Change?" www.ForeignAffairs.com, ESSAY, March/April 2019 Issue. https://www.foreignaffairs.com/articles/2019-02-12/less-zero?utm_medium=newsletters&utm_source=fatoday&utm_content=20190213&utm_campaign=FA%20Today%20021319%20Can%20Carbon-Removal%20Technologies%20Curb%20Climate%20Change?&utm_term=FA%20Today%20-%20112017

363 Lind, Jennifer, Wohlforth, William C., "The Future of the Liberal Order is Conservative: A Strategy to Save the System," www.ForeignAffairs.com, ESSAY, March/April 2019 Issue. https://www.foreignaffairs.com/articles/2019-02-12/future-liberal-order-conservative?utm_medium=newsletters&utm_source=fatoday&utm_content=20190215&utm_campaign=FA%20Today%20021519%20The%20Future%20of%20the%20Liberal%20Order%20Is%20Conservative&utm_term=FA%20Today%20-%20112017

364 Steil, Benn, "How to Win a Great-Power Competition: Alliances, Aid and Diplomacy in the Last Struggle for Global Influence," www.ForeignAffairs.com, February 9, 2018. https://www.foreignaffairs.com/articles/2018-02-09/how-win-great-power-competition

365 British Petroleum, *BP Statistical Review of World Energy*, Years covered 1965-2017. www.BP.com, June 2018. https://www.bp.com/content/dam/bp/business-sites/en/global/corporate/pdfs/energy-economics/statistical-review/bp-stats-review-2018-full-report.pdf

366 Ring, Edward, "California's Renewable Mandate Sets an Impossible Example for the World: It's debatable whether some 'renewables even produce net energy," www.CaliforniaGlobe.com, February 14, 2019. https://californiaglobe.com/governor/californias-renewables-mandate-sets-an-impossible-example-for-the-world/

367 Ring. Ibid. 2019.

368 Global Energy Consumption by fuel https://californiaglobe.com/governor/californias-renewables-mandate-sets-an-impossible-example-for-the-world/

369 Parke, Phoebe, "Why are 600 million Africans still without power?" www.CNN.com, April 1, 2016. https://www.cnn.com/2016/04/01/africa/africa-state-of-electricity-feat/index.html

370 U.S. Energy Information Administration *International Energy Outlook 2018*. Ibid. 2018.

371 Khasru, B.Z., "How China's rivalry with India is rippling across South Asia," www.SCMP.com, (South China Morning Post), July 20, 2018. https://www.scmp.com/comment/insight-opinion/article/2117674/how-chinas-rivalry-india-rippling-across-south-asia

372 Economic Times Contributors (ET), "View: Busting myths behind opposition to Adani mine," www.EconomicTimes.IndiaTimes.com, January 21, 2019. https://economictimes.indiatimes.com/industry/indl-goods/svs/metals-mining/view-busting-myths-behind-opposition-to-adani-mine/articleshow/67619641.cms

Chapter 7: Electrical Grid

373 DiChristopher, Tom, "Alexandria Ocasio-Cortez's Green New Deal would reshape the economy in 10 years. That could shock

the energy sector," www.CNBC.com, February 5, 2019. https://www.cnbc.com/2019/02/05/green-new-deal-could-break-parts-of-the-us-power-system.html

374 Electric Power Research Institute (EPRI), *Estimating the Costs and Benefits of the Smart Grid: A Preliminary Estimate of the Investment Requirements and the Resultant Benefits of a Full Functioning Smart Grid*. www.SmartGrid.gov, 2011 Technical Report. https://www.smartgrid.gov/files/Estimating_Costs_Benefits_Smart_Grid_Preliminary_Estimate_In_201103.pdf

375 Rhodes, Joshua D., "Old, dirty, creaky U.S. electric grid could cost $5 trillion to replace," www.Greenbiz.com, April 12, 2017. https://www.greenbiz.com/article/old-dirty-creaky-us-electric-grid-could-cost-5-trillion-replace

376 Financial Times (FT), "Maldives Counts the Cost of Debts to China," www.FT.com, February 10, 2019. https://www.ft.com/content/c8da1c8a-2a19-11e9-88a4-c32129756dd8

377 Mead, Walter Russell, "Europe's Challenge Is Decline, Not Trump: Even George Soros warns that the EU may 'go the way of the Soviet Union in 1991,'" www.WSJ.com, February 18, 2019. https://www.wsj.com/articles/europes-challenge-is-decline-not-trump-11550519599

378 Mead, Walter Russell, "How American Fracking Changes the World: Low energy prices enhance U.S. power at the expense of Moscow and Tehran," www.WSJ.com, November 26, 2018. https://www.wsj.com/articles/how-american-fracking-changes-the-world-1543276935

379 U.S. Energy Information Administration (EIA), Independent Statistics & Analysis, TODAY IN ENERGY, "California imports the most electricity from other states; Pennsylvania exports the most," www.EIA.gov, April 4, 2019. https://www.eia.gov/todayinenergy/detail.php?id=38912

380 Wikipedia, "Electrical grid," From Wikipedia the free encyclopedia, www.en.Wikipedia.com, February 12, 2019 (last page update). https://en.wikipedia.org/wiki/Electrical_grid

381 Kehinde, Ehineni, "Electrical Grid, Definition," www.StudentEnergy.org, Page accessed February 20, 2019. https://www.studentenergy.org/topics/electrical-grid

382 Rhame, Jay, "New-age economy can't grow when it relies on an outdated power grid," www.TheHill.com, March 28, 2018. https://thehill.com/opinion/energy-environment/380666-new-age-economy-cant-grow-when-it-relies-on-outdated-power-grid

383 Office of Electricity, U.S. Department of Energy, "Grid Modernization and the Smart Grid," www.Energy.gov, 2019. https://www.energy.gov/oe/activities/technology-development/grid-modernization-and-smart-grid

384 Office of Electricity, U.S. Department of Energy. Ibid. 2019.

385 Shellenberger, Michael, "Green New Deal Excludes Nuclear And Would Thus Increase Emissions – Just Like It Did In Vermont," www.Forbes.com, February 7, 2019. https://www.forbes.com/sites/michaelshellenberger/2019/02/07/green-new-deal-excludes-nuclear-and-would-thus-increase-emissions-just-like-it-did-in-vermont/#484b9889afd1

386 EnergySkeptic, "Peak Energy & Resources, Climate Change and the Preservation of Knowledge: 41 Reasons why wind power cannot replace fossil fuels," www.EnergySkeptic.com, December 14, 2018. http://energyskeptic.com/2018/wind/

387 United States Environmental Protection Agency (EPA), "Greenhouse Gas Emissions, Sources of Greenhouse Gas Emissions," www.EPA.gov, Page last updated October 9, 2018. https://www.epa.gov/ghgemissions/sources-greenhouse-gas-emissions

388 Shellenberger. Ibid. 2019. https://www.forbes.com/sites/michaelshellenberger/2019/02/07/green-new-deal-excludes-nuclear-and-would-thus-increase-emissions-just-like-it-did-in-vermont/#484b9889afd1

389 Stanton, Glenn T., "New Harvard Research Says U.S. Christianity Is Not Shrinking, But Growing Stronger," www.TheFederalist.com, January 22, 2018. http://thefederalist.com/2018/01/22/new-harvard-research-says-u-s-christianity-not-shrinking-growing-stronger/

390 Office of Electricity, U.S. Department of Energy. Ibid. 2019.

391 Wojick, David, "A brutal example of why 100% renewable energy can't work," www.Cfact.org, February 4, 2019. http://www.cfact.org/2019/02/04/a-brutal-example-of-why-100-renewables-cant-work/

392 Temple, James, Sustainable Energy Section, Massachusetts Institute of Technology (MIT), "California is throttling back record levels of solar – and that's bad news for climate goals," www.TechnologyReview.com, May 24, 2018. https://www.technologyreview.com/s/611188/california-is-throttling-back-record-levels-of-solarand-thats-bad-news-for-climate-goals/

393 Hadley, Ray, "Energy grid at 'crisis point as power prices surge 160 times the usual rate," www.2gb.com, June 13, 2018. https://www.2gb.com/energy-grid-at-crisis-point-as-power-prices-surge-160-times-the-usual-rate/

394 A Report by the American Physical Society (APS) (Physics and Physicists) on Public Affairs, *Integrating Renewable Electricity on the Grid*, (APS Physics, Washington D.C.), Report read and sourced February 20, 2019. https://www.aps.org/policy/reports/popa-reports/upload/integratingelec.pdf

395 Wikipedia, "Intermittent energy source," From Wikipedia, the free encyclopedia, www.en.Wikipedia.org, Page was last updated on February 20, 2018 when accessed for use as a source. https://en.wikipedia.org/wiki/Intermittent_energy_source

396 Office of Electricity, U.S. Department of Energy. Ibid. 2019.

397 Office of Electricity. U.S. Department of Energy. Ibid. 2019.

398 International Energy Agency (IEA), "Smart grids: Tracking Clean Energy Progress," www.IEA.org, January 25, 2019. https://www.iea.org/tcep/energyintegration/smartgrids/

399 Biello, David, "Solar Home Owners Battle Their Electric Companies," www.ScientificAmerican.com, November 2014. https://www.scientificamerican.com/article/solar-home-owners-battle-their-electric-companies/?redirect=1

400 International Energy Agency (IEA), Home page: The IEA is the global energy authority. www.IEA.org, IEA 2019. All Rights Reserved.
401 IEA. Ibid. 2019. https://www.iea.org/tcep/energyintegration/smartgrids/
402 Meadows, Sam, "The trouble with smart meters: the top five problems customers have," www.Telegraph.co.uk, August 20, 2018. https://www.telegraph.co.uk/bills-and-utilities/gas-electric/trouble-smart-meters-top-five-problems-customers-have/
403 U.S. Department of Energy (DOE), Electricity Delivery & Energy Reliability, American Recovery and Reinvestment Act of 2009, *2015 Progress Report for OE ARRA Smart Grid Demonstration Program Aggregation of RDSI, SGDP and SGIG Results*. (Renewable and the Distributed Systems Integration Program, Smart Grid Demonstration Program, Smart Grid Investment Grants, Washington D.C.), www.Energy.gov, May 2015. https://www.energy.gov/sites/prod/files/2016/12/f34/Activity%206%20Report_Public_Version_051415%20FINAL.pdf
404 Levinson, Marc, "Is the Smart Grid Really a Smart Idea," www.Issues.org, Vol. XXVII, No. 1, Fall 2010. https://issues.org/levinson/
405 Gerdeman, Dina, "Unplugged: What Happened to the Smart Grid?" www.HBSWK.HBS.edu (Harvard Business School), On Research & Ideas, March 8, 2012. https://hbswk.hbs.edu/item/unplugged-what-happened-to-the-smart-grid
406 Margonelli, Lisa, "What's Really Wrong With the Smart Grid," www.TheAtlantic.com, November 19, 2010. https://www.theatlantic.com/national/archive/2010/11/whats-really-wrong-with-the-smart-grid/66832/
407 Levinson. op. cit.. 2010.
408 Schumacher, E.F., *Small Is Beautiful: Economics as if People Mattered*, (Harper Perennial Modern Thought; Reprint Edition, New York, NY), October 19, 2010. https://www.amazon.com/Small-Beautiful-Economics-Mattered-Perennial/dp/0061997765

409 Environmental Progress, "Why the War on Nuclear Threatens Us All," www.EnvironmentalProgress.org, March 28, 2017. http://environmentalprogress.org/big-news/2017/3/28/why-the-war-on-nuclear-threatens-us-all

410 National Resources Defense Council (NRDC), "Energy efficiency is one of the most powerful weapons for combatting global climate change, boosting the economy, and ensuring that the air is safe to breathe," www.NRDC.org, Page accessed February 28, 2019. https://www.nrdc.org/issues/energy-efficiency

411 Mitchell, Patrick, Media Contact, American Council for an Energy-Efficient Economy (ACEEE), "ACEEE 2018 State Energy Efficiency Scorecard," www.ACEEE.org, October 4, 2018. https://aceee.org/press/2018/10/aceee-2018-state-energy-efficiency

412 Vermont's Green Mountain Power, "Our Mission," Home page explaining how they view energy and electricity. www.GreenMountainPower.com, 2019. https://greenmountainpower.com/about/

413 Angwin, Meredith, "Yes Vermont Yankee: A blog about Northeast energy issues, and in support of nuclear power," www.Yesvy.Blogspot.com, July 11, 2012. http://yesvy.blogspot.com/2012/07/carbon-dioxide-and-nuclear-energy-great.html#.XHgoJC2ZOgx

414 Shellenberger, Michael, "Green New Deal Excludes Nuclear And Would Thus Increase Emissions – Just Like It Did In Vermont," www.Forbes.com, February 7, 2019. https://www.forbes.com/sites/michaelshellenberger/2019/02/07/green-new-deal-excludes-nuclear-and-would-thus-increase-emissions-just-like-it-did-in-vermont/#646d29759afd

415 The Coalition For Energy Solutions, *Vermont Electric Power In Transition*, www.CoalitionforEnergySolutions.org, April 2010. http://www.coalitionforenergysolutions.org/vt_elec_pwr_in_transitionpr.pdf

416 Shellenberger. Ibid. 2019.

417 Robinson, Hannah, "Burlington, VT: Recognized by the United Nations as a Model of Sustainability," www.NRDC.org, July

15, 2015. https://www.nrdc.org/experts/hannah-robinson/burlington-vt-recognized-united-nations-model-sustainability

418 Sheppard, David, "Investors risk losing faith in returns on offer from 'Big Oil,'" www.FT.com (Financial Times), January 21, 2019. https://www.ft.com/content/8a56566c-0e90-11e9-b2f2-f4c566a4fc5f

419 Gordon, Meghan, "Permian oil pipelines EPIC, Cactus II caught in FERC backlog," www.SPGlobal.com, (S&P Global Platts), February 26, 2019. https://www.spglobal.com/platts/en/market-insights/latest-news/oil/022619-permian-oil-pipelines-epic-cactus-ii-caught-in-ferc-backlog

420 Holthaus, Eric, "Bernie's New Climate Change Plan Is an Environmentalist's Dream, Except for This One Things," www.Slate.com, December 7, 2015. SPECIAL NOTE: Sanders has doubled down on this plan by endorsing The Green New Deal. https://slate.com/news-and-politics/2015/12/bernie-sanders-climate-plan-calls-for-end-to-nuclear-energy.html

421 Bryce, Robert, "San Bernardino County Says No To Big Renewables," www.NationalReview.com, March 7, 2019. https://www.nationalreview.com/2019/03/renewable-energy-land-use-san-bernardino-county/

422 Nace, Ted, *CLIMATE HOPE: On the Front Lines of the Fight Against Coal*, (CoalSwarm, San Francisco, CA), www.CoalSwarm.org, 2010. http://coalswarm.org/wp-content/uploads/2015/06/ClimateHopeEntireText.pdf

423 Bryce, Robert, "Wind power is an attack on rural America," www.LATimes.com, February 27, 2017. https://www.latimes.com/opinion/op-ed/la-oe-bryce-backlash-against-wind-energy-20170227-story.html

424 Roth, Sammy, "California's San Bernardino County slams the brakes on big solar projects," www.LATimes.com, February 28, 2019. https://www.latimes.com/business/la-fi-san-bernardino-solar-renewable-energy-20190228-story.html

425 Royal, Todd, "Energy Storage Isn't Ready for Wide Deployment," www.FoxandHoundsDaily.com, November

15, 2018. http://www.foxandhoundsdaily.com/2018/11/energy-storage-isnt-ready-wide-deployment/

426 Wood Mackenzie, "*Performance review: Nuclear, Fossil Fuels, and Renewables during the 2019 Polar Vortex,*" www.WoodMac.com, February 7, 2019. https://www.woodmac.com/reports/power-markets-performance-review-nuclear-fossil-fuels-and-renewables-during-the-2019-polar-vortex-99948

427 Graham, Karen, "Polar vortex 2019 – How did the electrical grid hold up?" www.DigitalJournal.com, February 13, 2019. http://www.digitaljournal.com/news/environment/polar-vortex-2019-how-did-the-electrical-grid-hold-up/article/543155?utm_source=Sailthru&utm_medium=email&utm_campaign=Issue:%202019-02-14%20Utility%20Dive%20Newsletter%20%5Bissue:19428%5D&utm_term=Utility%20Dive

428 Wood Mackenzie. Ibid. 2019.

429 Wood Mackenzie. Ibid. 2019.

430 Roselund, Christian, "Wood Mackenzie looks at the polar vortex and 100% renewable energy," www.PV-Magazine.USA.com, February 12, 2019. https://pv-magazine-usa.com/2019/02/12/wood-mackenzie-looks-at-the-polar-vortex-and-100-renewable-energy/

431 Graham. Ibid. 2019.

432 Wood Mackenzie. Ibid. 2019.

433 Evarts, Eric C., "Polar vortex tests viability of renewable power," www.GreenCarReports.com, February 13, 2019. https://www.greencarreports.com/news/1121465_polar-vortex-tests-viability-of-renewable-power

434 Graham. Ibid. 2019.

435 Shellenberger, Michael, "The Only Green New Deals That Have Ever Worked Were Done With Nuclear, Not Renewables," www.Forbes.com, February 8, 2019. https://www.forbes.com/sites/michaelshellenberger/2019/02/08/the-only-green-new-deals-that-have-ever-worked-were-done-with-nuclear-not-renewables/#7dfc5bb17f61

Chapter Eight: Electric Vehicles

436 TERENCE BELL Updated October 23, 2018 https://www.thebalance.com/the-10-biggest-cobalt-producers-2014-2339726

437 https://www.worldatlas.com/articles/the-top-lithium-producing-countries-in-the-world.html

438 November 15, 2017 https://www.amnesty.org/en/latest/news/2017/11/industry-giants-fail-to-tackle-child-labour-allegations-in-cobalt-battery-supply-chains/

439 The Guardian, July 29, 2017 https://www.theguardian.com/environment/2017/jul/29/electric-cars-battery-manufacturing-cobalt-mining

440 Amnesty International https://www.amnesty.org/en/latest/news/2017/11/industry-giants-fail-to-tackle-child-labour-allegations-in-cobalt-battery-supply-chains/

441 The Motley Fool, January 19, 2014 https://www.fool.com/investing/general/2014/01/19/tesla-motors-dirty-little-secret-is-a-major-proble.aspx

442 Photo https://images.search.yahoo.com/yhs/search;_ylt=Awr9L taohcxcwrcA5dM2nI1Q;_ylu=X3oDM TBsZ29xY3ZzBHNlYwNzZWFyY2gEc2xrA2J1dHRvbg --;_ylc=X1MDMTM1MTE5NTcwMgRfcgMy BGFjdG4DY2xrBGNzcmNwdmlkA2hvQUxsREV3 TGpKTTBYN1hXdXhYaFFRbE5UUXVOd0FBQ UFEQ2RZYm4EZnIDeWhzLXB0eS1wdHlfcGF ja2FnZXMEZnIyA3NhLWdwBGdwcmlkA3RoS05 Xak5aU2JhUHJOMHhOd2UwQkEEbl9zdWdnAzA Eb3JpZ2luA21tYWdlcy5zZWFyY2gueWFob28uY29 tBHBvcwMwBHBxc3RyAwRwcXN0cmwzN0cmdDJsA zYyBHF1ZXJ5A0VsZWN0cm9tb3RpdmUlMjBmb3JjZSU yMGZyb20lMjBhJTIwVGVzbGElMjBsaXRoaXVtJTIwYm F0dGVyaWVzBHRfc3RtcAMxNTU2OTA3NDk0?p= Electromotive+force+from+a+Tesla+lithium+batteries &fr=yhs-pty-pty_packages&fr2=sb-top-images.search &ei=UTF-8&n=60&x=wrt&hsimp=yhs-pty_

packages&hspart=pty#id=34&iurl=http%3A%2F%2Fimages.hgmsites.net%2Fhug%2Ftesla-model-s-lithium-ion-battery-pack-in-rolling-chassis-photo-martin-gillet-via-flickr_100481091_h.jpg&action=click

443   https://images.search.yahoo.com/yhs/search?p=emf+around+tesla+lithium+batteries&fr=yhs-pty-pty_packages&hspart=pty&hsimp=yhs-pty_packages&imgurl=https%3A%2F%2Fwww.bloomberg.com%2Fgraphics%2F2017-lithium-battery-future%2Fimg%2Fcar-3.png#id=5&iurl=https%3A%2F%2Fwww.bloomberg.com%2Fgraphics%2F2017-lithium-battery-future%2Fimg%2F2017-lithium-battery-future-facebook.png&action=click

444   The Brussels Times, April 17, 2019 http://brusselstimes.com/business/technology/15050/electric-vehicles-emit-more-co2-than-diesel-ones,-german-study-shows

445   InsideEVs https://insideevs.com/features/342689/battery-electric-fast-charging-versus-time-explained/

446   Waste Management World https://waste-management-world.com/a/1-the-lithium-battery-recycling-challenge

447   Statistica https://www.statista.com/statistics/734953/global-projected-electric-vehicles-sales/

448   CNBC May 30, 2018 https://www.cnbc.com/2018/05/30/electric-vehicles-will-grow-from-3-million-to-125-million-by-2030-iea.html

449   SupplyChainDrive, May 3, 2019 https://www.supplychaindive.com/news/teslas-production-threatened-mineral-shortages-copper/554026/

450   Green Car Reports July 29, 2014 https://www.greencarreports.com/news/1093560_1-2-billion-vehicles-on-worlds-roads-now-2-billion-by-2035-report

Chapter Nine: Requirements for a Carbon-Free Society

451   U.S. Energy Information Administration (EIA), Independent Statistics & Analysis, TODAY IN ENERGY section, "EIA

forecasts renewables will be the fastest growing source of electricity generation," www.EIA.gov, January 19, 2019. Entire paragraph came from this source. https://www.eia.gov/todayinenergy/detail.php?id=38053

452 Dr. Linda Capuano, Administrator, U.S. Energy Information Administration, *International Energy Outlook 2018 (IEO2018)* for Center for Strategic International Studies. (U.S. Department of Energy, Washington, DC), www.EIA.gov, July 24, 2018. https://www.eia.gov/pressroom/presentations/capuano_07242018.pdf

453 Associated Press, "International Energy Agency: Nuclear Power Will Be Needed to Meet Climate Goals," www.ENR.com (Engineering News-Record), May 28, 2019. https://www.enr.com/external_headlines/story?region=enr&story_id=bI65yJYEqabBfQ_3HmJ3xFRAv9A1mRPChMuuAgF4kadaDxlbiNv9jMwsNWsNwMuPUIkyYtZkulJdZN_GPoQUvxIcV37D3hfK72BFbIaRJ0IsMVE7NbM2KqUnpFLSJGYu6RiLdDYQVup_UbO0UVSjzJIPOmkXFcnUnAP3-SY6URE*&images_premium=1&define_caption=1&oly_enc_id=8565F2119945D0S

454 Wikipedia.com, "Carbon," www.en.Wikipedia.com, January 13, 2019. https://en.wikipedia.org/wiki/Carbon

455 Ranken Energy Corporation, "Products made from petroleum: With over 6000 products and counting, petroleum continues to be a crucial requirement for all consumers," www.Ranken-Energy.com, 2017. Entire paragraph (except for Paleolithic Era quote) with a partial list of the 6,000 products and the graph is from this exhaustive source. https://www.ranken-energy.com/index.php/products-made-from-petroleum/

456 Grabianowski, Ed, "How Cave Dwellers Work," www.History.HowStuffWorks.com, July 1, 2008. https://history.howstuffworks.com/historical-figures/cave-dweller1.htm

457 U.S. Energy Information Administration (EIA), Independent Statistics & Analysis, FREQUENTLY ASKED QUESTIONS section, "What are petroleum products, and what is petroleum used for?" www.EIA.gov, Last updated April 6, 2018. Entire

paragraph from this source. https://www.eia.gov/tools/faqs/faq.php?id=41&t=6

458 Wei, Lingling, "China's Annual Economic Growth Rate Is Slowest Since 1990," www.WSJ.com, January 21, 2019. https://www.wsj.com/articles/china-annual-economic-growth-rate-is-slowest-since-1990-11548037761?mod=hp_lead_pos1&mod=article_inline

459 Feder, Judy, "Survey Points to Bullish Outlook for 2019, With Some Caveats," www.spe.org (Journal of Petroleum Technology), January 23, 2019. https://www.spe.org/en/jpt/jpt-article-detail/?art=5033

460 Feder. Ibid. 2019.

461 Chestney, Nina, "Oil and gas executives expect to boost spending this year: survey," www.Reuters.com, January 21, 2019. https://www.reuters.com/article/us-energy-investment-dnv/oil-and-gas-executives-expect-to-boost-spending-this-year-survey-idUSKCN1PF28X

462 Friedman, Ezra, "The EastMed Pipeline Project in Perspective," www.GlobalRiskInsights.com, January 6, 2019. https://globalriskinsights.com/2019/01/eastmed-pipeline-project-in-perspective/

463 Gorodelsky, Sonia, "Israel-Europe gas pipeline MoU signed: Energy Ministers from Israel, Greece, Italy and Cyprus agreed to push ahead with the 2,100 kilometer pipeline linking Israel and Italy," www.en.Globes.co.il, (Globes Israel's Business Arena), December 5, 2017. https://en.globes.co.il/en/article-israel-europe-gas-pipeline-mou-signed-1001214430

464 Friedman. Ibid. 2019.

465 U.S. Department of State, Office of the Spokesperson, Washington DC, "Joint Statement Regarding the Inaugural United States-Greece Strategic Dialogue," www.State.gov, December 13, 2018. https://www.state.gov/r/pa/prs/ps/2018/12/288079.htm

466 Williams, Garrath, "Thomas Hobbes: Moral and Political Philosophy," www.IEP.utm.edu, Internet Encyclopedia of

Philosophy: A Peer-Reviewed Academic Resource, Page accessed on January 31, 2019. https://www.iep.utm.edu/hobmoral/

467 Prem, Prejula, Wittels, Jack, "Rise of Shale Is Slowly Choking Off Decades-Old Gasoline Trade," www.Bloomberg.com, January 21, 2019. https://www.bloomberg.com/news/articles/2019-01-22/rise-of-shale-is-slowly-choking-off-decades-old-gasoline-trade

468 Alzhu, Chen, Meng, Meng, "Drill, China, drill: State majors step on the gas after Xi calls for energy security," www.Reuters.com, January 31, 2019. https://www.reuters.com/article/us-china-oil-exploration-analysis/drill-china-drill-state-majors-step-on-the-gas-after-xi-calls-for-energy-security-idUSKCN1PQ3PO

469 Doreen, Namala, Gupte, Eklavya, "South Sudan's crude oil output jumps as Unity state fields reopen," www.SPGlobal.com, (S&P Global Platts), January 22, 2019. https://www.spglobal.com/platts/en/market-insights/latest-news/oil/012219-south-sudans-crude-oil-output-jumps-as-unity-state-fields-reopen?utm_source=twitter&utm_medium=social&utm_content=news&utm_term=we-oil&hootpostid=956470926623bacdff4659625ffc9628

470 Crawford, Alex, special correspondent in Yambio, South Sudan, "Face-to-face with child soldiers told to rape and kill in South Sudan," www.News.Sky.com, January 28, 2019. https://news.sky.com/story/south-sudans-child-soldiers-haunted-by-rapes-and-murders-11615337

471 Wikipedia, "Derivatives (finance) definition," www.en.Wikipedia.com, January 11, 2019. https://en.wikipedia.org/wiki/Derivative_(finance)

472 Stapczynski, Stephen, Murtaugh, Dan, "The Future Is Now for LNG as Derivatives Trading Takes Off," www.Bloomberg.com, January 20, 2019. https://www.bloomberg.com/news/articles/2019-01-20/the-future-is-now-for-lng-as-derivatives-trading-takes-off?mod=djem_EnergyJournal

473 Stapczynski, Murtaugh. Ibid. 2019. Entire paragraph and terms that include "liquid LNG benchmark," and "spot trading," come from this source.

474 Stanway, David, "China firms funding coal plants offshore as domestic curb bite: study," www.Uk.Reuters.com, January 21, 2019. https://uk.reuters.com/article/us-china-coal/china-firms-funding-coal-plants-offshore-as-domestic-curbs-bite-study-idUSKCN1PG02P?mod=djem_EnergyJournal

475 Shearer, Christine, Researcher, *China at a Crossroads: Continued Support for Coal Power Erodes Country's Clean Energy Leadership.* www.IEEFA.org, January 2019. http://ieefa.org/wp-content/uploads/2019/01/China-at-a-Crossroads_January-2019.pdf

476 Shearer. Ibid. 2019.

477 Commodities, "Russia seals position as top crude oil supplier to China, holds off Saudi Arabia," www.Reuters.com, January 24, 2019. https://www.reuters.com/article/us-china-economy-trade-crude/russia-seals-position-as-top-crude-oil-supplier-to-china-holds-off-saudi-arabia-idUSKCN1PJ05W

478 Business News, "Russia says oil price war with U.S. would be too costly," www.UK.Reuters.com, January 23, 2019. https://uk.reuters.com/article/us-davos-meeting-russia-opec/russia-says-oil-price-war-with-u-s-would-be-too-costly-idUKKCN1PH1A9

479 Engdahl, F. William, "The Saudis Have Lost the Oil War," www.GlobalResearch.ca, June 1, 2016. https://www.globalresearch.ca/the-saudis-have-lost-the-oil-war/5533380

480 Robinson, Simon, Evans, Dominic, Zhdannikov, Dmitry, "Saudi Aramco eyes multi-billion dollar U.S. gas acquisitions: CEO," www.Reuters.com, January 22, 2019. https://www.reuters.com/article/us-davos-meeting-aramco/saudi-aramco-eyes-multi-billion-dollar-us-gas-acquisitions-ceo-idUSKCN1PG1W1

481 U.S. Energy Information Administration, Independent Statistics & Analysis, PETROLEUM & OTHER LIQUIDS section, "Drilling Activity Report," www.EIA.gov, Release Date: January 22, 2019. https://www.eia.gov/petroleum/drilling/

482 Dezember, Ryan, Yang, Stephanie, "Drillers Are Easing Off the Gas," www.WSJ.com, January 27, 2019. https://www.wsj.com/articles/drillers-are-easing-off-the-gas-11548597601?mod=djem_EnergyJournal

483 U.S Energy Information Administration, Office of Energy Analysis, U.S. Department of Energy, *Annual Energy Outlook 2019 with projections to 2050*, (Statistical Analytical Agency within the U.S. Department of Energy, Washington, DC), January 2019. https://www.eia.gov/outlooks/aeo/pdf/aeo2019.pdf

484 U.S. Energy Information Administration, *Annual Energy Outlook 2019 with projections to 2050*. Ibid. 2019.

485 Stein, Ronald, "California lawmakers' war on domestic oil and gas creating national security risk," www.cfact.org, April 22, 2019. https://www.cfact.org/2019/04/22/california-lawmakers-war-on-domestic-oil-and-gas-creating-national-security-risk/

486 U.S. Energy Information Administration, *Annual Energy Outlook 2019 with projections to 2050*. Page 152. Ibid. 2019.

487 Felix, Bate, Roelf, Wendell, "Oil major Total plans biggest exploration drive in years," www.Reuters.com, January 29, 2019. https://www.reuters.com/article/us-total-exploration/oil-major-total-plans-biggest-exploration-drive-in-years-idUSKCN1PN0QZ

488 Seba, Erwin, "Exxon OK's project to nearly double size of Texas refinery: sources," www.Reuters.com, January 28, 2019. https://www.reuters.com/article/us-total-exploration/oil-major-total-plans-biggest-exploration-drive-in-years-idUSKCN1PN0QZ

489 *National Geographic Magazine*, "A Blueprint for a Carbon-Free America," Explore what your state's energy mix will look with 100% renewable energy," www.NationalGeographic.com, Page accessed on January 29, 2019. https://www.nationalgeographic.com/climate-change/carbon-free-power-grid/#cover

490 Stein, Ronald, "California cannot run on "Renewables" alone," www.Cfact.org, September 1, 2018. http://www.cfact.org/2018/09/01/california-cannot-run-on-renewables-alone/

491 Leiden University, "Renewable energy sources can take up to 1000 times more space than fossil fuels," www.Phys.org, August 28, 2018. https://phys.org/news/2018-08-renewable-energy-sources-space-fossil.html

492 Fares, Robert, "Renewable Energy Intermittency Explained: Challenges, Solutions and Opportunities," www.blogs.ScientificAmerican.com, March 11, 2015. https://blogs.scientificamerican.com/plugged-in/renewable-energy-intermittency-explained-challenges-solutions-and-opportunities/

493 Fay, Marianne; Hallegatte, Stephane; Vogt-Schilb, Adrien; Rozenberg, Julie; Narloch, Ulf; Kerr, Tom. 2015. *Decarbonizing Development: Three Steps to a Zero-Carbon Future.* Climate Change and Development. (Washington, DC: World Bank. © World Bank.) License: CC BY 3.0 IGO. https://openknowledge.worldbank.org/handle/10986/21842

494 Federal Transit Administration, National Transit Database, "Monthly Module Adjusted Data Release," www.Transit.DOT.gov, November 2018. https://www.transit.dot.gov/ntd/data-product/monthly-module-adjusted-data-release

495 Greenhut, Steven, "Falling ridership will not dissuade the social engineers," www.OCRegister.com, January 25, 2019. https://www.ocregister.com/2019/01/25/falling-transit-ridership-will-not-dissuade-the-social-engineers/

496 Downey, Caroline, GREEN WATCH Section, "U.S. Achieves Largest Decrease in Carbon Emissions…Without the Paris Climate Accord," www.CapitalResearch.org (America's Investigative Think Tank), July 24, 2018. https://capitalresearch.org/article/u-s-achieves-largest-decrease-in-carbon-emissionswithout-the-paris-climate-accord/

497 Gold, Russell, *The Boom: How Fracking Ignited the American Energy Revolution and Changed the World*, Page 260-65 to verify the natural gas and Kyoto Protocol claim. (Simon & Schuster, New York, NY), April 21, 2015. https://www.amazon.com/Boom-Fracking-Ignited-American-Revolution/dp/1451692293/ref=asc_df_1451692293/?tag=hyprod-20&linkCode=df0&hvadid=312178235188&hvpos=1o1&hvnetw=g&hvrand=12150308387829367168&hvpone=&hvptwo=&hvqmt=&hvdev=c&hvdvcmdl=&hvlocint=&hvlocphy=9031167&hvtargid=pla-569982007563&psc=1&tag=&ref=&adgrpid=602588

71337&hvpone=&hvptwo=&hvadid=312178235188&hvpos=1o1&hvnetw=g&hvrand=12150308387829367168&hvqmt=&hvdev=c&hvdvcmdl=&hvlocint=&hvlocphy=9031167&hvtargid=pla-569982007563

498 News/Australia, Al-Jazeera, "Australia's conservatives set to secure majority government," www.aljazeera.com, May 20, 2019. https://www.aljazeera.com/news/2019/05/australia-conservatives-set-secure-majority-government-190520025604433.html

499 Bell, Larry, "Growing Iceland, Greenland glaciers make scientists gasp," www.cfact.org, May 19, 2019. https://www.cfact.org/2019/05/19/growing-iceland-greenland-glaciers-makes-scientists-gasp/

500 Greenhut. Ibid. 2019.

501 Ferris, Robert, "GM is going 'all-electric,' but it doesn't expect to make money off battery-powered cars until early next decade," www. CNBC.com, February 6, 2019. https://www.cnbc.com/2019/02/06/gm-doesnt-expect-to-make-money-off-electric-cars-until-next-decade.html

502 Goldberg, Jonah, "Green New Deal Backers Embrace Their Fantasies," www.Townhall.com, February 8, 2019. https://townhall.com/columnists/jonahgoldberg/2019/02/08/green-new-deal-backers-embrace-their-fantasies-n2541028?utm_source=thdaily&utm_medium=email&utm_campaign=nl&newsletterad=02/08/2019&bcid=f474ff7f07777dc0fd4d372af0dcd99b&recip=24783318

503 Panchadar, Arjun, "Tesla cuts jobs as it looks to make Model 3 more affordable," www.Reuters.com, January 18, 2019. https://www.reuters.com/article/us-tesla-layoffs-idUSKCN1PC0W0

504 Klare, Michael T., "Addicted to fossil fuels: Renewable energy sources are becoming mainstream, but that doesn't mean fossil fuels don't rule: By 2040, fossil fuels will still have a grip on a staggering 78 percent of the world's energy markets." www.Salon.com, July 24, 2016. https://www.salon.com/2016/07/24/addicted_to_fossil_fuels_renewable_energy_sources_are_

becoming mainstream but that doesnt mean fossil fuels dont rule partner/

505 Shellenberger, Michael, "The Only Green New Deals That Have Ever Worked Were Done With Nuclear, Not Renewables," www.Forbes.com, February 8, 2019. https://www.forbes.com/sites/michaelshellenberger/2019/02/08/the-only-green-new-deals-that-have-ever-worked-were-done-with-nuclear-not-renewables/#476c055f7f61

Chapter Ten: Energy and National Security

506 Paul Rogers and Katy Murphy, September 10, 2018, Mercury News 100% clean energy by 2045 https://www.mercurynews.com/2018/09/10/california-mandates-100-percent-clean-energy-by-2045/

507 https://www.eia.gov/todayinenergy/detail.php?id=38912

508 Products from Petroleum https://www.ranken-energy.com/index.php/products-made-from-petroleum/ Wikipedia, "Petroleum product," www.en.Wikipedia.org, Page accessed January 8, 2019. https://en.wikipedia.org/wiki/Petroleum_product

509 2018, Airport Authority 145 airports https://airport-authority.com/browse-US-CA

510 2017, U.S. Energy Information Administration 13 million gallons a day of aviation fuels https://www.eia.gov/state/seds/data.php?incfile=/state/seds/sep_fuel/html/fuel_jf.html&sid=CA

511 December 2017, California Department of Motor Vehicles California's 35 million registered vehicles https://www.dmv.ca.gov/portal/wcm/connect/5aa16cd3-39a5-402f-9453-0d353706cc9a/official.pdf?MOD=AJPERES&CONVERT_TO=url&CACHEID=5aa16cd3-39a5-402f-9453-0d353706cc9a

512 July 2017, California Department of Tax and Fee Administration 42 million gallons a day of gasoline for the 90 percent of registered vehicles in California that are NOT EV's https://insideevs.com/a-look-at-californias-plug-in-electric-car-sales-compared-to-rest-of-u-s/

513 2017, California Energy Commission California increased crude oil imports from foreign countries from 5% in 1992 to 56% in 2017 https://www.energy.ca.gov/almanac/petroleum_data/statistics/crude_oil_receipts.html

514 2015, Natural Gas Intelligence (NGI) largest shale reserves https://www.naturalgasintel.com/montereyinfo

515 December 20, 2015, Fox News Monterey Shale https://www.foxnews.com/politics/shale-oil-deposit-a-possible-boon-to-struggling-california-but-state-wary-enviros-opposed

516 April 4, 2014, SOS California, http://soscalifornia.org/california-relies-on-imported-oil/

517 U.S. Energy Information Administration, Independent Statistics & Analysis, "Review of Emerging Resources: U.S. Shale Gas and Shale Oil Play," www.eia.gov, July 11, 2011. https://www.eia.gov/analysis/studies/usshalegas/

518 SOS California http://soscalifornia.org/faq/

519 2017, California Energy Commission California imported crude oil from foreign countries at the rate of more than 354 million barrels annually https://www.energy.ca.gov/almanac/petroleum_data/statistics/crude_oil_receipts.html

520 December 16, 2018, Average Crude Oil Spot Price https://ycharts.com/indicators/average_crude_oil_spot_price

521 Keith Crane, Andreas Goldthau, Michael Toman, Thomas Light, Stuart Johnson, Alireza Nader, Angel Rabasa, Harun Dogo, 2009, Rand Corporation Rand research study https://www.rand.org/pubs/research_briefs/RB9448/index1.html

522 2018 report by the U.S. House of Representatives Committee on Science, Space, and Technology https://www.heartland.org/template-assets/documents/publications/House%20Science%20Committe%20Russian%20Attempts%20to%20Influence%20U.S.%20Domestic%20Energy%20Markets.pdf

523 Kotkin, Joel, "The first shots in the climate wars," www.OCRegister.com, December 9, 2018. https://www.ocregister.com/2018/12/09/the-first-shots-in-the-climate-wars/

524 February 2, 2018, U.S. Energy Information Administration, https://www.eia.gov/todayinenergy/detail.php?id=34792

525 California Energy Commission – Tracking Progress, page 2 https://www.energy.ca.gov/renewables/tracking_progress/documents/Greenhouse_Gas_Emissions_Reductions.pdf

526 2017, California Department of Tax and Fee Administration California fuel consumption is at the highest level in years. Motor Vehicle 10-year report. https://www.cdtfa.ca.gov/taxes-and-fees/spftrpts.htm

527 2018, Airport Authority 145 airports https://airport-authority.com/browse-US-CA

528 December 2017, California Department of Motor Vehicles 35 million registered vehicles https://www.dmv.ca.gov/portal/wcm/connect/5aa16cd3-39a5-402f-9453-0d353706cc9aofficial.pdf?MOD=AJPERES&CONVERT_TO=url&CACHEID=5aa16cd3-39a5-402f-9453-0d353706cc9a

529 August 2018, U.S. Energy Information Administration California household users are paying more than 40% more, and industrial users are paying more than 100% than the national average for electricity https://www.eia.gov/state/?sid=CA#tabs-5

530 August 2018, U.S. Energy Information Administration U.S. Energy Information Administration https://www.eia.gov/state/?sid=CA#tabs-5

531 December 2018, Gas Buddy $1.00 more per gallon of fuel https://www.gasbuddy.com/Charts

532 Jim Mladenik and Kendra Seymour, July 25, 2018, Stillwater Associates https://stillwaterassociates.com/projecting-the-costs-of-californias-cap-trade-and-low-carbon-fuel-standard-programs/?utm_source=August+2018+Newsletter&utm_campaign=Newsletter_08_2018&utm_medium=email

533 U.S. Department of Housing and Urban Development https://www.hudexchange.info/resources/documents/2018-AHAR-Part-1.pdf

534 State by State Poverty rates, geographically adjusted, places California highest in the nation https://en.wikipedia.org/wiki/List_of_U.S._states_and_territories_by_poverty_rate

535 California spends more than $100 billion going toward welfare https://www.marketwatch.com/story/no-other-state-comes-close-to-california-when-it-comes-to-welfare-spending-2017-11-28

536 Gary Beevers, 2010, the United Steel, Paper and Forestry, Rubber, Manufacturing, Energy, Allied Industrial and Service Workers International Union (USW), page 54 The HF or MHF technology is currently in use at 50 US refineries (page 54 of the link) http://assets.usw.org/resources/hse/pdf/A-Risk-Too-Great.pdf

537 Joel Kotkin, *July 3, 2018, Presidential Fellow in Urban Futures at Chapman University and executive director of the Center for Opportunity Urbanism* permanent spikes in fuel costs and higher GHG emissions https://www.city-journal.org/html/californias-climate-extremism-16002.html

538 August 2018, U.S. Energy Information Administration California household users are paying more than 40% more, and industrial users are paying more than 100% than the national average for electricity https://www.eia.gov/state/?sid=CA#tabs-5

539 Lomberg, Bjorn, Director of the Copenhagen Consensus Center, "Are Electric Cars Really Green," via PragerU for YouTube.com, www.prageru.com & www.youtube.com, August 13, 2017. https://www.youtube.com/watch?v=OrmVk5OA2QE

540 Mark Kane, February 20, 2016, Insideevs.com more than 50% of all electric vehicles in the country are registered in California https://insideevs.com/a-look-at-californias-plug-in-electric-car-sales-compared-to-rest-of-u-s/

541 2017, California Energy Commission California fuel consumption is at the highest level since 2009 https://www.energy.ca.gov/almanac/transportation_data/gasoline/piira_retail_survey.html

542 July 2018, Statistica.com California's imports and exports of goods https://www.statista.com/statistics/234201/imports-and-exports-of-goods-of-california/

543 September 12, 2018, U.S. Energy Information Administration <u>the United States is now the largest global crude oil producer</u> https://www.eia.gov/todayinenergy/detail.php?id=37053

544 Erin De Santiago, <u>80,000 gallons of fuel per day, per liner</u> https://cruises.lovetoknow.com/wiki/How_Much_Fuel_Does_a_Cruise_Ship_Use

545 Joel Kotkin, July 3, 2018, City Journal.org <u>California contributes less than 1% of the world's emissions.</u> https://www.city-journal.org/html/californias-climate-extremism-16002.html

546 Paul Rogers and Katy Murphy, September 10. 2018, Mercury News <u>100% clean energy by 2045</u> https://www.mercurynews.com/2018/09/10/california-mandates-100-percent-clean-energy-by-2045/

547 Bill Fletcher and Marc Joffe, January 10, 2017, California Policy Center <u>With California already having trillions of debt obligations</u> https://californiapolicycenter.org/californias-total-state-local-debt-totals-1-3-trillion/

548 Paul Rogers and Katy Murphy, September 10. 2018, Mercury News <u>100% clean energy by 2045</u> https://www.mercurynews.com/2018/09/10/california-mandates-100-percent-clean-energy-by-2045/

549 Paul Rogers and Katy Murphy, September 10. 2018, Mercury News <u>100% clean energy by 2045</u> https://www.mercurynews.com/2018/09/10/california-mandates-100-percent-clean-energy-by-2045

550 August 2018, U.S. Energy Information Administration <u>electricity generation by Nuclear and Natural Gas</u> https://www.eia.gov/state/?sid=CA#tabs-4

551 Dr. Sarma Pisupati, Professor, Department of Energy and Mineral Engineering, College of Earth and Mineral Sciences <u>International Energy outlook</u> https://www.e-education.psu.edu/egee102/node/1929

552 2017, California Energy Commission <u>Solar and wind represented a small portion of electricity generation in 2016</u> https://www.energy.ca.gov/almanac/electricity_data/total_system_power.html

553 Wikipedia renewables at this time unable to power the huge California economy on a continuously uninterruptible basis https://en.wikipedia.org/wiki/Energy_in_California#/media/File:California_Electricity_Generation_Sources_Pie_Chart.svg

554 Dr. Sarma Pisupati, Professor, Department of Energy and Mineral Engineering, College of Earth and Mineral Sciences Energy consumption in the USA per the EIA https://www.e-education.psu.edu/egee102/node/1929

555 May 16, 2018, U.S. Energy information Administration, https://www.eia.gov/energyexplained/?page=us_energy_home

556 August 2018, U.S. Energy Information Administration California household users are paying more than 40% more, and industrial users are paying more than 100% than the national average for electricity https://www.eia.gov/state/?sid=CA#tabs-5

557 Goreham, Steve, "100 percent renewable energy-Poor policy for electricity ratepayers," www.cfact.org, October 18, 2018. http://www.cfact.org/2018/10/30/100-percent-renewable-energy-poor-policy-for-electricity-ratepayers/

558 August 2018, U.S. Energy Information Administration U.S. Energy Information Administration https://www.eia.gov/state/?sid=CA#tabs-5

559 California Climate Investment Programs administered through different California agencies. https://ww3.arb.ca.gov/cc/capandtrade/auctionproceeds/2019_cci_annual_report.pdf

560 Jim Mladenik and Kendra Seymour, July 25, 2018, Stillwater Associates More costs onto fuels are projected by 2030 from cap and trade and the low-carbon fuel standard that may add another $1.00 to $2.00 per gallon to fuel https://stillwaterassociates.com/projecting-the-costs-of-californias-cap-trade-and-low-carbon-fuel-standard-programs/?utm_source=August+2018+Newsletter&utm_campaign=Newsletter_08_2018&utm_medium=email

561 January 2017, U.S. Interagency Council on Homelessness homeless https://www.usich.gov/tools-for-action/map/#fn[]=1500&f

n[]=2900&fn[]=6100&fn[]=10100&fn[]=14100&year=2017&all_types=true&state=CA

562 Anjar Priandoyo, September 2, 2015, priandoyo.wordpress.com world's energy consumption forecasted out to 2030 https://priandoyo.wordpress.com/2015/09/02/summary-energy/

563 Annual Energy Outlook 2018, February 6, 2018, U.S Energy Information Administration, Energy Information Administration (EIA) https://www.eia.gov/outlooks/aeo/

Chapter Eleven: The Weaponization of Energy

564 O'Sullivan, Meghan, "IGA-412: The Geopolitics of Energy," Course taught at the Harvard Kennedy School of Government. Entire paragraph – except the last sentence - is based off this course syllabus. Page accessed January 5, 2019. https://www.hks.harvard.edu/courses/geopolitics-energy

565 Wikipedia, "Petroleum product," www.en.Wikipedia.org, Page accessed January 8, 2019. https://en.wikipedia.org/wiki/Petroleum_product

566 Hanson, Victor Davis, "Actually 2018 Was A Pretty Good Year," www.Townhall.com, January 3, 2010. https://townhall.com/columnists/victordavishanson/2019/01/03/actually-2018-was-a-pretty-good-year-n2538358

567 Hanson, Victor Davis, "Actually 2018 Was A Pretty Good Year," www.Townhall.com, January 3, 2010. https://townhall.com/columnists/victordavishanson/2019/01/03/actually-2018-was-a-pretty-good-year-n2538358

568 Hanson. Ibid. 2019. Entire paragraph references Dr. Hanson's article as a source.

569 Boak, Josh, "US employers went on a surprising hiring spree in December," www.APNEws.com (Associated Press), January 4, 2019. https://apnews.com/f3925762c6f845dfab936b45c28b4176

570 Rapier, Robert, "OPEC Is Losing Its Stranglehold On Oil Prices," www.OilPrice.com, January 5, 2019. https://oilprice.com/Energy/

Crude-Oil/OPEC-Is-Losing-Its-Stranglehold-On-Oil-Prices.html

571   Brown, Jonathan, "Nato boss claims Russia has secretly infiltrated green groups fighting fracking," www.Independent.co.uk, June 19, 2014. https://www.independent.co.uk/environment/nato-boss-claims-russia-has-secretly-infiltrated-green-groups-fighting-fracking-9549975.html

572   Mooney, Kevin, "Russian-funded environmental group gave millions to anti-fracking groups," www.WashingtonExaminer.com (Within the article there is a report from the US Congress' Science, Space and Technology Committee that is the research for Mr. Mooney's piece.), June 14, 2018. https://www.washingtonexaminer.com/opinion/russian-funded-environmental-group-gave-millions-to-anti-fracking-groups

573   Krauss, Clifford, "Russia Uses Its Oil Giant, Rosneft, as a Foreign Policy Tool," www.NYTimes.com, (New York Times), October 29, 2017. https://www.nytimes.com/2017/10/29/business/energy-environment/russia-venezula-oil-rosneft.html

574   The Economist Intelligence Unit, Russia Energy, "More than oil, gas is Russia's main strategic asset," www.EIU.com, December 11, 2017. Link gives amount proven, recoverable Russian energy reserves of oil and natural gas to use as a leveraged weapon against the west. http://www.eiu.com/industry/article/816211465/more-than-oil-gas-is-russias-main-strategic-asset/2_3

575   Simple English Wikipedia, "Geopolitics," www.Wikipedia.com, Page accessed January 5, 2019. https://simple.wikipedia.org/wiki/Geopolitics

576   Blank, Stephen, "Russia has weaponized the energy sector in war against the West," www.TheHill.com, October 17, 2017. https://thehill.com/opinion/international/355742-russias-has-weaponized-the-energy-sector-in-war-against-the-west

577   Dickinson, Peter, "Can the West Prevent the Slow Strangulation of Ukraine? Creeping Russian Aggression Cannot Go Unchecked," www.ForeignAffairs.com, December 5, 2018. https://www.foreignaffairs.com/articles/ukraine/2018-12-05/

can-west-prevent-slow-strangulation-ukraine?cid=nlc-fafatoday-20181213

578 Bay, Austin, "Russia's Pinprick War in Ukraine Has Global Implications," www.Townhall.com, November 21, 2018. https://townhall.com/columnists/austinbay/2018/11/21/russias-pinprick-war-in-ukraine-has-global-implications-n2536316?utm_source=thdaily&utm_medium=email&utm_campaign=nl&newsletterad=&bcid=f474ff7f07777dc0fd4d372af0dcd99b&recip=24783318

579 Wikipedia, "Crimea," Entire paragraph based off of Wikipedia page. Page accessed on January 5, 2019. https://en.wikipedia.org/wiki/Crimea

580 Meredith, Sam, "Ukraine declares martial law amidst intensifying standoff with Russia," www.CNBC.com, November 26, 2018. https://www.cnbc.com/2018/11/26/russia-ukraines-proposal-of-martial-law-adds-instability-to-standoff.html

581 Hirsh, Michael, "How Putin Is Perfecting His Border Plan," www.ForeignAffairs.com, November 28, 2018. https://foreignpolicy.com/2018/11/28/putins-near-perfect-plan/

582 Wikipedia.com, "Occupied territories of Georgia," www.Wikipedia.com, Page accessed on December 13, 2018. https://en.wikipedia.org/wiki/Occupied_territories_of_Georgia

583 Stein, Ronald, "Is California becoming a national security risk? www.cfact.org, November 13, 2018. https://thehill.com/opinion/international/355742-russias-has-weaponized-the-energy-sector-in-war-against-the-west

584 Kaufman, Alexander C., "Al Gore's Stupendous Wealth Complicates His Climate Message. That Can Change," www.HuffingtonPost.com, October 3, 2017. https://www.huffingtonpost.com/entry/al-gore-wealth_us_599709f2e4b0e8cc855d5c09

585 Walters, Dan, "Warm and fuzzy book (*The Browns of California*) about Browns falls short," www.CalMatters.org, August 5, 2018. Link provided to show article and book detail how Pat and Jerry Brown made millions off fossil fuels. https://calmatters.org/articles/commentary/warm-and-fuzzy-book-about-browns-falls-short/

586   Lomberg, Bjorn, "Arnold Schwarzenegger Is Wrong On Climate Change," www.Forbes.com, December 12, 2015. https://www.forbes.com/sites/bjornlomborg/2015/12/12/when-politicians-speak-their-minds-facts-still-matter/#31c83a6c3d62

587   Barbaro, Michael, Davenport, Coral, "Aims of Donor Are Shadowed by Past in Coal," www.NYTimes.com, July 4, 2014. https://www.nytimes.com/2014/07/05/us/politics/prominent-environmentalist-helped-fund-coal-projects.html

588   Greenhut, Steven, from the magazine, "Well-Heeled and Wrongheaded in California: Tom Steyer spend millions to stop energy exploration," www.City-Journal.org, Summer 2014. https://www.city-journal.org/html/well-heeled-and-wrongheaded-california-13673.html

589   Hoft, Jim, "10 YEARS AGO TODAY – Al Gore Predicted North Pole Would Be COMPLTELY ICE FREE in Five Years," www.TheGatewayPundit.com, December 13, 2018. https://www.thegatewaypundit.com/2018/12/10-years-ago-today-al-gore-predicted-north-pole-would-be-completely-ice-free-in-five-years/

590   Moore, Stephen, "Follow the (climate change) Money," www.Townhall.com, December 18, 2018. https://townhall.com/columnists/stephenmoore/2018/12/18/follow-the-climate-change-money-n2537638?utm_source=thdaily&utm_medium=email&utm_campaign=nl&newsletterad=12/18/2018&bcid=f474ff7f07777dc0fd4d372af0dcd99b&recip=24783318

591   Stanford Engineering Staff, Stanford Earth, "The impact of climate change on human behavior," www.Earth.Stanford.edu, October 15, 2018. https://earth.stanford.edu/news/impact-climate-change-human-behavior

592   Koerth-Baker, Maggie, "Human Behavior Might Be The Hardest Part Of Climate Change To Predict," www.FiveThirtyEight.com, November 27, 2018. https://fivethirtyeight.com/features/human-behavior-might-be-the-hardest-part-of-climate-change-to-predict/

593 Williams, Walter, "Global Warming," www.Townhall.com, March 11, 2015. https://townhall.com/columnists/walterewilliams/2015/03/11/global-warming-n1967847

594 Galen, Rich, "Climate Change," www.Townhall.com, December 14, 2015. https://townhall.com/columnists/richgalen/2015/12/14/climate-change-n2093325

595 Shellenberger, Michael, "Had They Bet On Nuclear, Not Renewables, Germany & California Would Already Have 100% Clean Energy," www.Forbes.com, September 11, 2018. https://www.forbes.com/sites/michaelshellenberger/2018/09/11/had-they-bet-on-nuclear-not-renewables-germany-california-would-already-have-100-clean-power/#23be0205e0d4

596 Driessen, Paul, "We are still in" totalitarians flunk basic reality," www.CanadaFreePress.com, December 16, 2018. (SPECIAL NOTE: Mr. Driessen is a former member of the Sierra Club and Zero Population Growth). https://canadafreepress.com/article/we-are-still-in-totalitarians-flunk-basic-reality

597 Krieger, Lisa M., "Why fossil fuel emissions are increasing – again: Stanford: Strong global economies are driving energy use," www.MercuryNews.com (Bay Area News Group), December 5, 2018. https://www.mercurynews.com/2018/12/05/why-fossil-fuel-emissions-are-increasing-again/

598 Energy Skeptic, Peak Energy & Resources, Climate Change, and the Preservation of Knowledge, "41 Reasons why wind power cannot replace fossil fuels," www.EnergySkeptic.com, December 14, 2018. http://energyskeptic.com/2018/wind/

599 Wilson, Robert, The Energy Collective Group, "Can You Make a Wind Turbine Without Fossil Fuels," www.EnergyCentral.com, February 25, 2014, https://www.energycentral.com/c/ec/can-you-make-wind-turbine-without-fossil-fuels

600 Assessment, Stratfor Worldview, "How the U.S. Is Complicating India's Relationship With Iran," www.Worldview.Stratfor.com, December 14, 2018. https://worldview.stratfor.com/article/how-us-complicating-indias-relationship-iran?utm_campaign=B2C%20%7C%20Newsletter%20%7C%20060818

&utm_source=hs_email&utm_medium=email&utm_content=68364505&_hsenc=p2ANqtz-8lnU_FPqeIXgS2xE56Gc829PnlktctKHUh4wRsv9qc96I1hI4-BLyonPD9mQnMiV6jbS2DPLHZR1PE9lrpHj4wxTrpbA&_hsmi=68365124

601 Hanson, Victor Davis, *The Second World War: How The First Global Conflict Was Fought And Won*, (Basic Books, Hachette Book Group, New York, NY), PART SEVEN: ENDS, Chapter 20, pages 503-30. October 17, 2017. https://www.amazon.com/Second-World-Wars-Global-Conflict/dp/0465066984/ref=sr_1_2?ie=UTF8&qid=1544664246&sr=8-2&keywords=victor+davis+hanson+the+second+world+wars

602 Royal, Todd, "Can the EU Its Russian Energy Habit? www.GeopoliticalMonitor.com, January 4, 2018. https://www.geopoliticalmonitor.com/can-the-eu-shake-its-russian-energy-habit/

603 Royal, Todd, "The U.S. is in a geopolitical mess over the Nord Stream 2 pipeline," www.cfact.org, October 25, 2018. http://www.cfact.org/2018/10/25/the-u-s-is-in-a-geopolitical-mess-over-the-nordstream-2-pipeline/

604 Buck, Tobias, "Nord Stream 2: Gas pipeline from Russia that's dividing Europe," www.IrishTimes.com, July 21, 2018. https://www.irishtimes.com/news/world/europe/nord-stream-2-gas-pipeline-from-russia-that-s-dividing-europe-1.3571552

605 Gotev, Georgi, "Green MEP denounces Gazprom's bullying tactics over Nord Stream 2," www.Euractiv.com, February 24, 2016. https://www.euractiv.com/section/energy/news/green-mep-denounces-gazproms-bullying-tactics-over-nord-stream-2/

606 Reuters Commodities, "Russia's Gazprom says offshore part of TurkStream is complete," www.Reuters.com, November 19, 2018. https://www.reuters.com/article/us-turkey-russia-gas-pipeline/russias-gazprom-says-offshore-part-of-turkstream-is-complete-idUSKCN1NO1KS

607 Sprener, Sebastian, "Turkey defiant on purchase of Russian S-400 anti-missile weapon," www.DefenseNews.com, July 11, 2018. https://www.defensenews.com/smr/nato-priorities/2018/07/11/

turkey-defiant-on-purchase-of-russian-s-400-anti-missile-weapon/

608 Nedos, Vassilis, "U.S. Senator: Turkey must choose between US F-35 jets and Russian S-400," www.Ekathimerini.com, January 4, 2019. http://www.ekathimerini.com/236236/article/ekathimerini/news/us-senator-turkey-must-choose-between-us-f-35-jets-and-russian-s-400

609 Kiley, Sam, "Vladimir Putin must be delighted with his useful idiots in the West," www.CNN.com, July 18, 2018. https://www.cnn.com/2018/07/18/opinions/vladimir-putin-and-his-useful-idiots-opinion-intl/index.html

610 Epstein, Alex, *The Moral Case For Fossil Fuels*, (Portfolio / Penguin Book, New York, NY), Chapter 7, Pages 151-176. November 13, 2014. https://www.amazon.com/Moral-Case-Fossil-Fuels/dp/1591847443/ref=sr_1_1?ie=UTF8&qid=1544665798&sr=8-1&keywords=alex+epstein+the+moral+case+for+fossil+fuels

611 Inozemsev, Vladislav, "Summer of Summitry: The Putin Moment," www.The-American-Interest.com, July 15, 2018. https://www.linkedin.com/pulse/companies-leaving-california-increase-study-urges-more-joseph-vranich/

612 Blank. Ibid. 2017.

613 Berman, Ilan, "Understanding Putin's Paranoid Style: The answer, one of Russia's leading opinion centers has concluded, has everything to do with a pervasive sense of cultural siege," www.NationalInterest.com, September 1, 2018. https://nationalinterest.org/blog/buzz/understanding-putin's-paranoid-style-30322

614 Miller, Chris, "The Surprising Success of Putinomics: Behind Putin's Formula for Holding Onto Power," www.ForeignAffairs.com, February 7, 2018. https://www.foreignaffairs.com/articles/russian-federation/2018-02-07/surprising-success-putinomics

615 Blank. Ibid. 2017.

616 Rogan, Tom, "In Belarus' energy rage against Vladimir Putin, America's opportunity," www.WashingtonExaminer.com, December 13, 2018. https://www.washingtonexaminer.com/

opinion/in-belarus-energy-rage-against-vladimir-putin-americas-opportunity

617 Blank. Ibid. 2017.

618 Vakhshouri, Sara, Atlantic Council Review of the *America First Energy Plan*, titled, *The America First Energy Plan: Renewing the Confidence of American Energy Producers*, www.AtlanticCouncil.com, August 17, 2017. https://www.atlanticcouncil.org/publications/issue-briefs/america-first-energy-plan

619 Borland, Justin, "How An Oil Boom in West Texas Is Reshaping the World," www.Time.com, January 3, 2019. http://time.com/5492648/permian-oil-boom-west-texas/

620 S. Nye, Jr., Joseph, "Soft Power: The Means to Success in World Politics," www.ForeignAffairs.com, CAPSULE REVIEW May/June 2004 Issue. https://www.foreignaffairs.com/reviews/capsule-review/2004-05-01/soft-power-means-success-world-politics

621 Shellenberger, Michael, "We Don't Need Solar And Wind To Save The Climate – And It's A Good Thing, Too," www.Forbes.com, May 8, 2018. https://www.forbes.com/sites/michaelshellenberger/2018/05/08/we-dont-need-solar-and-wind-to-save-the-climate-and-its-a-good-thing-too/#1048f9f6e4de

622 Mai-Duc, Christine, "Tom Steyer makes moves toward presidential bid," www.LATimes.com, November 20, 2018. https://www.latimes.com/politics/la-pol-ca-steyer-20181120-story.html

623 Xuetong, Yan, "The Age of Uneasy Peace: Chinese Power in a Divided World," *Foreign Affairs Magazine* Comment Section, January/February 2019 Issue, www.ForeignAffairs.com,

624 Vranich, Joseph, Spectrum Location Solution, *It's Time for Companies to Leave California's Toxic Business Climate*, A Report examining California's increasingly hostile business environment and the state's $77 billion losses from company out-of-state migrations from January 1, 2008 to December 31, 2016. www.SpectrumLocationSolutions.com, December 2018. https://www.linkedin.com/pulse/companies-leaving-california-increase-study-urges-more-joseph-vranich/

625   Hethcock, Bill, "1,800 companies left California in a year – with most bound for Texas," www.BizJournals.com, https://www.bizjournals.com/dallas/news/2018/12/13/1-800-companies-left-california-in-a-year-with.html

626   Hethcock, Bill, "Fortune 500 company (McKesson Corp.,) to move headquarters from California to DFW," www.BizJournals.com, November 30, 2018. https://www.bizjournals.com/dallas/news/2018/11/30/mckesson-relocates-headquarters-to-north-texas.html

627   Brands, Hal, "New Threat to the U.S.: the Axis of Autocracy (Russia, China, Iran), www.Bloomberg.com, April 19, 2018. https://www.bloomberg.com/opinion/articles/2018-04-19/china-russia-and-iran-are-forming-an-axis-of-autocracy

628   Stewart, Scott, *Stratfor Worldview Threat Lens 2019 Annual Forecast: An Excerpt.* www.Worldview.Stratfor.com, December 11, 2018. Please see the map graphic titled, "Iran Proxies and Previous Areas of Operations." https://worldview.stratfor.com/article/threat-lens-2019-annual-forecast-excerpt

629   Xuetong. Ibid. 2019.

630   China, Kara, Frank, Jacqui, Silverstein, Sara, "The legendary economist who predicted the housing crisis says the US will win the trade war," www.BusinessInsider.com, November 30, 2018. https://www.businessinsider.com/gary-shilling-legendary-economist-trade-war-outlook-says-us-will-win-2018-10

631   Lung, Natalie, "Trade War Damage to China's Economy Is Already Done, Citi Says," www.Bloomberg.com, December 11, 2018. https://www.bloomberg.com/news/articles/2018-12-12/trade-war-damage-to-china-s-economy-is-already-done-citi-says

632   European Commission Press Release, "EU-Japan trade agreement on track to enter into force in February 2019. www.Europa.eu, December 12, 2018. http://europa.eu/rapid/press-release_IP-18-6749_en.htm

633   Blas, Javier, "Texas Is About to Create OPEC's Worst Nightmare," www.Bloomberg.com, November 20, 2018. https://www.bloomberg.com/news/articles/2018-11-21/

opec-s-worst-nightmare-the-permian-is-about-to-pump-a-lot-more

634 Amadeo, Kimberly, "OPEC Oil Embargo, Its Causes, and the Effects of the Crisis," www.TheBalance.com, November 6, 2018. https://www.thebalance.com/opec-oil-embargo-causes-and-effects-of-the-crisis-3305806

635 Resnick-Ault, Jessica, "Oil dives on fears of glut, global economic slowdown," www.Reuters.com, December 17, 2018. https://www.reuters.com/article/us-global-oil/us-oil-prices-drop-1-percent-on-oversupply-fears-idUSKBN1OH03J

636 U.S. Energy Information Administration, Independent Statistics & Analysis, "Short-Term Energy Outlook (STEO)," www.EIA.com, December 2018. https://www.eia.gov/outlooks/steo/pdf/steo_full.pdf

637 Mead, Walter Russell, "How American Fracking Changes the World: Low energy prices enhance U.S. power at the expense of Moscow and Tehran," www.WSJ.com, November 26, 2018. https://www.wsj.com/articles/how-american-fracking-changes-the-world-1543276935

638 Zenne, Michael, "Here's Why Russian Bombers Are in Venezuela. And Why the U.S. Is So Angry About It," www.Time.com, December 13, 2018. http://time.com/5478644/venezuela-russian-bombers/

639 Krauss. Ibid. 2017.

640 American Petroleum Institute (API), "Liquefied Natural Gas Export | America's Opportunity and Advantage | Why Export LNG?" www.API.org, Page accessed on December 18, 2018. https://lngexports.com/#/?section=why-export-lng

641 Clemente, Jude, "Europe Needs More U.S. Liquefied Natural Gas," www.Forbes.com, December 7, 2018. https://www.forbes.com/sites/judeclemente/2018/12/07/europe-needs-more-u-s-liquefied-natural-gas/#56e2a4361acf

642 Nedos, Vassilis, "U.S. officials sends clear message to Turkey over Cyprus drilling," www.Knews.Kathimerini.com.cy, December 17, 2018. http://focus-fen.net/opinion/2018/12/16/5282/

kathimerini-us-official-sends-clear-message-to-turkey-over-cyprus-drilling.html

643   Strategy International, International Global Affairs, International Security, Strategy, Tactics and Defense, "The emergence of Turkey as a regional power & the Middle East disruption & reset," www.StrategyInternational.org, December 14, 2018. https://strategyinternational.org/the-emergence-of-turkey-as-a-regional-power-the-middle-east-disruption-reset/

644   Krauss. Ibid. 2017.

645   Blank. Ibid. 2017.

646   Faucon, Benoit, Said, Summer, "Kuwait, Saudis Close to Oil-Field Pact, After U.S. Intervention: Oil production in Saudi-Kuwait neutral zone could restart in the first quarter of 2019," www.WSJ.com, December 12, 2019. https://www.wsj.com/articles/kuwait-saudis-close-to-oil-field-pact-after-u-s-brokers-deal-11544627624

647   Wood Mackenzie News Release, "Major LNG buyers' uncontracted demand to quadruple by 2030," www.WoodMac.com, (Wood Mackenzie), December 13, 2018. https://www.woodmac.com/press-releases/major-lng-buyers-uncontracted-demand-to-quadruple-by-2030/

648   The New Arab & agencies, "Qatar to invest $20 billion in US energy sector," www.Alaraby.co.uk, December 16, 2018. https://www.alaraby.co.uk/english/news/2018/12/16/qatar-to-invest-20-billion-in-us-energy-sector

649   Yergin, Daniel, *The Prize: The Epic Quest for Oil, Money & Power*, (Free Press, a Division of Simon & Schuster, Inc., New York, NY), December 23, 2008. https://www.amazon.com/Prize-Epic-Quest-Money-Power/dp/1439110123

650   Yergin, Daniel, *The Quest: Energy, Security and the Remaking of the Modern World*, (Penguin Books, New York, NY), September 26, 2012. https://www.amazon.com/Quest-Energy-Security-Remaking-Modern/dp/0143121944ref=pd_lpo_sbs_14_img_0?_encoding=UTF8&psc=1&refRID=3S9GFGTC7YRTFE00GZ6Z

651 Institute for New Economic Thinking, A Series of Debates, "Is Green Growth Possible?" www.ineteconomics.org, December 2018. https://www.ineteconomics.org/perspectives/collections/is-green-growth-possible-a-debate

652 Rose, Gideon, "Who Will Run the World," www.ForeignAffairs.com, January/February 2019 Issue, https://www.foreignaffairs.com/articles/2018-12-11/who-will-run-world

653 Friedman Lissner, Rebecca, Rapp-Hooper, Mira, "The Liberal Order Is More Than a Myth," www.ForeignAffairs.com, July 31, 2018. https://www.foreignaffairs.com/articles/china/2018-11-13/how-counter-chinas-influence-south-pacific?cid=int-flb&pgtype=hpg

654 Global Data Report, *H2 2018 Production and Capital Expenditure Outlook for Key Planned and Announced Upstream Projects in FSU – Russia Accounts for Most of Capex in Region.* www.GlobalData.com, December 2018. https://www.globaldata.com/store/report/gdge0265mar--h2-2018-production-and-capital-expenditure-outlook-for-key-planned-and-announced-upstream-projects-in-fsu-russia-accounts-for-most-of-capex-in-region/

655 U.S. President Donald Trump, U.S. Secretary of Defense James Mattis, *National Defense Strategy 2018*, U.S. Department of Defense, www.nssarchives.us, January 19, 2018. http://nssarchive.us/national-defense-strategy-2018/

656 Edel, Charles, "How to Counter China's Influence in the South Pacific," www.ForeignAffairs.com, November 13, 2018. https://www.foreignaffairs.com/articles/china/2018-11-13/how-counter-chinas-influence-south-pacific?cid=int-flb&pgtype=hpg

657 Ring, Edward, "How Globalism is the Real Authoritarianism," www.AmericanGreatness.com, December 16, 2018. https://amgreatness.com/2018/12/16/how-globalism-is-the-real-authoritarianism/

658 The World Bank | DataBank | "Population estimates and projections," www.Databank.WorldBank.org, 2018. http://databank.worldbank.org/data/source/population-estimates-and-projections

659 Dudley, Bob, Group chief executive, British Petroleum (BP), *BP Statistical Review of World Energy*, www.BP.com, June 2018.

https://www.bp.com/content/dam/bp/en/corporate/pdf/energy-economics/statistical-review/bp-stats-review-2018-full-report.pdf

660 von Clausewitz, Carl, *On War*, Volume 1, Chapter 1: What is War? Translated by Colonel J.J. Graham. New and Revised edition with Introduction and Notes by Colonel F.N. Maude, in Three Volumes, (Kegan Paul, Trench, Trubner & C, London, England), www.oll.libertyfund.org, 1918. https://oll.libertyfund.org/pages/clausewitz-war-as-politics-by-other-means

661 Roth, Sammy, "California is aiming for 100% clean energy. But Los Angeles might invest billions in fossil fuels," www.LATimes.com, December 20, 2018. https://www.latimes.com/business/la-fi-100-clean-energy-gas-plants-20181220-story.html

662 Domonoske, Camila, "California Sets Goal Of 100 Percent Clean Electric Power By 2045," www.NPR.org, (US National Public Radio), September 10, 2018. https://www.npr.org/2018/09/10/646373423/california-sets-goal-of-100-percent-renewable-electric-power-by-2045

663 Ring, Edward, "Alternatives to the Nihilistic Futility of Mass Immigration," www.AmericanGreatness.com, December 1, 2018. https://amgreatness.com/2018/12/01/alternatives-to-the-nihilistic-futility-of-mass-immigration/

664 Novak, Michael, *The Spirit of Democratic Capitalism*, (Madison Books, Lanham, MA), Introduction, pages 16-17. December 29, 1990. https://www.amazon.com/Spirit-Democratic-Capitalism-Michael-Novak/dp/0819178233/ref=sr_1_1?ie=UTF8&qid=1545324496&sr=8-1&keywords=the+spirit+of+democratic+capitalism

665 Nikolskaya, Polina, Osborn, Andrew, "Russia's Putin accuses U.S. of raising risk of nuclear war," www.Reuters.com, December 20, 2018. https://www.reuters.com/article/us-russia-putin-nuclear/russias-putin-accuses-us-of-raising-risk-of-nuclear-war-idUSKCN1OJ11R

666 Jaiani, Vasil, "6 Unintended Consequences From The West's Passive Response To The Ukraine Invasion," www.Forbes.com, March 5, 2015. https://www.forbes.com/sites/

realspin/2014/03/05/6-unintended-consequences-from-the-wests-passive-response-to-the-ukraine-invasion/#7779753914b1

Chapter Twelve: Climate Change

667 Oregon Global Warming Petition Project http://www.petitionproject.org/

668 https://ntotrickszone.com/2013/05/17/atmospheric-co2-concentrations-at-400-ppm-are-still-dangerously-low-for-life-on-earth/

669 December 21, 2018, Wikipedia, https://en.wikipedia.org/wiki/Human

670 August 10, 2015, Meritnation.com, https://www.meritnation.com/blog/history-of-earth-on-24-hour-clock/

671 Alexa Halford, Brett Carter, and Julie Currie, September 8, 2017, Newsweek sun that goes through 11-year cycles of solar activity of massive sunspots and solar flares https://www.newsweek.com/solar-minimum-sun-activity-solar-flare-baffling-scientists-661695

672 Matt Williams, February 10, 2017, Universe Today majority of the Earth's surface is covered by oceans https://www.universetoday.com/25756/surface-area-of-the-earth/

673 https://greatclimatedebate.com/co2-is-not-causing-global-warming/

674 Enten, Henry, "The Political Rhetoric Around Climate Change Change…Er, Global Warming," www.FiveThirtyEight.com, June 4, 2014.

675 Sixteen scientists via opinion page in *Wall Street Journal*, "No Need to Panic About Global Warming: There's No Compelling Scientific Argument for Drastic Action to 'decarbonize' the World's Economy," WSJ.com, January 27, 2012. http://www.wsj.com/articles/SB10001424052970204301404577171531838421366

676 WiseEnergy.org, "Sample Books Related to Anthropogenic Global Warming," www.WiseEnergy.org, March 24, 2019. http://wiseenergy.org/Energy/AGW/Sample_AGW_Books.pdf

677 Williams, Walter, "Global Warming," www.Townhall.com, March 11, 2015. https://townhall.com/columnists/walterewilliams/2015/03/11/global-warming-n1967847

678 Galen, Rich, "Climate Change," www.Townhall.com, December 14, 2015. https://townhall.com/columnists/richgalen/2015/12/14/climate-change-n2093325

679 CFACT Europe, "700 Papers Supporting Climate Realism," www.Cfact.org, April 26, 2010. https://www.cfact.org/2010/04/26/700-papers-supporting-climate-realism/

680 CFACT Europe, "Over 450 Peer-Reviewed Scientific Papers Challenging Man-Made Global Warming," www.Cfact.org, October 30, 2009. https://www.cfact.org/2009/10/30/450-peer-reviewed-scientific-papers-support-climate-realism/

681 Cass, Oren, "Who's The Denier Now?" www.NationalReview.com, May 1, 2017. https://www.nationalreview.com/magazine/2017/05/01/climate-change-science-ignored/

682 World Tribune Staff, "Survey finds majority of scientists are global warming doubters," www.TheTribunePapers.com, March 7, 2019. http://www.thetribunepapers.com/2019/03/07/survey-finds-majority-of-scientists-are-global-warming-doubters/

683 Oregon Global Warming Petition Project http://www.petitionproject.org/

684 By Associated Press, "Key Greenland glacier growing again after shrinking for years, NASA study shows," www.NBCNews.com, March 26, 2019. https://www.nbcnews.com/mach/science/key-greenland-glacier-growing-again-after-shrinking-years-nasa-study-ncna987116

685 Khazendar, Ala, et al., "Interruption of two decades of Jakobshavn Isbrae acceleration and thinning as regional ocean cools," www.Nature.com, March 25, 2019. https://www.nature.com/articles/s41561-019-0329-3

686 Steele, Jim, "A Sea Level Rise Conundrum – Greenland's Cycles," www.WattsUpWithThat.com, March 21, 2019. https://wattsupwiththat.com/2019/03/21/a-sea-level-rise-conundrum-greenlands-cycles/

687 Balasubramanian, A., Professor, University of Mysore, *Elements of Climate and Weather*, www.ResearchGate.net, August 2017. https://www.researchgate.net/publication/319181402_ELEMENTS_OF_CLIMATE_AND_WEATHER

688 Jayaraj, Vijay, "Global Cooling: The Real Climate Threat," www.AmericanThinker.com, March 14, 2019. https://www.americanthinker.com/articles/2019/03/global_cooling_the_real_climate_threat.html

689 Lindzen, Richard, "Climate Change: What do Scientists Say?" www.YouTube.com via www.PragerU.com, April 18, 2016. https://www.youtube.com/watch?v=OwqIy8Ikv-c

690 Jayaraj. Ibid. 2019.

691 Nova, Joanne, "NASA hides page saying the Sun was the primary climate driver, and clouds and particles are more important than greenhouse gases," www.JoanneNova.com, via www.ZeroHedge.com, March 2019. http://joannenova.com.au/2019/02/nasa-hides-page-saying-the-sun-was-the-primary-climate-driver-and-clouds-and-particles-are-more-important-than-greenhouse-gases/

692 Jayaraj. Ibid. 2019.

693 Prigg, Mark for DailyMail.com, "A year on the sun: Stunning animation reveals the 'deathly quiet' of 2018 as the solar minimum approaches," www.DailyMail.co.uk, January 30, 2019. https://www.dailymail.co.uk/sciencetech/article-6649689/A-year-sun-Animation-reveals-deathly-quiet-2018-solar-minimum-approaches.html

694 Space Weather Prediction Center, National Oceanic and Atmospheric Administration (NOAA), "Solar Cycle 24 Status and Solar Cycle 25 Upcoming Forecast," www.SWPC.NOAA.gov, April 26, 2018. https://www.swpc.noaa.gov/news/solar-cycle-24-status-and-solar-cycle-25-upcoming-forecast

695 Jayaraj. Ibid. 2019.

696 Australian Government, Bureau of Meteorology, Space Weather Services, "Monthly Sunspot Numbers," www.SWS.BOM.gov.au, March 3, 2019. https://www.sws.bom.gov.au/Solar/1/6

697 Jayaraj. Ibid. 2019.

698 Sing, A.K., Bhargawa, Asheesh, "Prediction of declining solar activity trends during solar cycles 25 and 26 and indication of other solar minimum," www.Link.Springer.com, January 15, 2019. https://link.springer.com/article/10.1007/s10509-019-3500-9

699 Herring, Joe, "Green Insanity Is Flooding Towns and Destroying Lives," www.AmericanThinker.com, March 24, 2019. https://www.americanthinker.com/articles/2019/03/green_insanity_is_flooding_towns_and_destroying_lives.html

700 Devore, Chuck, "Trump's Right About California Fires: It Wasn't Climate Change; Two New California Laws Prove It," www.Forbes.com, November 27, 2018. https://www.forbes.com/sites/chuckdevore/2018/11/27/trumps-right-about-californias-fires-it-wasnt-climate-change-two-new-california-laws-prove-it/#2f4b2da222e3

701 Hamlin, Larry, "Cal Fire reports pinpoints thinning of forests to reduce Ca. wildfire risks," www.WattsUpWithThat.com, March 7, 2019. https://wattsupwiththat.com/2019/03/07/cal-fire-report-pinpoints-thinning-of-forests-to-reduce-ca-wildfire-risks/

702 California Department of Forestry and Fire Protection, *Community Wildfire Prevention & Mitigation Report*, in response to Executive Order N-05-19, www.Assets.DocumentCloud.org, February 22, 2019. https://assets.documentcloud.org/documents/5759583/Cal-Fire-2019-Community-Wildfire-Prevention-and.pdf

703 Cal Fire. Ibid. 2019.

704 Cal Fire. Ibid. 2019.

705 Thanawala, Sudhin, "California officials focus on forest management after fires," www.APNews.com, March 5, 2019. https://www.apnews.com/7cf25d7c1c8148e381fbb593c185e88c

706 Connor, Alex, "That anti-straw movement? It's all based on one 9-year-old's suspect statistic," www.USAToday.com, July 18, 2018. https://www.usatoday.com/story/news/2018/07/18/anti-straw-movement-based-unverified-statistic-500-million-day/750563002/

707 Gray, Alex, "90% of plastic polluting our oceans comes from just 10 rivers," www.WeForum.org, June 8, 2018. https://www.weforum

.org/agenda/2018/06/90-of-plastic-polluting-our-oceans-comes-from-just-10-rivers/

708 Golden, C. Douglas, "10 Failed Global Warming Predictions That You Need To Know About," www.WesternJournal.com, August 8, 2018. https://www.westernjournal.com/ct/10-failed-global-warming-predictions/

709 McAleer, Phelim, "How Enviros Lie About America (And Why)," www.Townhall.com, March 7, 2019. https://townhall.com/columnists/phelimmcaleer/2019/03/07/how-enviros-lie-about-america-and-why-n2542743

710 McAleer. Ibid. 2019.

711 McAleer. Ibid. 2019.

712 Mead Walter Russell, "NATO Is Dying, but Don't Blame Trump: Germany reneges on defense commitments, thumbing its nose at the alliance," www.WSJ.com, March 25, 2019. https://www.wsj.com/articles/nato-is-dying-but-dont-blame-trump-11553555665

713 Peterson, Matthew J., "Total Political War," www.AmericanGreatness.com, March 23, 2018. https://amgreatness.com/2018/03/23/total-political-war/

714 Romel, Valentina, Reed, John, "The Asian Century is set to begin," www.FT.com (Financial Times), March 25, 2019. https://www.ft.com/content/520cb6f6-2958-11e9-a5ab-ff8ef2b976c7

715 Bromley, Bud, "CO2 is not causing (statistically relevant) global warming," www.GreatClimateDebate.com, January 15, 2019. https://greatclimatedebate.com/co2-is-not-causing-global-warming/

716 Sorman, Guy, From the Magazine, "Climate Science's Myth-Buster," www.City-Journal.org, Winter 2019. https://www.city-journal.org/global-warming

Index

A

abundant, 64, 72
affordable, xv, 1, 18, 26, 29, 37, 50, 60, 62, 67, 71, 85, 90, 92, 105–6, 117, 121, 125, 127, 131, 148, 162, 164, 175–76, 180–81, 197–98, 202
Africa, xvii, 39, 51, 68, 77, 88, 114, 116, 122, 140, 165, 198, 201–3, 229
airlines, 11, 181
allies, 10, 29, 31–32, 37, 39–40, 187
anti-fracking, 47, 171, 193
Axis Powers, 29–30, 32, 39–40, 187

B

batteries, 9, 14, 22, 48, 105–6, 124, 126, 128–29, 132, 135, 138–45, 182

C

catastrophic, xvii, 13, 99, 206, 220, 223
China, xiv, xvii, 21–22, 34–35, 37, 43, 48, 51, 60–64, 66–73, 75–82, 85, 88, 91–92, 116–17, 120, 147, 152, 154–55, 187–89, 197–203, 227
clean energy, 6, 22, 83, 127–28, 134, 161, 179–80, 196

climate change, xvii, 69, 193, 217, 220–21, 224, 227–28
coal-fired power plants, xvi, 35, 60, 66–68, 71, 76, 78–79, 105, 112, 116, 129, 164, 193
coal power, 155
cobalt, 22, 110, 140–42, 144, 182
consequences, xvii, 17–18, 32, 71, 79, 123, 171–72, 197, 204
cruise liners, 12–13, 26, 179, 182

D

dark side, 140
deaths, xvii, 1, 16–17, 26, 71
diesel engine, 1–2, 11, 20–21, 46, 49, 167, 181, 195

E

electricity, xii, 4, 6–7, 9, 21, 26, 28, 36, 45, 47–49, 56–57, 62, 64, 68, 74, 84–85, 87, 90, 92–94, 100, 104–8, 113, 116–18, 120–21, 123–31, 133–35, 137–38, 142, 149–51, 158–60, 162–65, 174, 179–80, 182–86, 188, 197
electric vehicles, xiii, xvii, 7–8, 12, 48, 64, 92, 110, 139–43, 146–47
energy density, 1, 8–9, 13, 90

Energy Information Administration (EIA), xii, 3, 9, 22, 28, 86, 88, 108, 116, 121, 148, 156, 174, 177, 183

F

flexible, xv, 29, 37, 60, 67, 71, 85, 90, 92, 102, 117, 119, 121, 131, 148, 162, 180, 197–98, 202
fracking, 43, 47, 61, 72, 98, 189–90, 196

G

Global Warming, 217
Gore, Albert Arnold, Jr. (Al Gore), xvi–xvii, 27, 46, 103, 109, 113, 178, 192, 203, 217, 223, 226, 229
green technology, 140
grid, 118, 120–22, 124, 126, 128–30, 133–36

I

India, xiv, xvii, 48, 50–51, 60–63, 67–68, 73–82, 88, 116–17, 194, 198, 201–3, 227, 229
Iran, 43, 46, 73, 79, 117, 187–89, 195, 198, 200, 203, 227

J

jet engine, xvii, 26

L

lithium, 110, 140, 142, 144–45, 182

M

merchant ships, 12–13
militaries, xii, 2, 9–11, 13–14, 18, 20, 26–27, 29, 36, 42, 44, 49, 64, 81, 85, 90, 92, 105, 113, 116–17, 121, 148–49, 167, 173, 178–79, 182, 186–87

Modi, Narendra, 77

N

national security, 167, 169, 173, 176, 178, 197, 204, 227
natural gas, 21, 52, 101–2, 162–63, 165, 180, 187, 199–200
nuclear, 6, 36, 57, 76, 131, 180

O

oil import, 158

P

Paris Accord, 45–47, 49, 51, 60–61, 171, 187
poverty, 71
Putin, Vladimir, 35, 153, 171, 189, 191–96, 203–4

R

reliable, xi, xiv–xv, 1, 10, 18, 29, 36, 39, 48, 50, 52, 62, 67, 71, 80, 85, 90, 92, 94, 99, 105, 117, 121–22, 125, 127, 131, 148, 153, 162, 165, 175–76, 180, 188, 197–98, 201–2
renewable electricity, xvii, 20, 64, 70, 83–86, 92, 97–98, 104, 107–8, 133, 137–38
Russia, 35, 37, 43, 46–47, 79, 155, 182, 187–91, 194, 197–203, 227

S

scalable, xv, 10, 29, 37, 50, 60, 62, 67, 71, 85, 90, 92, 105–6, 116, 121, 125, 131, 148, 153, 162, 180, 197–98, 202
Schwarzenegger, Arnold, xvii, 27, 46, 178, 192, 203, 217
smart grid, xvii, 118–21, 125–31, 136–37, 283

South America, 79, 122, 140, 144, 199
space, 160
Steyer, Tom, xvii, 27, 46, 131, 178, 192–93, 197, 203, 217, 223, 226, 229

T

trucking, xii, 2, 9, 11–12, 28, 45, 47, 90, 178, 182, 186

V

vehicles, 9, 12, 48, 58, 146–47, 177

W

weaponization, viii, 117, 187–88, 196, 198, 200–204
World War, 10, 29–33, 35, 37, 113, 187

X

Xi Jingping, 64, 69, 154–55, 203–4